Economic Conditions
and
Welfare Reform

Sheldon H. Danziger

Editor

1999

W.E. Upjohn Institute for Employment Research
Kalamazoo, Michigan 49007-4686

Library of Congress Cataloging-in-Publication Data

Economic conditions and welfare reform / Sheldon Danziger, editor.
   p. cm.
  Includes bibliographical references and index.
  ISBN 0–88099–200–X (cloth : alk. paper). — ISBN 0–88099–199–2
  (paper : alk. paper)
   1. Public welfare—Economic aspects—United States—Congresses. 2. Welfare
recipients—United States—Economic conditions—Congresses. 3. United
States—Economic conditions—1981—Congresses. I. Danziger, Sheldon.
HV91 .E26 1999
361.973—dc21   99–049277

The facts presented in this study and the observations and viewpoints expressed are the sole responsibility of the authors. They do not necessarily represent positions of the W.E. Upjohn Institute for Employment Research.

Cover design by J.R. Underhill
Index prepared by Diane Worden.
Printed in the United States of America.

The Authors

Timothy J. Bartik is a Senior Economist at the W.E. Upjohn Institute for Employment Research in Kalamazoo, Michigan.

Rebecca M. Blank is Henry Carter Adams Professor of Public Policy, Professor of Economics, and Dean of the School of Public Policy at the University of Michigan.

Maria Cancian is an Associate Professor in the La Follette Institute of Public Affairs and the School of Social Work at the University of Wisconsin-Madison.

Howard A. Chernick is a Professor in the Department of Economics of Hunter College and in the Graduate Center, City University of New York.

Sheldon H. Danziger is Henry J. Meyer Collegiate Professor in the School of Social Work and a Professor in the School of Public Policy at the University of Michigan.

Randall W. Eberts is Executive Director of the W.E. Upjohn Institute for Employment Research in Kalamazoo, Michigan.

David N. Figlio is an Assistant Professor in the Department of Economics at the University of Florida.

Robert H. Haveman is John Bascom Professor of Economics and Public Affairs at the University of Wisconsin-Madison.

Harry J. Holzer is a Professor in the Department of Economics, Michigan State University.

Thomas Kaplan is a Senior Scientist with the Institute for Research on Poverty at the University of Wisconsin-Madison.

Phillip B. Levine is an Associate Professor in the Department of Economics of Wellesley College.

Therese J. McGuire is a Professor with the Institute of Government and Public Affairs and the College of Urban Planning and Public Affairs, University of Illinois at Chicago.

Daniel R. Meyer is an Associate Professor of Social Work at the University of Wisconsin-Madison.

Robert A. Moffitt is a Professor in the Department of Economics at Johns Hopkins University.

LaDonna A. Pavetti is a Senior Researcher with Mathematica Policy Research, Inc.

Geoffrey L. Wallace is an Assistant Professor in the Department of Economics and the Robert M. La Follette Institute of Public Affairs at the University of Wisconsin-Madison.

Barbara L. Wolfe is Director of the Institute for Research on Poverty and a Professor of Economics and Preventive Medicine at the University of Wisconsin-Madison.

James P. Ziliak is an Associate Professor in the Department of Economics at the University of Oregon.

Contents

Introduction

What Are the Early Lessons?

Sheldon Danziger
University of Michigan

The papers in this volume were commissioned and presented at a conference held in November 1998 in Washington, D.C. The Joint Center for Poverty Research at the University of Chicago and Northwestern University organized the conference, which was funded by the Office of the Assistant Secretary for Planning and Evaluation (ASPE) at the Department of Health and Human Services. Assisting me in planning the conference were Greg Duncan of Northwestern University and Donald Oellerich of ASPE. Special thanks are due to the conference discussants and participants, who provided valuable suggestions for the revisions that are published here, and to Julie Balzekas and Diane Kallenback for excellent staff assistance.

Based on early analyses of the effects of the 1996 welfare reform act, this introduction focuses on three key questions: Why are caseloads falling? How are recipients faring? How are the states responding?

REFORMING WELFARE

Welfare reform has generated a great deal of interest in the 1990s. No other domestic policy has generated such intense media coverage, popular discussion, and policy debate. This round of welfare reform began when presidential candidate Clinton gave a 1992 campaign speech calling for dramatic changes in welfare policy: "No one who works full-time and has children at home should be poor anymore. No one who can work should be able to stay on welfare forever." Shortly after Clinton took office, he appointed an interagency task force to turn this promise into legislation. At the time, few expected the years of contentious debate that ensued. In the summer of 1994, the Clinton administration issued its welfare reform plan; it was set aside after the Republican victory in the 1994 elections. A Republican welfare reform plan that had been part of the "Contract with America" shaped much of the subsequent debate. In August 1996, amid great controversy, Congress passed and the president signed P.L. 104-93, the Personal Responsibility and Work Opportunity Reconciliation Act (PRWORA).

Since 1996, much attention has focused on the effects of PRWORA. In this volume, economists and policy analysts use the best data that are currently available and sophisticated research techniques to answer some key policy questions. Their goal is to evaluate what has happened to date and what is likely to happen as the business cycle ebbs and flows in the coming years. In particular, the authors were asked to use their analyses to predict what is likely to happen to welfare caseloads, to recipient well-being, and to state budgets and policies when the next recession arrives. The authors present their estimates and predictions, but they leave it to the reader to weigh the available evidence and decide how successful PRWORA has been in its first few years of "ending welfare as we know it" and to consider how welfare reform might be further reformed when the 1996 act comes up for re-authorization.

The 1996 act represents a dramatic change in the way cash assistance and services are delivered to single mothers and their children. The Aid to Families with Dependent Children (AFDC) program had evolved over the previous 60 years to provide cash benefits to all who met state and federal eligibility criteria. Benefit levels were set by the states, but total costs for this entitlement program were shared between the states and the federal government. The Temporary Assistance for Needy Families (TANF) program, which replaced AFDC, now provides greater discretion to the states concerning eligibility criteria, work requirements, and other programmatic rules. In return, the federal government provides a block grant of fixed size to each state and no longer shares in the cost increases or decreases associated with rising or falling caseloads. The provisions of TANF are discussed in detail in this volume, especially in the chapters of Part III.

Welfare reform has led to a more rapid decline in the cash assistance caseload than most analysts would have predicted in 1996 when the act was signed. In part, this is because few analysts predicted that the economy would continue to grow so rapidly with so little inflation and with such low unemployment rates. As the papers in Part I discuss, welfare caseloads began falling several years before PRWORA became law, but caseload declines have accelerated since that time.

Consider the trend in the number of welfare recipients (first under AFDC, now under TANF) from 1960 to December 1998 (Figure 1). The caseload rose rapidly in the aftermath of the "War on Poverty" from about 4 million persons in the mid 1960s to about 10 million by the early 1970s; it then fluctuated between 10 and 12 million until the early 1990s, when it rose to about 14 million. By December 1998, the caseload had declined to about 7.5 million, 47 percent below the level of January 1994 and 38 percent below the level of August 1996.[1] The four papers in Part I of this volume analyze the causes of these caseload fluctuations, primarily through 1996, due to data constraints.

Reducing caseloads is a major goal of welfare reform, but it is not the only goal. One issue that has not been resolved in the few years since PRWORA was enacted is how recipients who have left the rolls are faring in the labor market. How interested are employers in hiring them? What kinds of jobs are they getting? How much are they earning? The tight labor markets and low unemployment rates of the late 1990s provide the best possible environment for welfare recipients who are entering the labor market. As a result, the caseload declines have been accompanied by increased employment among unmarried mothers. However, the increased employment has not led to increased economic well-being for some former recipients, and some of the most disadvantaged single mothers have been unable to find jobs. The two papers in Part II address these issues.

Some other recent studies that have focused on all single mothers, regardless of welfare participation, are relevant to understanding the overall labor market context in which welfare reform is proceeding. First, more unmarried mothers are working. According to Gary Burtless (1998), by 1998 the employment-to-population ratio of unmarried mothers—divorced, separated, and never-married women—had caught up with that of married mothers, at about 66 percent. This ratio rose

4

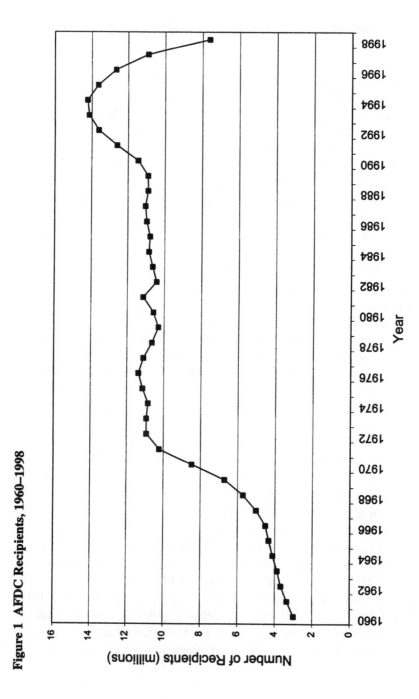

Figure 1 AFDC Recipients, 1960–1998

only 2.2 percentage points in the 14 years prior to 1993, but rose 11.5 points between that year and 1998.

Second, the poverty rate for single mothers remains quite high, in part because welfare caseloads have fallen much faster than the poverty rate. Consider the trend in the official poverty rate for families with female householders and no husband present (the group from which most welfare recipients are drawn). According to the Census Bureau (P-60, no. 201), the 1997 rate (35.1 percent) is about the same as the 1989 rate (35.9 percent) and the 1979 rate (34.9 percent). This suggests that many of those who are leaving the cash assistance rolls remain poor. It is possible, however, that the data for 1998 and 1999, when available, will show that poverty rates have fallen further as the economy has continued to grow and caseloads have continued to fall during these years.

On the other hand, the experience in the year following PRWORA suggests caution. Wendell Primus (1999) documents that disposable income increased on average for all single mothers between 1993 and 1997. Yet, the poorest fifth of single-mother families, many of whom are current or former welfare recipients, had less disposable income in 1997 than in 1995. The disposable income of the next fifth of these families was unchanged over these two years because declines in income from public assistance programs offset increased earnings and benefits from the Earned Income Tax Credit.

Although there has been some discussion about how families that were receiving cash assistance are faring, much greater attention has been given by policymakers and the media to caseload declines. A few studies on how families are faring have recently appeared, and many more will appear in the next few years. It takes time to gather and evaluate this evidence, as it is more difficult to follow families leaving welfare and find out about their incomes than it is to count the number of families remaining on the welfare rolls. Several continuing studies and the Cancian et al. study (Chapter 6 in this volume) suggest that reductions in caseloads do not mean that most families who leave the rolls are "making it." Recipients are looking harder for jobs in response to the increased policy pressure than were recipients prior to 1996; and, in part because the labor market is so tight, many are getting jobs. Greater numbers of recipients have left the rolls than are getting jobs, however.

In addition, in some states, recipients have been terminated from the rolls because of rule changes, not because they are finding jobs. For example, a report in *The New York Times* ("West Virginia Trims Welfare, but Poor Remain," March 7, 1999) noted that West Virginia had begun to count child Supplemental Security Income (SSI) benefits as income for TANF recipients, rendering them ineligible for TANF benefits regardless of their ability to find work. A court ruling subsequently overturned this policy. Yet, this demonstrates that some states have instituted administrative rule changes that have reduced caseloads, with little regard for the employability of the affected recipients. For example, some states are pursuing diversion policies that attempt to minimize the number of applicants who enter the rolls, and other states, sanction policies that attempt to maximize exit from the rolls.

To date, all studies, including those in this volume (which were completed in early 1999) can provide only short-term responses to the questions posed here. Because it has only been three years since welfare reform was passed and because macroeconomic conditions have been unusually good, we do not yet know how families who have left the rolls will fare in the long run or in ordinary or recessionary economic periods. Some recipients who have left the rolls, even if they now have earnings below their former welfare benefit level, may gain additional hours of work and/or wage increases if they stay employed. Of course, their current situation might be better than their long run prospects because the labor market is so tight.

Over the next few years, we will learn much more about the issues analyzed in this volume. For now, however, the chapters that follow tell us about what we have learned so far and speculate about what might happen in the long run. In particular, the authors consider what is likely to happen during an economic slowdown: How responsive are caseloads to changes in economic conditions and policy changes? How are recipients likely to fare as employer willingness to hire them fluctuates over the business cycle? What policy changes might state governments undertake? I now turn to a brief summary of the chapters. Parts I, II and III are organized around the three broad questions: Why are caseloads falling? How are recipients faring? How are the states responding?

WHY ARE CASELOADS FALLING?

The four chapters in Part I analyze trends in welfare caseloads in recent years, with particular emphasis on sorting out how much of the caseload changes—increases in the late 1980s and early 1990s, followed by decreases—can be attributed to macroeconomic conditions and how much to welfare reform policy changes. A careful reading of all four papers, each of which uses different data or different estimation strategies, shows how difficult it is to explain caseload changes.

In their chapter, David Figlio and James Ziliak attempt to reconcile a controversy about the relative effects of changes in the unemployment rate and pre-TANF changes in state welfare policies on the welfare caseload. In 1997, a paper by staff members of the President's Council of Economic Advisers (CEA) attributed more than one-third of the decline in caseloads between 1993 and 1996 to declining unemployment and less than one-third to state waiver policies. Another 1997 paper by Ziliak, Figlio, and colleagues attributed a greater share to the former and a smaller share to the latter. In their replication of the CEA model, about one-third of the caseload decline is again attributed to the economy, but only about one-sixth to waivers; their preferred models attribute about half to three-quarters of the change to the economy, but virtually none to welfare reform. Figlio and Ziliak conclude that these differences are due to the fact that the CEA uses a static model, while they prefer a dynamic one, and that "the primary consequence of controlling for caseload dynamics is to reduce the role of welfare reform relative to the macroeconomy in generating the decline in AFDC caseloads." They also point out that welfare reform has played a larger role in the post-PRWORA caseload decline than it did prior to 1996.

Geoffrey Wallace and Rebecca Blank analyze trends in both AFDC and food stamp caseloads for the 1980–1996 period. They document a significant unexplained increase in both caseloads, even after they control for a broad range of economic, demographic, political, and policy-related variables. During the 1994–1996 period, about half of the AFDC caseload change is attributed to the unemployment rate and about one-fifth to state welfare waivers, but for the 1994–1998 period, a much smaller part of the decline is due to unemployment rate changes. They conclude that, based on their historical estimates, "the expected effect of any future one-point increase in unemployment will be to increase TANF caseloads by 4 to 6 percent and food stamp case-loads by 6 to 7 percent." This suggests that a severe recession that raises the unemployment rate by 3–4 percentage points, to 7.5–8 per-cent, would leave welfare caseloads well below the levels reached in the early 1990s. They conclude that the 1996 welfare reform seems to have achieved a large reduction in caseloads independent of the state of the economy.

Robert Moffitt applies the CEA methodology not to time series data, but to micro data from the 1976–1996 Current Population Sur-veys. This allows him to focus more directly on specific population groups such as less-educated women, who are most likely to be affected by welfare reform, and to examine not only changes in welfare caseloads, but also changes in earnings and family income. He finds that state welfare waivers reduced AFDC participation rates among women without high school degrees and increased their labor force attachment, but had little effect on their earnings. Women who were high school graduates fared better: their AFDC participation rates fell, their work effort increased, and their earnings also increased.

In the last chapter of Part I, Timothy Bartik and Randall Eberts extend the kinds of models estimated by the CEA, Figlio and Ziliak, and Wallace and Blank to include measures of economic conditions other than unemployment rates, notably labor demand factors. They focus on state employment growth, the wage premium associated with an area's industrial mix, the educational requirements implied by the industrial mix, and the extent to which a state's industries tend to employ welfare recipients. They find that a welfare recipient faces greater barriers to employment than does a typical worker because of low educational attainment and greater volatility in industries that tend to hire recipients, and that caseloads are higher in states with higher concentrations of industries that hire more educated workers. They conclude that the national trend toward higher educational require-ments in many industries can account for some of the increase in wel-fare caseloads in the late 1980s and early 1990s.

HOW ARE RECIPIENTS FARING?

The two chapters in Part II focus on the labor market, first on recipient work and earnings outcomes and then on employer willingness to hire welfare recipients. The findings are similar to those in the Moffitt and Bartik/Eberts chapters; i.e., the least-skilled have the hardest time making it in the labor market.

Maria Cancian and her colleagues review evidence from several data sources about the post-welfare work effort and the economic well-being of former recipients. Although most former recipients can find some work, most cannot get and keep full-time, year-round work. In their analysis of pre-TANF data from the National Longitudinal Survey of Youth, in each of the five years after exit, about two-thirds worked. However, in any of these years, only about one-sixth to about one-quarter worked full-time, full-year. The same was true in the post-TANF Wisconsin administrative data they analyze; during the first year after leaving the rolls, about two-thirds of leavers worked. They also found that most former recipients (at least in the first few years) will earn relatively low wages, between $6.50 and $7.50 per hour. This is not surprising, given that welfare recipients have low skills and that the real wages of less-skilled workers have fallen dramatically over the past quarter century and have not increased much during the current economic boom.

This finding about the wage prospects of less-skilled workers is not new. It was the motivation for the proposal of the first Clinton administration "to make work pay and end welfare as we know it." This suggests that former welfare recipients will continue to need government income supplements if they are to support their family at incomes above the poverty line. The expanded Earned Income Tax Credit (EITC) has a very important role here, as does post-welfare access to subsidized child care, health care, and food stamps. As the Cancian et al. chapter cautions, "Even consistent work may not suffice for self-support if wages are low . . . The relatively modest growth in wages for this sample is inconsistent with the suggestion that even if former welfare recipients start in low-paying jobs, they will soon move on to jobs that pay wages that can support a family above the poverty line." The good news in Wisconsin for the sample of families that had left the welfare rolls is that twice as many of them were above the poverty line relative to those remaining on the rolls. Yet, only 27 percent of those who left cash assistance and did not return escaped poverty, and only about one-third of all leavers obtained the income level they received just before they left welfare.

An additional caveat is in order. The first wave of data from a panel study of welfare recipients being conducted at the University of Michigan[2] shows that women remaining on welfare have characteristics, not evaluated in most studies of recipients, that make their labor market prospects more problematic than those of all single mothers and even those of recipients who have already left the rolls. The study examined 14 potential barriers to employment, including major depression, post-traumatic stress disorder, maternal health, child health, labor market skills, perceived experiences of discrimination, and several standard human capital measures. It found that about 75 percent of single mothers who received cash welfare in February 1997 and had zero or one of these barriers were working in Fall 1997, whereas only about 40 percent of those with four or more barriers were working. As welfare caseloads continue to decline, this suggests that the recipients who remain will be the least employable.

Harry Holzer presents evidence from his survey of a large sample of employers in several metropolitan areas in Michigan. He concludes that labor market tightness has a substantial effect on employer demand for welfare recipients. Like Cancian et al., he finds that most welfare recipients can get some work when labor markets are very tight, as they have been in the late 1990s. In fact, many of the employers whom Holzer interviewed in Fall 1997 told him that they were willing to hire welfare recipients in 1998, although many had not yet done so. Thus, a recession is likely to significantly reduce employer demand for less-skilled workers in general and welfare recipients in particular, because, at the time of the interviews, the employers expected labor market tightness to increase and they were already having difficulty filling current vacant positions. Holzer estimates that a recession would reduce demand for recipients by 25 to 40 percent from current levels, suggesting that the employment experience of recipients may provide a classic example of the "last hired, first fired" syndrome. In addition, he finds that employers are more receptive to many public interventions on behalf of welfare recipients (such as tax credits for hiring or training workers) because of current labor market tightness and their difficulty in finding qualified workers.

HOW ARE THE STATES RESPONDING?

The three chapters in Part III all focus on what states are doing now and how they are likely to respond when a recession comes. This is unchartered territory, as PRWORA has given states a fixed block grant along with greater discretion. The block grant provides states in each year with an amount of federal funds that is the higher of the 1994 or 1995 level or the average for the 1992–1994 period. Because welfare caseloads were much higher during these years than they now are, this has produced a financial windfall for the states. However, as the authors discuss, the federal government will not share the increased welfare costs associated with a recession as it did in the past.

LaDonna Pavetti analyzes how states have begun to implement the new work-oriented welfare system in a "resource-rich" environment. Given available resources and declining caseloads, many states have provided expanded job search assistance and support services to many more recipients than was the case prior to PRWORA. The challenge when the economy turns down, according to Pavetti, is that state resources will be fixed, the number of recipients seeking assistance will increase, jobs will be harder to find, and time limits will have come into effect in a greater number of states. She concludes that given the emphasis on mandatory work, it may be necessary to broaden the definition of what constitutes participation in a work activity. Alternatives include increased use of vocational education or training programs, participation in community work experience or public service employment programs, or volunteer activities in the community.

Pavetti's concerns are important given the difficulty of many former recipients in finding stable employment in the tight labor market of 1998 and 1999. She suggests that states should begin experimenting with community service employment or work-for-your-welfare policy options now, while caseloads are still declining and resources are plentiful. The next recession is likely to occur when some single mothers will have already exhausted their lifetime eligibility for TANF benefits. It will be easier to pilot these programs now when the labor market is good than to reach the next recession without this kind of safety net in place.[3]

In his chapter, Phillip Levine examines how much states will likely be forced to spend on additional welfare payments in the event of a recession. He concludes that costs will rise by $7–14 billion, depending on the severity of the recession, and this will impose a serious financial burden on some states. He also shows that the rules governing how states can draw funds from the federal contingency fund are such that many states will receive little relief. Levine uses the states' experiences with the unemployment insurance system to predict how states are likely to handle the burden imposed by the increased cyclicality of their welfare spending. His simulations suggest that some states will have a very hard time saving for a rainy day.

Howard Chernick and Therese McGuire speculate about how states might respond now that the open-ended matching grant program of AFDC has been changed to a fixed block grant. They analyze the long-run spending responses of governments to other matching and block grants and past variations in state revenues and expenditures over the business cycle. They argue that because PRWORA's maintenance-of-effort requirement limits a state's spending reduction to 20 or 25 percent of the 1994 level, and because caseloads have already declined by so much, the shift to TANF's block grant has not led to immediate cuts in benefit levels. Over time, benefits are likely to be, at most, 10 percent lower as a consequence of the price increase for public assistance that is associated with PRWORA's elimination of matching grants. This reduction does not lend support to the idea that there will be a "race to the bottom" in state benefit levels. They estimate that in a recession comparable in magnitude to the 1990–1991 recession, most states should be able to avoid drastic spending cuts. However, in the past, some states have sharply reduced their welfare spending in response to a downturn, and some states now have tax systems that make their revenues especially sensitive to economic downturns. Some states, like California, are considered likely to face difficult problems by both the Levine and the Chernick/McGuire analyses.

SUMMARY

Taken together, the chapters in this volume suggest that, in its first few years, the 1996 welfare reform has been more successful in some dimensions (notably, reducing caseloads) than in others (raising disposable income). Much of the success to date is due to a booming economy and to a fiscal environment in which states have more funds to spend per recipient than they had in the past. Nonetheless, even under these optimal economic and fiscal conditions, some recipients have already "slipped through the cracks." The end of entitlement has meant that some single mothers, with poor labor market prospects and no other means of support, have not received the benefits they would have under the pre-PRWORA welfare system. Indeed, there are concerns that some recipients have lost not only their cash assistance, but also the food stamp and Medicaid benefits to which they are still entitled.

The chapters collectively raise a cautionary flag that, given current rules, much of the success achieved to date may disappear during the next recession. The cyclical effects on state budgets will be greater during the next recession than they were during previous ones. Then, some single mothers will have reached their lifetime benefit limit and will require benefit extensions/exemptions; others will not be able to get benefits to which they are eligible without some changes in diversion/sanction policies; and both groups may need access to community service jobs if they are to avoid serious material hardships.

The authors analyze some of the key issues that Congress and the next administration should consider when the 1996 act comes up for re-authorization, and they provide a road map for "reforming welfare reform" to avoid problems that are inherent in current law. State policymakers would also be well-served if they began to make contingency plans in response to the authors' projections. To end on an optimistic note, the relative success of welfare reform in reducing caseloads may have created the fiscal and political context that will allow the reforming of welfare reform in order to better serve those who need further assistance, especially those who have fallen through the cracks in the new safety net.

Notes

1. For the most recent caseload statistics by state, see the web site of the Administration for Children and Families, www.acf.dhhs.gov/news/stats/caseload.htm.
2. Sandra Danziger, Mary Corcoran, Sheldon Danziger, Colleen Heflin, Ariel Kalil, Judith Levine, Daniel Rosen, Kristin Seefeldt, Kristine Siefert, and Richard Tolman. "Barriers to the Employment of Welfare Recipients." University of Michigan School of Social Work, April 1999, www.ssw.umich.edu/poverty/pubs.html.
3. For a discussion of current state and local efforts in this area, see Clifford Johnson, "Publicly-Funded Jobs for Hard-to-Employ Welfare Recipients," Center on Budget and Policy Priorities, March 1, 1999, www.cbpp.org.

References

Burtless, Gary. 1998. "Can the Labor Market Absorb Three Million Welfare Recipients." *Focus* 19(3). Institute for Research on Poverty, University of Wisconsin-Madison.

Primus, Wendell. 1999. Testimony before the Subcommittee on Human Resources of the Committee on Ways and Means, U.S. House of Representatives, May 27.

U.S. Department of Commerce, Bureau of the Census. 1998. *Poverty in the United States: 1997.* Current Population Reports, P60-201. Washington, D.C.: U.S. Government Printing Office.

Part I
Why Are Caseloads Falling?

Welfare Reform, the Business Cycle, and the Decline in AFDC Caseloads

David N. Figlio
University of Florida

James P. Ziliak
University of Oregon

The past decade has witnessed unprecedented changes in both the caseload size and administration of the Aid to Families with Dependent Children (AFDC) program. Welfare caseloads increased nationwide by about 26 percent from 1990 to the peak in early 1994, and then declined by 35 percent as of the third quarter of 1998. With the lone exception of Hawaii, every state has experienced caseload reductions, ranging from a 13 percent drop in Alaska to an 86 percent drop in Wisconsin. Two factors are widely credited for these declines: strong economic growth and a fundamental transformation of the welfare system (Blank 1998; Council of Economic Advisers 1997; Ziliak et al. 1997). Since 1993, nearly 18 million new jobs have been created, unemployment rates have fallen to their lowest level in a generation, and employers of low-wage workers are arguably facing the tightest labor market in 50 years (Maharaj 1998). During this same period, the U.S. Department of Health and Human Services (HHS) became more liberal in granting waivers from federal AFDC requirements, permitting states to experiment in earnest with their welfare systems. These experiments culminated in the passage of the Personal Responsibility and Work Opportunity Reconciliation Act of 1996 (PRWORA). PRWORA created a new federal block-grant program called Temporary Assistance for Needy Families (TANF) to replace AFDC; the new program eliminates individual entitlement to cash assistance and gives states wide latitude in setting program parameters.

While it is generally incontrovertible that the business cycle and welfare reform underlie the dramatic decline in the AFDC program, the relative contribution of each factor is in dispute. While the Council of

17

Economic Advisers (CEA) presents a number of specifications, their preferred estimate suggests that the business cycle accounts for 44 percent of the decline in AFDC caseloads from 1993–1996, while welfare waivers account for 31 percent of the decline. Alternatively, Ziliak et al., using higher-frequency data and a more dynamic specification, attribute nearly two-thirds of the decline to the robust economy but nearly nothing to welfare reform.

Because the policy implications from the CEA and Ziliak et al. differ significantly, it is important to delineate the methodological differences in order to make more informed fiscal and welfare policy. For example, if AFDC cases only weakly respond to business-cycle conditions, then we would expect the welfare-program budget surpluses that many states have enjoyed recently to persist even into a recessionary period. Alternatively, if caseloads are strongly countercyclical, then states that have failed to save for a "rainy day" may face difficult fiscal constraints during the next cyclical downturn. In addition, any interrelationship between welfare reform and the macroeconomy may become disentangled when the economy turns toward recession. Bishop (1998) presented evidence that most of the increase in labor force participation rates since 1994 is among single women with children. If a large share of these women are former welfare recipients and the recent success of welfare reform is tied to the robust economy, then the movement from welfare to work could be much weaker in a sluggish economy.

Our purpose here is threefold. First, we conduct an extensive reconciliation between the findings in Ziliak et al. and those of the CEA.[1,2] Specifically, using the data and sample period employed by the CEA, we examine the relative impacts of the business cycle and welfare reform on the 1993–1996 caseload decline via numerous modeling choices, including using recipients versus cases as the outcome of interest, using year dummies versus a cubic trend to control for macroeconomic factors, using controls for welfare benefits, using weights in the regression model, using different sample periods, using first differences instead of levels, and using a dynamic framework. Second, we turn our attention to the issue of how welfare recipiency might respond in the event of a recession. To address this question, we employ the preferred dynamic specifications that arise from the reconciliation and simulate how caseloads respond to alternative "shocks" to the unemployment rate. Third, we examine the possibility of interactions between the macroeconomy and welfare reform.

Our reconciliation suggests that the differences in results between Ziliak et al. and the CEA emanate largely from the treatment of dynamics. These dynamics surface in the form of sluggish adjustment of current caseloads to past caseloads, from lags in the response of caseloads to changes in unemployment rates, and from nonstationarities in caseloads (especially at monthly frequencies). The primary consequence of controlling for caseload dynamics is to reduce the role of welfare reform relative to the macroeconomy in generating the decline in AFDC caseloads. Once we control for dynamics, we attribute up to 75 percent of the 1993–1996 caseload decline to the macroeconomy and at most 1 percent to welfare reform.

Moreover, the simulations underscore both the importance of controlling for dynamics and the cyclical sensitivity of welfare recipiency. We find that the implied long-run effect of a 1-percentage-point increase in the unemployment rate is 2.5 and 6 times the static estimate in levels and first differences, respectively. In addition, we find that a 2-percentage-point increase in the unemployment rate leads up to an 11.7 percent increase in welfare recipiency after four years, while a 4-percentage-point increase yields a 23.4 percent increase in recipiency. Finally, the results from interactions between the macroeconomy and welfare reform indicate that pre-TANF welfare reform requires a robust economy (i.e., low unemployment rates) in order to have a negative impact on recipiency rates.

REVIEW OF CASELOAD LITERATURE

Research on modeling aggregate AFDC caseloads is a relatively recent addition to the welfare literature. This stands in contrast to the large microeconometric literature that focuses either on the determinants of AFDC participation or the duration of welfare spells (Danziger, Haveman, and Plotnick 1981; Moffitt 1992). A few previous papers have considered the impact of economic stimuli on caseload levels without examining the concurrent effects of welfare reform.[3] The purpose of most of these studies has been to develop models that can accurately forecast changes in the number of families receiving AFDC over time. They tend to use time series data and focus on a single state, and in some cases on a single city (New York). The study by Peskin, Tapogna, and Marcotte (1993) for the Congressional Budget Office is a notable exception in their application of quarterly time-series data for national AFDC-Basic and AFDC-UP (unemployed parents) caseloads.[4] They employed a distributed lag model, permitting the business cycle to have a dynamic impact on caseloads, and found that both Basic and UP caseloads exhibit strong countercyclical movements. Specifically, their model predicts that a 1-percentage-point increase in the employment gap (the percentage difference between potential and actual employment) leads to a 0.5 percent decline in Basic and a 1.7 percent decline in UP caseloads in that quarter.

Moffitt (1987) used cross-sectional and time-series data separately to study the large run-up in AFDC recipiency in the late 1960s. For the cross-sectional analysis, he employed a static model of AFDC participation for 1967, 1973, and 1979, where participation is a function of measured demographics, AFDC program parameters, and the unemployment rate. The model predicts that most of the run-up is unexplained by economic and demographic factors. Instead, Moffitt attributed the increase to non-economic factors, such as court-ordered and legislative decisions that made eligibility easier and an increased willingness to participate in the program, possibly due to a reduction in the stigma associated with benefit receipt.

More recently, researchers have turned to state-level administrative data to model the impact of both the business cycle and welfare reform on AFDC caseloads. The advantage of the state panel-data approach is that it fosters identification of the business-cycle and welfare-reform effects by exploiting spatial differences across states and time-series differences within states. Because the focus of this paper is in reconciling the results from this literature, we provide a more detailed summary of the methods.

The Council of Economic Advisers (1997) employed annual state-level panel data for 1976–1996 to model per capita AFDC recipiency rates. The dependent variable combines AFDC recipients, not cases, in both the Basic and UP programs; this implicitly assumes that the business-cycle and welfare-reform responses between the two groups are identical. The CEA modeled per capita recipiency as a function of the business cycle, waivers from federal welfare programs, program parameters, and unobserved state fixed effects and trends. To capture the impact of the business cycle, the CEA used current and one-period-lagged state unemployment rates; the lag controls for any delays between the timing of unemployment and the receipt of welfare. The waiver variables were defined as the fraction of the year that the (full-state) waivers are approved. In some specifications the waivers were aggregated as "any statewide waiver," while in others they were disaggregated as "JOBS sanctions," "time limits," "work requirements," "family cap," and "earnings disregards." In several specifications, the CEA included both contemporaneous waiver variables and one-period "lead" waivers. The latter was an attempt to control for political rational expectations on the part of welfare recipients, signifying that welfare benefits were soon to be threatened. The AFDC program parameter was the AFDC maximum-benefit guarantee for a family of three, which is used to capture the "price" of welfare. Lastly, the state fixed effects and trends controlled for permanent differences in labor-force composition and welfare populations, as well as trending differences across states.

In their preferred results (Council of Economic Advisers 1997, Table 2, Column 6), the CEA found that contemporary unemployment has little effect on AFDC recipiency, but that a 1-percentage-point increase in lagged unemployment increases recipiency by almost 5 percent. The waiver effects are mixed—there is no significant current effect from the variable "any statewide waiver," but the lead effect suggests that states with any anticipated federal waiver could expect a 6 percent decline in annual recipiency rates. The conclusions were reversed for the "JOBS sanctions" variable: the current effect suggests a 7 percent decline, but there is no significant lead effect.

The specifications in Blank (1998) are similar to the CEA's, with a few notable exceptions. She used annual state panel data from 1979–1995 and estimated separate models for AFDC-Basic and AFDC-UP caseload levels. In addition to the explanatory variables used by the CEA, Blank controlled for a second lag in unemployment, along with interstate differences in median and 20th percentile wages, racial composition, female headship, age composition, average years of schooling, and political affiliation of the governor and state legislature.

Overall, Blank's estimates of the effects of the business cycle and welfare waivers do not differ substantively from the CEA's (see Blank 1998, Table 2, Column 1). The net effect of a 1-percentage-point increase in unemployment leading to a 3.8 percent increase in cases is comparable to the CEA's estimate of 4.07 percent. When Blank included a lead waiver (Blank 1998, Table 3, column 2) she estimated that "any statewide waiver" leads to about an 12.8 percent reduction in caseloads; again, this is similar to the CEA's overall estimate of about 12.5 percent (summing up the current and lead coefficients). It is important to note how closely the results mimic each other even though Blank's pertain to Basic cases while the CEA's pertain to total recipients. Blank did find that the UP program is more responsive to macroeconomic and policy variables than the Basic program; however, since UP cases are only about 6 percent of the total, pooling the samples adequately represents the majority of cyclical and welfare-reform movements in cases. Unlike the CEA, Blank did not prefer the models with lead waiver variables, because the latter likely capture other factors changing in the states (prior to waiver approval) and not true program effects.

The paper by Ziliak et al. (1997) differs in several dimensions from those of the CEA and Blank. The period under study was shorter (1987–1996), the data were monthly as opposed to annual state-level data, and the empirical specification was more parsimonious in control variables because there is very little within-year variation in measured demographics. The dependent variable was per capita AFDC-Total caseloads, while the measures of the business cycle were either employment per capita or the unemployment rate. The welfare waiver dummy variables (1 = month waiver was approved) were broken down into four categories: work requirements, time limits, work pays (e.g., higher earnings disregard), and responsibility (e.g., family cap). Finally, there were controls for state fixed effects and time trends, as well as month-of-year dummy variables to control for seasonality in caseloads and employment.

Two additional methodological differences in Ziliak et al. are that the model was estimated in first differences and it had a richer dynamic structure. Ziliak et al. provided evidence that monthly caseloads are nonstationary in levels but stationary in first-differences. Moreover, they introduced dynamics into the model in the form of state dependence (6 lags of the dependent variable), lagged business cycles (11 lags of employment per capita), and an "implementation lag" for the welfare waivers. The implementation lag was defined as the number of months since approval and was designed to capture the fact that it may take several months or even years to revamp the program with the reforms in place.

The results and subsequent policy implications of Ziliak et al. differ markedly from those in the CEA and Blank. Ziliak et al. gave much more weight to the business cycle relative to welfare reform in explaining the recent decline. The small overall effect of welfare waivers arises because the type of waiver that a state adopts matters for aggregate caseload levels: some are caseload-decreasing while others are caseload-enhancing. In simulations of the dynamic model, they showed that work requirements and responsibility waivers significantly reduce caseloads, yet waivers that make work more attractive increase caseloads by nearly the same percentage. Ziliak et al. conducted a limited reconciliation of their results with those of the CEA and Blank and concluded that the key difference arose through the modeling of dynamics.

In the following sections, we expand on the reconciliation begun in Ziliak et al. One issue that we do not address econometrically is the effect of lead waivers. As mentioned above, Blank did not believe that the lead variables signal true program effects. Martini and Wiseman (1997) went even further in their critique of the CEA's use of lead effects, arguing that many of the waivers are not "threatening" per se and the one waiver that might be perceived as threatening, "JOBS sanctions," has no significant lead effect. Moreover, they claimed that it is unlikely that welfare recipients would respond one year in advance of waiver approval when the approval date is so uncertain, and that if lead effects are to be interpreted literally, then all states without waivers as of August 1995 should be coded with a lead effect anticipating PRWORA. However, the latter would be unreasonable, because passage of PRWORA was uncertain up to a month before President Clinton signed it into law. Additionally, Ziliak et al. presented evidence that lead effects disappear in annual first-difference models. Because of these limitations, we do not explore the role of lead waivers further. Consequently, our reconciliation focuses on the CEA's specification 2, which does not control for lead waiver effects.

RECONCILING THE CEA AND ZILIAK ET AL.

The data used in this study are the same as those employed by the CEA. Although Ziliak et al. used state-level monthly data, for the purposes of the reconciliation it is most instructive to use the same data as the CEA in order to abstract from data issues and focus on modeling choices. The annual state-level panel data are for the 1976–1996 federal fiscal years and contain information on AFDC recipients, state unemployment rates, state population, real AFDC maximum benefits for a family of three, and statewide welfare waivers. In addition to the CEA data, we collected information on caseload levels by state and year. The reader is referred to the CEA technical report (1997) for more extensive details about the data.

We begin our reconciliation by replicating specification 2 from Table 2 of the CEA. This static model regresses the log of AFDC recipients per capita on the unemployment rate, the real maximum AFDC benefit for a family of three, year dummies, and state-specific fixed effects and trends. The year dummies control for macroeconomic factors that affect all states in a given year, such as federal expansions in the Earned Income Tax Credit or oil-price shocks. Meanwhile, the controls for time-invariant state fixed effects and for state-specific trends are intended to capture not only fixed unobserved state-specific propensities to take up welfare, but also slow-moving state-specific trends in demographics such as fertility rates, marital status, and migration patterns. Thus, the static model for each state i ($i = 1, \ldots,$ 51) in period t ($t = 1, \ldots, 21$) is

Eq. 1 $R_{it} = \mu + \alpha UR_{it} + \beta W_{it} + \theta B_{it} + \gamma_t + \delta_i + \lambda_i t + \varepsilon_{it}$,

where

   R_{it} = the natural log of per capita AFDC recipients
   UR_{it} = the unemployment rate
   W_{it} = the welfare reform indicator that equals the fraction of a year (based on the approval date) that "any statewide waiver" is in effect
   B_{it} = the real maximum AFDC benefit for a family of three
   γ_t = a vector of year effects

δ_i = the time-invariant state-specific deviation from the overall constant μ

$\lambda_i t$ = the state-specific trend,

ε_{it} = a random error.

To control for possible heteroskedasticity, the regression is weighted by state population.

In column 1 of Table 1, we present the base-case, weighted-least-squares estimates of the effects of the business cycle and welfare reform on per capita AFDC recipients (CEA's specification 2). The results suggest that a 1-percentage-point increase in the unemployment rate will yield a 3.1 percent increase in per capita AFDC recipients. Alternatively, states with a statewide welfare waiver experience a 5.5 percent decline in AFDC recipiency relative to states without a waiver.[5] The point estimates are useful for decomposing the fraction of the 1993–1996 decline in recipients attributable to the business cycle and to welfare reform. The estimates indicate that the robust economy accounted for 31 percent of the decline, while welfare reform accounted for 16 percent.

Recipients versus Caseloads

The first step towards reconciling the results from Ziliak et al. with those from the CEA involves the choice of dependent variable. Ziliak et al. used AFDC caseloads per capita as the dependent variable, rather than the number of AFDC recipients. Cases may be preferred to recipients because the latter confounds the number of households receiving AFDC with the within-household fertility behavior. In addition, the number of cases may better represent the underlying household behavioral response to changes in economic conditions and welfare reform, because it is the adult who makes the decision about whether or not to participate in AFDC. In most situations, there is only one adult per AFDC household, while there may be several children, so the caseload correlates most closely with the number of decision makers. Lastly, there appears to be more political interest in understanding the factors that affect the number of cases than those that determine the number of recipients per se. In fact, most welfare reform waivers are designed to affect the caseload rather than the number of recipients.

Table 1 Sensitivity of Static Estimates of the Impact of Welfare Reform and the Business Cycle on per Capita AFDC Recipients in the pre-TANF Period[a]

Variable	Col. 1[b]	2	3	4	5	6	7	8	9
Unemployment rate	3.092	2.882	2.647	3.216	3.620	3.007	-0.978	1.018	1.424
	(0.264)	(0.245)	(0.220)	(0.262)	(0.244)	(0.267)	(0.457)	(0.235)	(0.266)
Any waiver	-5.450	-5.414	-8.183	-5.062	-6.327	-3.314	-1.451	-.911	-0.123
	(1.947)	(1.815)	(2.067)	(1.921)	(2.272)	(2.091)	(1.529)	(1.181)	(1.254)
% of 1993–1996 decline due to the economy	30.5	29.5	26.1	31.7	35.7	29.7	-9.7	10.0	14.1
% of 1993–1996 decline due to welfare reform	15.8	15.7	23.7	14.6	18.3	9.6	4.2	2.6	0.4

[a] All coefficients are multiplied by 100. Standard errors are in parentheses. The data are annual and pertain to all 50 states and the District of Columbia. Unless noted otherwise, all regressions are based on fiscal years 1976–1996, use total recipients, are weighted by the state population, use levels, and have controls for the real maximum benefit guarantee for a family of 3, state-specific fixed effects, state-specific trends, and year dummies.

[b] Col. 1 = CEA (1997) specification 2.   Col. 6 = Blank (1998) sample period
Col. 2 = AFDC caseloads   Col. 7 = Ziliak et al. (1997) sample period
Col. 3 = cubic trend   Col. 8 = first differences
Col. 4 = no AFDC benefits   Col. 9 = unweighted first differences
Col. 5 = unweighted

To test the sensitivity of the model estimates to the choice of dependent variable, we report the results from a model of AFDC case-loads in column 2 of Table 1. The estimates are nearly identical, especially for the welfare waivers, to those from the model with AFDC recipients reported in column 1. This indicates that the differences between the CEA and Ziliak et al. are not due to the use of a different dependent variable.[6]

Year Dummies versus Cubic Trend

The next dimension that differentiates the models of the CEA and Ziliak et al. is in the way that they controlled for period-specific macro-economic factors that are common to all states. The CEA used annual year dummies; Ziliak et al. used a cubic trend because they used monthly data, and rather than append 120 month dummies to the regression, they parameterized the national trends with a cubic polynomial in order to capture the fall (1987–1990), rise (1990–1993), and subsequent fall (1993–1996) in caseloads. It is not clear *a priori* whether the use of a cubic trend is likely to favor the business cycle or welfare reform relative to year dummies.

Column 3 reports the sensitivity of the model estimates to the use of a cubic trend rather than year dummies. Relative to column 1, it appears that the cubic trend imputes less of an effect to the economy and considerably more to welfare reform; that is, the fraction of the 1993–1996 decline attributable to the economy falls to 26 percent and the fraction attributable to welfare reform rises to 24 percent. This suggests that, if anything, the specification used by Ziliak et al. is likely to favor welfare reform relative to the economy. Since Ziliak et al. attributed a smaller effect to welfare reform relative to the CEA, it is clear that the choice of a cubic trend cannot explain the discrepancy in results.

Benefits versus No Benefits

Unlike the studies by the CEA and Blank, Ziliak et al. did not include welfare benefit levels as a regressor because of the lack of suitable instruments that could deal with the possible simultaneity with recipiency. It is sensible to think that while benefit levels might explain welfare recipiency, the size of the caseload might also affect the benefit level. Indeed, the simultaneity between welfare benefits and recipiency has been shown by Figlio, Kolpin, and Reid (forthcoming), Gramlich and Laren (1984), and Shroder (1995). Nonetheless, it is instructive to examine the sensitivity of the estimated business-cycle and welfare-reform effects to the inclusion of welfare benefits, even though they may be endogenous.

Column 4 of Table 1 presents a reduced-form version of the base-case model in which welfare benefits are omitted. As shown, the estimated welfare-reform and business-cycle effects differ trivially whether one includes or omits welfare benefits. Again, this suggests that controlling for welfare benefits, even if endogenous but treated as if they are exogenous, does not lead to substantive differences between Ziliak et al. and the CEA.

Weighted versus Unweighted

Both the CEA and Blank weighted their regression models; the CEA used total population and Blank used the population of women between the ages of 15 and 45 (under the assumption that the latter are more likely at risk for entering AFDC). On the other hand, Ziliak et al. did not weight their regression model. In general, weighting a regression model is recommended in situations of nonrandom sampling, nonspherical disturbances, or random parameter heterogeneity (Deaton 1997, pp. 67–73). Since all 50 states and the District of Columbia are represented in the data, they clearly are not subject to problems associated with nonrandom sample-selection bias. The disturbances may, however, be nonspherical, most likely in the form of heteroskedasticity (and serial correlation in the absence of controls for caseload dynamics). Nonetheless, it not clear that the only source of heteroskedasticity arises from population as assumed in the CEA and Blank. A more agnostic approach is to assume that the form of heteroskedasticity is unknown and to simply adjust standard errors using the Eicker-Huber-White correction.

Martini and Wiseman (1997) criticized the CEA for weighting by arguing that if states are viewed as "laboratories" for waiver experiments, then each state should be given equal weight. Indeed, we have no *a priori* reason to believe that a state's population factored into

HHS's decision-making process for welfare waivers. Martini and Wiseman's argument suggests that the impact of waivers is homogeneous across states, and if so, then unweighted regression is superior to weighted regression on efficiency grounds. If, instead, we expect the responses to the experiments to be different across states, then weighting like that of the CEA and Blank produces consistent estimates when the parameter heterogeneity is unrelated to the other variables in the regression model (i.e., random coefficients). If this is a correct parameterization of the unobserved heterogeneity, then the usual weighted-least-squares standard errors are incorrect, although this obviously has no effect on the parameter estimates (Deaton 1997, p. 73). Indeed, as long as the model is correctly specified, there should be no significant difference between weighted and unweighted parameter estimates. If, however, the model is misspecified (e.g., through a lack of controls for caseload, business-cycle, and welfare-reform dynamics), then weighted and unweighted parameter estimates may diverge.

In column 5 of Table 1, we report unweighted business-cycle and welfare-reform estimates. Weighting by population in column 1 has the effect of reducing the estimated impact of both the business cycle and welfare waivers. The fraction of the 1993–1996 decline attributable to the economy rises from 31 to 36 percent, while the fraction attributable to welfare reform rises from 16 to 18 percent when moving from weighted to unweighted regression analysis. The downward effect that weighting has on the waiver estimates is most likely due to the fact that the larger states had both relatively smaller caseload declines and later (or no) pre-TANF waiver approvals. Likewise, these larger states also experienced less-pronounced reductions in their unemployment rates. Because the share of the caseload decline due to the business cycle and welfare reform between the weighted and unweighted models differs by about 17 percent, this suggests that the static model in Eq. 1 is misspecified. However, because the proportionate increase attributable to the economy and to welfare reform is nearly identical, weighting the regression model is not likely the primary source of difference between the CEA and Ziliak et al.

Sample Period

The CEA's estimates were based on federal fiscal years 1976–1996, while Blank used 1977–1995 fiscal years and Ziliak et al. used 1987–1996 fiscal years (although the latter used monthly, not annual, data). Because many states did not receive a welfare waiver until 1995 or 1996, it is possible that ending the sample in 1995 (as Blank did) would lead to a lower welfare-reform estimate. However, her estimated business-cycle effect should be quite comparable to that of the CEA because both samples include the dramatic contraction and subsequent expansion of the 1980s. The sample used in Ziliak et al., on the other hand, included the entire pre-TANF waiver period (like the CEA) but misses the substantial cyclical movements of the late 1970s and early 1980s. This suggests that Ziliak et al. and the CEA should have comparable welfare-reform estimates, but that the Ziliak et al. business-cycle effect may be either dampened or strengthened relative to the CEA, depending on the relative changes in caseloads associated with economic fluctuations.[7]

Columns 6 and 7 in Table 1 present business-cycle and welfare-reform estimates for the sample periods used by Blank and Ziliak et al., respectively. In general, the results confirm prior expectations, especially with regard to the 1977–1995 sample used by Blank. The fraction of the decline attributable to the economy using Blank's sample period is about 30 percent, compared with the 31 percent in the base model (Column 1). Alternatively, the fraction due to welfare reform is a much lower 9.6 percent due to the termination of the sample at the same time that many states were still in the process of receiving waiver approvals. The results in column 7 based on the Ziliak et al. sample, however, are somewhat perverse, in that a negative 9.7 percent share is attributed to the economy and only a 4.2 percent share to welfare reform. In annual data, we expect the Ziliak et al. sample may yield a smaller share to the economy than the CEA, but not a negative share.[8]

The differences in the point estimates in columns 1 and 7 seem too pronounced to be explained simply by different aggregate macroeconomic conditions between 1976 and 1987. Indeed, further analysis indicates that the differences (at least for the welfare waivers) are explained to a large extent by three states: Florida, Iowa, and Michigan. Eliminating those three states yields welfare waiver coefficients of −1.69 for the CEA sample period and −2.22 for the Ziliak et al. sample period. However, the coefficient on unemployment remains negative in the Ziliak et al. sample. What is special about Florida, Iowa, and Michigan that by eliminating them from the sample makes the welfare-waiver effects comparable across sample periods? From 1987–1992, these three states saw a 19 percent increase in the caseload, while the rest of the country saw a slightly larger increase of 22 percent. However, from 1976–1987, the two sets were much different: the three states saw an increase of 11 percent when the rest of the country saw a reduction of 7 percent. As a result, from 1976–1992, these three states saw an increase of 30 percent while the rest of the country saw an increase of 15 percent. From 1992–1996, the three states saw a decline of 16 percent while the rest of the country saw a decline of 12 percent. Put differently, Florida, Iowa, and Michigan saw a bigger deviation from trend in the welfare-reform years than did the rest of the country. This suggests that the sample period matters in the annual static model, but it is not clear whether the CEA's period is preferable to the Ziliak et al. period, because the differences in welfare-reform estimates are driven by a few states.

Levels versus First Differences

The CEA model in Eq. 1 above is estimated in levels; however, Ziliak et al. estimated their model in first differences. It is important to note that asymptotically fixed effects and first differences should provide the same point estimates as long as the model is well specified. The two estimators could diverge if there is measurement error in the regressors or if there are misspecified dynamics either in the form of a nonstationarity in caseloads or in state dependence. Ziliak et al. presented evidence that nonstationarity in AFDC caseloads is likely to be a problem, especially at the monthly level but also in annual data; indeed, formal augmented Dickey-Fuller tests cannot reject the null hypothesis of a unit root at the 5 percent level. In many panel-data applications, nonstationarity is less problematic because the asymptotics are based on the cross-sectional dimension (e.g., Holtz-Eakin, Newey, and Rosen 1988, p. 1373). However, in the CEA and Ziliak et al. papers, the cross-sectional dimension was only 51, which is substantially less than "large" as typically implied in panel-data asymptotics, and thus suggests that nonstationarity cannot be dismissed out of hand.

Columns 8 and 9 in Table 1 present weighted and unweighted first-difference estimates, respectively. Both specifications yield substantially lower point estimates relative to the levels models. The fraction of the 1993–1996 decline attributable to the economy falls to 10 (14) percent, while the fraction attributable to welfare reform falls to a meager 2.6 (0.4) percent in the weighted (unweighted) model. Because of the substantial difference in parameter estimates, this suggests that the static model in Eq. 1 suffers from some form of misspecification, whether it be nonstationarity, lack of controls for state dependence, measurement error, or some combination of the three. Ziliak et al. argued that the difference is due to nonstationarity and state dependence in caseloads; however, they did not address the possibility of measurement error. It may be the case that measurement error in state unemployment rates is exacerbated in the monthly data relative to annual and in first-differences relative to fixed effects as noted by Griliches and Hausman (1986). If that is the case, then Ziliak et al. should be biasing their estimates of the effect of the macroeconomy toward zero relative to the CEA by estimating the first-difference model with monthly data. This bias, however, is in the opposite direction to that argued by those who believe the Ziliak et al. model is somehow biased toward the macroeconomy. We do not formally address the issue of measurement error here, but instead proceed with the maintained assumption in CEA, Blank, and Ziliak et al., i.e., that unemployment rates are not measured with error.

Static versus Dynamic Specifications

We now extend the static model in Eq. 1 to allow a detailed parameterization of dynamics. As shown in Ziliak et al., these dynamics are manifest both in the form of state dependence in caseloads and in lagged responses to cyclical movements in the economy. Specifically, even after controlling for heterogeneity in the form of state-specific fixed effects and trends, previous AFDC recipiency may have a direct impact on future recipiency, i.e., recipiency may sluggishly adjust to changing economic and political conditions. In addition, we expect lagged unemployment to be important as well because welfare recipients are likely to be the last ones hired during an economic recovery and thus may not instantaneously move from welfare to work.

We consider two variants of the dynamic model, one in levels and the other in first differences. The dynamic levels estimating equation is

$$\text{Eq. 2} \quad R_{it} = \mu + \sum_{s=1}^{s} \rho_s R_{it-s} + \sum_{j=0}^{j} \alpha_j UR_{it-j} + \beta W_{it}$$

$$+ \theta B_{it} + \gamma_t + \delta_i + \lambda_i t + \varepsilon_{it}$$

and the dynamic first-difference estimating equation is

$$\text{Eq. 3} \quad \Delta R_{it} = \sum_{s=1}^{S} \rho_s \Delta R_{it-s} + \sum_{j=0}^{J} \alpha_j \Delta UR_{it-j} + \beta \Delta W_{it}$$

$$+ \theta \Delta B_{it} + \tilde{\gamma}_t + \lambda_i + \Delta \varepsilon_{it}$$

where all variables are defined as in Eq. 1 and where $\tilde{\gamma}_t$ in Eq. 3 is a re-normalized vector of year effects. Notice that in Eq. 2 and 3 the lag lengths for recipiency and the unemployment rate are not restricted to be the same. One can approach the issue of lag length either by starting broadly and then eliminating lags to improve model fit or by starting with a short lag structure and adding additional lags. We use the latter approach, in conjunction with the Schwarz criterion, and find that four lags of recipiency rates and unemployment rates provides the best model fit.

In Table 2 we present the estimates of the dynamic models for a variety of specifications, including levels and first differences, weighted and unweighted, and the Ziliak et al. sample period. Column 1 presents weighted estimates of Eq. 2, which is the dynamic analogue to the weighted static CEA model in Table 1. The estimates reveal a strong degree of state dependence and lagged responses to changes in the unemployment rate. Important here is the change in the fractions of the decline attributable to the macroeconomy and to welfare reform in the dynamic context: we now attribute about 48 percent of the decline to the economy and –6.7 percent to welfare reform. The negative impact of welfare reform follows from the positive coefficient on "any waiver." A positive coefficient on welfare reform is not implausible if one considers that the variable "any waiver" is an aggregate of all waiver types,

Table 2 Sensitivity of Dynamic Estimates of the Impact of Welfare Reform and the Business Cycle on per Capita AFDC Recipients in the pre-TANF Period[a]

Variable	Levels models				First difference models			
	Col. 1	2	3	4	5	6	7	8
Recipients ($t-1$)	118.737	114.263	73.108	62.218	53.429	46.889	42.166	37.384
	(3.542)	(5.332)	(6.828)	(7.933)	(3.638)	(5.077)	(7.010)	(7.534)
Recipients ($t-2$)	-51.848	-45.374	-37.426	-33.053	-15.044	-12.532	-19.022	-17.454
	(5.463)	(6.192)	(8.564)	(8.459)	(4.022)	(4.559)	(7.534)	(7.333)
Recipients ($t-3$)	9.761	11.883	-0.937	3.368	5.456	8.277	-6.607	-1.954
	(5.275)	(5.165)	(9.592)	(7.745)	(3.983)	(3.874)	(8.825)	(7.131)
Recipients ($t-4$)	-6.533	-9.856	-7.456	-6.545	-5.890	-8.168	-13.519	-8.679
	(3.265)	(3.481)	(8.380)	(6.060)	(3.270)	(3.319)	(8.828)	(6.335)
Unemployment rate (t)	0.835	1.594	-0.443	-0.032	0.809	1.434	-0.534	0.014
	(0.216)	(0.275)	(0.523)	(0.428)	(0.219)	(0.281)	(0.534)	(0.446)
Unemployment rate ($t-1$)	0.541	0.258	-0.055	0.159	1.105	1.259	-0.160	0.023
	(0.262)	(0.297)	(0.456)	(0.350)	(0.205)	(0.226)	(0.460)	(0.350)
Unemployment rate ($t-2$)	-0.035	-0.108	0.433	0.521	0.603	0.611	0.671	0.659
	(0.259)	(0.279)	(0.427)	(0.336)	(0.210)	(0.227)	(0.425)	(0.318)
Unemployment rate ($t-3$)	0.437	0.292	0.562	0.426	0.653	0.480	0.760	0.614
	(0.253)	(0.270)	(0.419)	(0.340)	(0.202)	(0.215)	(0.427)	(0.372)
Unemployment rate ($t-4$)	0.393	0.527	0.623	0.807	0.712	0.581	0.993	0.872
	(0.197)	(0.216)	(0.507)	(0.406)	(0.204)	(0.218)	(0.496)	(0.409)
Any waiver	1.056	-0.175	0.887	0.604	0.610	0.505	1.477	1.415
	(0.772)	(0.906)	(0.927)	(1.088)	(0.929)	(1.274)	(0.974)	(1.194)

% of 1993–1996 decline due to the economy	47.5	56.4	18.3	30.5	68.9	75.5	22.9	30.7
% of 1993–1996 decline due to welfare reform	−6.7	1.1	−4.2	−2.8	−3.1	−2.5	−5.6	−5.7

[a] All coefficients are multiplied by 100. Standard errors are in parentheses. The data are annual and pertain to all 50 states and the District of Columbia. Unless noted otherwise, all regressions are based on fiscal years 1976–1996, use total recipients, are weighted by the state population, are in levels, and have controls for the real maximum benefit guarantee for a family of 3, state-specific fixed effects, state-specific trends, and year dummies.

[b] Col. 1 = base case
Col. 2 = unweighted
Col. 3 = Ziliak et al. sample period
Col. 4 = unweighted + Ziliak et al. sample period

Col. 5 = base case
Col. 6 = unweighted
Col. 7 = Ziliak et al. sample period
Col. 8 = unweighted + Ziliak et al. sample period

and a positive effect simply implies that the weighted impact of case-load-increasing waivers (e.g., higher earnings disregards and asset limits) dominates caseload-decreasing waivers. Ziliak et al., in their dynamic model of monthly data, disaggregated waiver types into work requirements, time limits, work incentives, and responsibility waivers and also permitted lag effects of waivers, yet still found that, for the nation as a whole, the economy accounts for 66 percent of the 1993–1996 decline and welfare reform for –9 percent. This suggests that the results in Table 2 are not an artifact of the aggregated "any waiver" specification. Consequently, controlling for dynamics in welfare recipiency enhances the role of the economy and reduces the role of welfare reform in accounting for the decline in welfare utilization between 1993 and 1996.

We also reconsider several of the model specifications reported in Table 1; in particular, in the static model we found that there are differences depending on whether one weights the regression. In column 2 (Table 2) we report the results from the unweighted analogue to column 1. As in the static model, the contributions of both the macroeconomy and welfare reform increase relative to the weighted model, although the share attributable to welfare reform is effectively zero. We also noted that the results are sensitive to sample period. Hence, in columns 3 and 4, we present weighted and unweighted parameter estimates from the Ziliak et al. sample period. While the welfare reform effects are quite comparable (columns 3 and 4 relative to columns 1 and 2), the share of the decline attributable to the economy falls substantially.[9] This result underscores the potential pitfall of using a relatively short time horizon to identify business-cycle effects. Again, however, it is important to emphasize that this criticism does not apply directly to the Ziliak et al. paper, as they used 120 months rather than 10 years.

Lastly, we address the issue of levels versus first differences in columns 5 to 8. Recall that dynamics might arise not only from state dependence and lagged responses to unemployment rates, but also through nonstationarity. Columns 5 and 6 indicate that first differences increase the fraction of the decline attributable to the robust economy a further 45 percent over the col. 1 weighted model (to 69 percent) and by 34 percent over the col. 2 unweighted model (to 76 percent). Interestingly, though, the first-difference specifications do little to the welfare reform estimates. Consequently, while the dynamic first-difference specification enables the model to identify a larger role for the macroeconomy relative to a dynamic levels model, this is not accomplished at the expense of welfare reform, but instead from other previously unobserved factors in the model (such as state-specific trends).[10]

In summary, we conclude from our reconciliation that the majority of the difference in model estimates between the CEA and Ziliak et al. arises from the treatment of dynamics. These dynamics surface in the form of nonstationarities in caseloads, sluggish adjustment of current caseloads to past caseloads, and lags in the response of caseloads to changes in unemployment rates. First-differencing to eliminate a possible nonstationarity permits the dynamic model to attribute a larger role to the macroeconomy relative to a static or dynamic levels model. However, after differencing the dynamic model, weighting the regression no longer has a substantive impact on the parameter estimates. The primary consequence of controlling for caseload dynamics is to reduce the role of welfare reform relative to the macroeconomy in accounting for the decline in AFDC recipiency. Our preferred model specification indicates that the macroeconomy accounted for three-quarters of the 1993–1996 decline in welfare recipients, while welfare reform had a negligible impact.

WHAT WILL HAPPEN TO RECIPIENCY RATES IN THE NEXT RECESSION?

A key issue confronting policymakers is how welfare caseloads might respond in the event of a recession. If AFDC cases only respond weakly to business-cycle conditions, then we would expect the welfare-program budget surpluses that many states have enjoyed recently to persist even into a recessionary period. Alternatively, if caseloads are strongly countercyclical, then states who have failed to save for a "rainy day" may face difficult fiscal constraints during the next cyclical downturn. Moreover, if the robust economy has fostered implementation of welfare reform, then when the economy turns toward recession this interrelationship may become disentangled. To address these issues, we use several of the dynamic models from Table 2 to examine the responsiveness of recipiency rates to alternative "shocks" to unemployment. We then investigate the extent to which the economy and welfare reform are interrelated and the implications of this link in the event of a recession.[11]

Dynamic Short-Run and Long-Run Simulations

In Table 3 we present both short-run and long-run impacts of alternative unemployment rate increases on recipiency rates. Specifically, based on the parameter estimates from the dynamic models in Table 2, we solve for the long-run, steady-state impact of the unemployment rate on recipiency rates. We then simulate the impact of unemployment rate increases of 1 to 5 percentage points four years into the future; these simulations are possibly more reasonable estimates given that the long-run steady state is rarely attained. While our preferred model in Table 2 is the unweighted, dynamic first-difference column 6, we also present simulation results for the weighted and unweighted dynamic levels models (from columns 1 and 2, as well as the weighted, dynamic first-difference model in column 5).

The first column of Table 3 contains the implied long-run effect of a 1-percentage-point increase in the unemployment rate on welfare recipiency. This effect ranges from 6.26 percent in the weighted, dynamic first-difference model to 8.81 percent in the unweighted, dynamic levels model. Interestingly, although the short-run effect of the unemployment rate on recipiency is higher in the first-differences models relative to levels, the levels models imply a larger long-run effect because the adjustment to the long-run equilibrium is more attenuated in levels. Most important, however, the long-run equilibrium estimates underscore the importance of controlling for dynamics in modeling AFDC recipiency. In the static models of Table 1, the short-run and long-run effects coincide. However, the estimates in Table 3 reinforce the fact that the static model is a misspecification, because the long-run estimates in levels are 2.5 times their static counterparts in Table 1, while the long-run estimates in first differences are 5–6 times the static estimates.

The remaining five columns in Table 3 present estimates four years into the future of increases of various magnitudes in the unemployment

Table 3 Simulated Long-Run and Four-Year Impacts of Alternative Unemployment Rate Increases on Welfare Recipient Rates (%)

Specification	Implied long-run effect of 1 p. pt.[a]	Four-year impact from an unemployment rate increase of				
		1 p. pt.	2 p. pt.	3 p. pt.	4 p. pt.	5 p. pt.
Weighted levels	7.29	3.7	7.4	11.1	14.8	18.5
Unweighted levels	8.81	4.4	8.8	13.1	17.5	21.9
Weighted 1st difference	6.26	5.3	10.7	16.1	21.4	26.8
Unweighted 1st difference	6.66	5.9	11.7	17.6	23.4	29.3

[a] p. pt. = percentage point(s).

rate. For example, after four years, the unweighted first-difference model predicts that a 1-percentage-point increase in the unemployment rate will lead to a 5.9 percent increase in welfare recipients, while a 3-percentage-point increase generates a 17.6 percent increase. In these simulations, the first-difference models yield a larger effect on recipients than the levels models. This arises because the first-difference models yield larger short-run effects relative to levels, and simulations based on a four-year time horizon are dominated by short-run influences. The simulations suggest that welfare caseloads are quite cyclically sensitive, and that if the economy were to make a substantive turn for the worse, many states may experience a surge in welfare recipients.

Interactions between Welfare Reform and the Macroeconomy

An issue neglected up to this point is the potential role of an interaction between welfare reform and the robust economy since 1993 in fostering the rapid decline in AFDC caseloads. We address the possibility of interactions between welfare reform and the business cycle in the context of the dynamic levels and first-differences models in Eq. 2 and 3. Specifically, we consider interactions between the "any waiver" variable with the contemporaneous unemployment rate and then with the full set of current and lagged unemployment rates. If economic activity stimulates the caseload reductions associated with welfare reforms *and if this effect is independent of the "natural" relationship between the business cycle and the welfare caseload*, the coefficients on these interactions will be positive.[12]

In Table 4, we present estimates of the interaction between welfare reform and the macroeconomy on per capita AFDC recipients in the pre-TANF period. For ease of presentation, we suppress the coefficients on the lagged dependent variable and the current and lagged unemployment rates; we present the waiver coefficient along with the interactions. In addition, because the partial effect of welfare reform is dependent on the level of the unemployment rate, we compute the impact of welfare reform after four years in situations with a sustained unemployment rate of 2, 4, 6, or 8 percent. Finally, we also present the *p*-value on the (joint) significance of the interaction term(s); that is, for models with one interaction, the *p*-value refers to the *t*-statistic, while for models with several interactions the p-value refers to a Wald test of the null hypothesis that the interactions are jointly zero.

In the weighted, dynamic levels model column 1, we confirm our prior expectation of a positive interacted effect between the macroeconomy and welfare reform.[13] This interaction is highly significant, with a p-value of 0.00. The model predicts that after four years, welfare reform leads to a 5.6 percent reduction in per capita recipients in states with an unemployment rate of 2 percent, while it leads to an increase of 2.8 percent in states with an unemployment rate of 8 percent. Comparable estimates are found in the fully interacted (column 2) as well as in the multiple-interaction difference specifications (columns 6 and 8), while evidence of a caseload-decreasing effect of welfare reform is less obvious in the unweighted levels models and the single-interaction first-difference specifications. Taken as a whole, the estimates in Table 4 suggest that pre-TANF welfare reform require a robust economy (i.e., low unemployment rates) in order to have a negative impact on recipiency rates.

A Lagniappe

While our primary focus in this paper is to provide a reconciliation between the CEA and Ziliak et al. estimates of the effect of welfare reform and the macroeconomy on per capita AFDC recipients in the pre-TANF period, there is much policy interest in understanding the sources of caseload declines after passage of PRWORA in August 1996. A difficulty in applying the model described here to the post-TANF period is correctly defining the welfare-reform variable, because the reform applies to all states (unlike the pre-TANF waiver programs). Nonetheless, one possible strategy is to use the date of waiver approval for those states that obtained waivers and to use the date of approval for the TANF plan for those states without waivers. We did this, and then updated our data to include observations from the 1997 and 1998 federal fiscal years and re-ran the dynamic levels and first-difference models in Eq. 2 and 3.

The estimates of the impact of the macroeconomy on recipiency rates are nearly identical to those reported in Tables 2 and 3. For instance, the estimated long-run effect of a 1-percentage-point increase in the unemployment rate is 6.55 percent in both the weighted and

42

Table 4 Estimates of the Interaction between Welfare Reform and the Business Cycle on per Capita AFDC Recipients in the pre-TANF Period[a]

Variable	Levels models					First-difference models		
	Col. 1[b]	2	3	4	5	6	7	8
Any waiver	-5.324	-10.787	-4.155	-4.497	-0.895	-5.427	0.312	-1.686
	(2.359)	(3.292)	(2.822)	(3.467)	(3.162)	(6.249)	(4.730)	(6.137)
Any waiver × unemployment rate (t)	1.013	-0.161	0.752	0.713	0.232	-1.080	0.035	0.426
	(0.354)	(0.998)	(0.476)	(1.078)	(0.466)	(1.460)	(0.739)	(1.318)
Any waiver × unemployment rate (t−1)		0.693		-1.328		-2.387		-5.039
		(1.492)		(1.561)		(2.709)		(2.428)
Any waiver × unemployment rate (t−2)		0.816		2.221		7.051		7.895
		(1.324)		(1.376)		(2.611)		(2.410)
Any waiver × unemployment rate (t−3)		0.390		-0.359		-0.983		-0.944
		(1.016)		(1.129)		(1.834)		(1.975)
Any waiver × unemployment rate (t−4)		-0.006		-0.523		-1.890		-2.055
		(0.678)		(0.642)		(1.361)		(1.311)
				Percentage change in recipients after four years				
Unemployment rate of								
2%	-5.6	-5.2	-4.5	-1.4	-0.2	-0.1	0.1	1.1
4%	-1.3	-2.7	-1.9	0.3	0.0	2.0	0.2	2.7
6%	0.8	-0.3	0.6	2.1	0.2	4.0	0.2	4.4
8%	2.8	2.2	3.2	3.9	0.4	6.0	0.2	6.0

Wald test of significance of interactions

P-value	0.00	0.00	0.11	0.08	0.62	0.00	0.96	0.00

[a] All coefficients are multiplied by 100. Standard errors are in parentheses. The data are annual and pertain to all 50 states and the District of Columbia for fiscal years 1976–1996. Each regression controls for 4 lags of per capita recipients, 4 lags of unemployment rates, the real maximum benefit guarantee for a family of 3, state-specific fixed effects, state-specific trends, and year dummies.

[b] Cols. 1 and 2 = weighted   Cols. 5 and 6 = weighted
Cols. 3 and 4 = unweighted   Cols. 7 and 8 = unweighted

unweighted dynamic differences model. However, the welfare-reform variable is uniformly negative in both the levels and differences models, although the effects are relatively small and statistically insignificant. These updated estimates are suggestive, though, that welfare reform has played a larger independent role on the decline in recipiency rates in the post-PRWORA period. The finding of an enhanced welfare reform effect in the post-PRWORA period is fully expected, as our prior, stated in Ziliak et al. (1997), is that welfare reform should take more time to affect caseloads than the period covered in the CEA, Blank, and Ziliak et al. studies.

CONCLUSION

Our reconciliation with the previous caseload literature suggests that the differing conclusions emanate largely from the treatment of dynamics. These dynamics surface in the form of nonstationarities in caseloads, sluggish adjustment of current caseloads to past caseloads, and lags in the response of caseloads to changes in unemployment rates. The primary consequence of controlling for caseload dynamics is to reduce the role of welfare reform relative to the macroeconomy in generating the decline in AFDC caseloads. Our preferred specification, an unweighted, dynamic first-difference model, predicts that the macroeconomy accounted for about 75 percent of the 1993–1996 decline in recipiency rates, while the effect of welfare reform was negligible. We find that the implied long-run effect of a 1-percentage-point increase in the unemployment rate is 2.5 to 6 times the static estimate in levels and first differences. In addition, we find that recipiency rates (caseloads) are quite cyclically sensitive: a 2-percentage-point increase in the unemployment rate leads to an 11.7 percent increase in welfare recipiency after four years, while a 4-percentage-point increase yields a 23.4 percent increase in recipiency.

Further underscoring the important role that the macroeconomy plays in determining caseloads, the analysis suggests that welfare reform efforts have been greatly aided by the simultaneous presence of a robust economy. Bishop (1998) presented evidence that most of the increase in labor force participation rates since 1994 are among single women with children. If a large share of these women are former welfare recipients, then the results here suggest that the movement from welfare to work would be much weaker in a sluggish economy. However, even in the presence of economic growth, many welfare recipients may face substantial personal barriers to employment (Danziger et al. 1998).

This raises the broader task of delineating the goals of welfare reform. Reducing the caseload may be worthy in its own right if one's objective is to reduce the size of government spending, and the results here present evidence on the influence of the macroeconomy and welfare reform in achieving that goal. However, if the objective is to reduce poverty, then the results of this study do not directly speak to the outcomes of former welfare recipients. Unfortunately, many states are not following their former welfare cases; thus, a better understanding of welfare reform is incumbent upon correcting this deficiency.

Notes

We thank our discussant, Robert Moffitt, Sheldon Danziger, Greg Duncan, and Joe Stone for extensive comments on earlier versions of this manuscript. In addition, we are grateful to Jeffrey Russell for excellent research assistance, to Gilbert Crouse at the U.S. Department of Health and Human Services for providing us with the national caseload data, and to Phil Levine for providing the data used in the Council of Economic Adviser's report. Financial support from the U.S. Department of Health and Human Services and the Joint Center for Poverty Research is gratefully acknowledged. All remaining errors are our own. Address correspondence to: James P. Ziliak, Department of Economics, 1285 University of Oregon, Eugene, OR 97403-1285; phone, (541) 346-4681; fax, (541) 346-1243; e-mail, jziliak@oregon.uoregon.edu.

1. For reasons discussed below, the replication of the CEA actually focuses on their specification 2 of Table 2, which predicts a 31 percent share of the decline to the business cycle and a 15 percent share to welfare reform.
2. To a lesser extent we reconcile the results with Blank (1998) as well. Blank focused primarily on the 1990–1993 run-up in caseloads and argued that the economy does not explain this unexpected run-up. Instead, she attributed the increase to a rise in child-only cases, an increase in take-up rates, and a long-term, yet unexplained, increase in eligibility.
3. See Peskin, Tapogna, and Marcotte (1993) for a complete list of these studies.
4. The Basic program, which comprises about 95 percent of total cases, consists of single parents (mainly women) and their children. The UP program permits both parents to be present, although the primary income earner must be under fiscal

stress, e.g., must work less than 100 hours in a month. The UP program was available only in about one-half of the states prior to the Family Support Act of 1988, which mandated all states to offer the program by 1990. However, HHS stopped making the distinction between the Basic and UP programs as of June 1997 because many states only maintain a single program under PRWORA.

5. The estimated welfare-waiver coefficient differs slightly from that reported in the CEA. The discrepancy arises from a miscoded waiver for West Virginia in the original CEA data, as noted in Levine and Whitmore (1998). The different coefficients, coupled with a slightly different weighting scheme, results in our simulations yielding a bit more of the share of the 1993–1996 decline to welfare reform than did the CEA.

6. Blank (1997) differed from the CEA and Ziliak et al. by conducting her analysis for the Basic and UP programs separately. The estimates reported here are very similar to those reported by Blank for the Basic program, but the UP program is much more cyclically sensitive. This suggests that examining total recipients is not misleading if one is interested in movements in the largest segment of the program or in forecasting aggregate recipients in general.

7. Importantly, though, Ziliak et al. actually attributed a larger share to the economy and a smaller share to welfare reform. This is partly due to their use of monthly data, which picks up high-frequency movements in the business cycle, and from the use of a dynamic model as described below.

8. In results not tabulated, we estimated column 7 without weighting the regression model and found the business cycle to have a small, but positive, share of the 1993–1996 decline in recipients.

9. The estimates in columns 3, 4, 7, and 8 are only meant to be suggestive, because the relatively short time horizon may make the coefficients of the lagged dependent variables susceptible to the so-called Nickell bias (Nickell 1981), that is, the bias (toward zero) in the lagged dependent variable that arises from the correlation between the lagged dependent variable and the model's error term. Ziliak et al. argued that this bias is negligible in their sample of monthly data since $T = 120$; however, the annualized version of the Ziliak et al. sample in Table 2 only has $T = 10$. The CEA sample, however, has $T = 21$ and thus again the Nickell bias is likely to be of smaller concern. The latter seems verified in that the results in columns 5 and 6 are quite similar to the results in Ziliak et al.

10. One further difference between Ziliak et al. and the CEA is that Ziliak et al. introduced a "time since waiver approval" variable. We examined a comparable specification in the context of the annual models here without any substantive change in the conclusions. If anything, the share attributable to welfare reform was more negative.

11. There might be some concern that with passage of PRWORA in August 1996, a structural change took place in the relationship between unemployment rates and welfare caseloads. If so, then out-of-sample forecasts based on pre-PRWORA data might be unreliable. We investigated this possibility in the context of a dynamic model of AFDC caseloads using state-level monthly data through March

1998. We interacted the five lags of the unemployment rate with a dummy variable that equaled 1 for any month after September 1996 (the sample began in October 1980) and could not reject the null hypothesis of no change in the unemployment rate coefficients after PRWORA. Hence, this suggests that there was no structural change in the relationship between unemployment rates and welfare caseloads.

12. It might be the case that tests of complementarities between the business cycle and welfare reform are better conducted within a state, as opposed to among states. The reason for this would be that within-state analyses offer a more natural experiment—the welfare reform policy should be relatively uniform within states (rather than among states) and other contemporaneous political and social factors are more likely to be constant within a state. This suggests that the tests conducted here are likely biased against finding complementarities.

13. Levine and Whitmore (1997) found a statistically insignificant impact on the interacted term in their static model. We confirmed their result, but we also found that the interaction was strongly statistically significant without weights. This again underscores the likely misspecification of a static model.

References

Bishop, John. 1998. *Is Welfare Reform Succeeding?* Working paper, Cornell University.

Blank, Rebecca. 1998. *What Causes Public Assistance Caseloads to Grow?* Working paper no. 2, Joint Center for Poverty Research, University of Chicago .

Council of Economic Advisers. 1997. *Technical Report: Explaining the Decline in Welfare Receipt, 1993–1996.* U.S. Council of Economic Advisers. URL: http://www.whitehouse.gov/WH/EOP/CEA/Welfare/Technical_Report.html.

Danziger, Sandra, Mary Corcoran, Sheldon Danziger, Colleen Heflin, Ariel Kalil, Judith Levine, Daniel Rosen, Kristin Seefeldt, Kristine Siefert, and Richard Tolman. 1998. *Barriers to the Employment of Welfare Recipients.* Working paper, University of Michigan.

Danziger, Sheldon, Robert Haveman, and Robert Plotnick. 1981. "How Income Transfers Affect Work, Savings, and the Income Distribution: A Critical Review." *Journal of Economic Literature* 19(3): 975–1028.

Deaton, Angus. 1997. *The Analysis of Household Surveys: A Microeconometric Approach to Development Policy.* Baltimore: Johns Hopkins University Press.

Figlio, David, Van Kolpin and William Reid. Forthcoming. "Do States Play Welfare Games?" *Journal of Urban Economics.*

Gramlich, Edward and Deborah Laren. 1984. "Migration and Income Redistribution Responsibilities." *Journal of Human Resources* 31(1): 489–511.

Griliches, Zvi, and Jerry Hausman. 1986. "Errors in Variables in Panel Data." *Journal of Econometrics* 31: 93–118.

Holtz-Eakin, Douglas, Whitney Newey, and Harvey Rosen. 1988. "Estimating Vector Autoregressions in Panel Data." *Econometrica* 56(1): 1371–1396.

Levine, Phillip B., and Diane M. Whitmore. 1998. "The Impact of Welfare Reform on the AFDC Caseload." *Proceedings of the National Tax Association's Ninetieth (1997) Annual Conference,* Washington, D.C.: National Tax Association, pp. 24–33.

Maharaj, Davan. 1998. "Restaurant, Retail Jobs Go Begging." *The Los Angeles Times,* October 5.

Martini, Alberto, and Michael Wiseman. 1997. "Explaining the Recent Decline in Welfare Caseloads: Is the Council of Economic Advisers Right?" Photocopy, The Urban Institute.

Moffitt, Robert. 1987. "Historical Growth in Participation in Aid to Families with Dependent Children: Was There a Structural Shift?" *Journal of Post-Keynesian Economics* 9(3): 347–363.

Moffitt, Robert. 1992. "Incentive Effects of the U.S. Welfare System: A Review." *Journal of Economic Literature* 30(1): 1–61.

Nickell, Stephen. 1981. "Biases in Dynamic Models with Fixed Effects." *Econometrica* 49: 1399–1416.

Peskin, Janice, John Tapogna, and David Marcotte. 1993. "Forecasting AFDC Caseloads, with an Emphasis on Economic Factors." Congressional Budget Office, Staff memorandum, July.

Shroder, Mark. 1995. "Games the States Don't Play: Welfare Benefits and the Theory of Fiscal Federalism." *Review of Economics and Statistics* 77(1): 183–190.

Ziliak, James P., David N. Figlio, Elizabeth E. Davis, and Laura S. Connolly. 1997. *Accounting for the Decline in AFDC Caseloads: Welfare Reform or Economic Growth?* Discussion paper no. 1151–97, Institute for Research on Poverty, University of Wisconsin-Madison.

What Goes Up Must Come Down?
Explaining Recent Changes in Public Assistance Caseloads

Geoffrey Wallace
University of Wisconsin–Madison

and

Rebecca M. Blank
University of Michigan

Over the past decade, public assistance caseloads have increased rapidly to a historical high point and then decreased with even greater speed to their lowest level in decades. Several recent papers have focused on the rise in Aid to Families with Dependent Children (AFDC) caseloads in the early 1990s and the turn around in the mid 1990s. This research indicates that both macroeconomic factors and program factors appear to be important for these changes. A key question is whether these recent declines are permanent and how much they might turn around in a more sluggish economy. This paper is focused on the relationship between recent caseload changes and the overall economy, comparing estimates from a wide variety of models using both annual and monthly data. By using monthly data, which is available through late 1998, we also present several rough estimates of the impact of welfare reform after 1996.

The Food Stamp program has also experienced major program changes, although it has remained relatively unchanged for single mothers and their children who once participated in AFDC. This paper also provides a detailed comparative analysis of AFDC/TANF caseload changes with food stamp caseload changes.

The welfare reform legislation of 1996 has been cited as a primary reason why AFDC/TANF caseloads began a steep decline in the mid 1990s. This legislation, which states were required by law to implement by July 1997, abolished the AFDC program and replaced it with the TANF block grant, giving states much greater discretion over the design of cash assistance and related work programs for low-income families. The extent of change in state public assistance programs following this legislation has been enormous. Virtually all states have implemented major changes in the way in which they determine eligibility, require and support work effort, and organize their public assistance offices.[1]

These program changes occurred in a very strong labor market. At the end of 1998, the unemployment rate was at a 30-year low. Among workers who lacked a high school diploma, unemployment was near 7 percent, after being in the double digits for years. This has led many observers to suggest that program reform may be less important to the decline in caseloads than many states are claiming. The widespread availability of jobs should have produced a steep decline in caseloads even in the absence of program changes. The question of how much caseload decline can be explained by economic factors is particularly important in forecasting future caseload changes. If the decline is largely due to tight labor markets, it may be more reversible in a future economic downturn than if the decline is due to tightened eligibility rules or greater "diversion" activities (keeping people off public assistance by providing one-time assistance or requiring participation in job search activities).

Figure 1 shows AFDC/TANF and food stamp caseloads from 1980 through 1998. Note that food stamp caseloads are consistently about twice as high as AFDC/TANF caseloads.[2] This reflects the broader eligibility rules in the Food Stamp program. The unusual trends in the past decade are clearly apparent in this figure. AFDC caseloads, which were largely flat from the mid 1970s through 1990, rose by 27 percent between 1990 and 1994, but between 1994 and mid 1998 they fell by 40 percent. In June of 1998, they were at their lowest level since 1972.

Food stamp caseloads follow a remarkably similar trend. They decline slightly faster than AFDC caseloads in the mid 1990s, in part because the legislation that abolished AFDC also cut access to food stamps among a number of immigrant groups and limited their availability to families without children. But they have continued to decline even after the implementation of these changes.

The rapidity of these changes is almost unprecedented. Indeed, the caseload increases of the early 1990s were one reason behind growing support for welfare reform. In turn, the caseload declines that have

Figure 1 AFDC/TANF and Food Stamp Caseloads

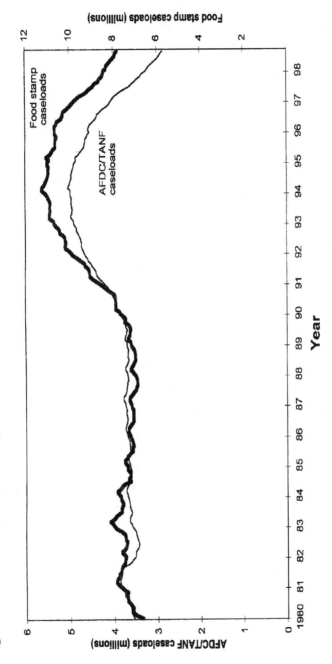

occurred since the enactment of welfare reform have been unexpectedly large in the opinion of most observers. Many of the new state-designed programs funded under the TANF block grant involve time limits and extensive sanctioning policies, as well as efforts at diversion, all of which might be expected to cause caseload declines. These program changes, however, lead to an important caveat: estimates that use historical evidence on the AFDC program to predict future changes in TANF-funded programs are probably unreliable. This is particularly true with regard to macroeconomic effects. As more persons reach time limits or are sanctioned, or as state dollars are more limited, people may be less able to return to the rolls in an economic downturn. The long-term effect of current program changes on the responsiveness of caseloads to a future economic slowdown is hard to foresee with any certainty, although this is a key policy concern.

EXISTING RESEARCH ON CASELOAD CHANGE

Several recent studies have investigated the determinants underlying the caseload changes in AFDC. A host of early studies focus on state-specific data or on data from only a few years.[3] More recent studies have used panel data on caseloads across many years. This includes work by the Council of Economic Advisers (1997), Blank (1997b), Ziliak et al. (1998), and Levine and Whitmore (1998). Table 1 provides a brief comparison of this research. Except for the Blank study, these papers have focused almost entirely on the effect of economic variables and of program-related variables on caseloads. The Blank study went further in trying to utilize a host of demographic and political variables, although these appear to make little difference in her results on the impact of the economy or of programs. Blank's was also the only study to differentiate between the AFDC-Basic program for single parents and the AFDC-UP (unemployed parents) program, a much more limited program for married-couple families.[4]

One topic of concern in these studies is to understand the effect of AFDC "waivers," which allowed states to run experimental welfare programs prior to the 1996 welfare reform legislation. These waivers differed greatly across states, but typically included some combination

Table 1 Major Research on Caseload Change

Study	Data	Dependent variable	Included variables	Results on key variables
Blank (1997b)	Annual state panel 1977–95	ln(AFDC caseloads female pop. ages 15–44) (Also separates this into AFDC-Basic and AFDC-UP caseloads)	Economic (including unemployment) Program (including waivers and AFDC benefits) Demographic Political State effects Year effects	Estimated share of caseload change due to economic factors: • 23% in 1990–94 • 51% in 1994–95
	Monthly state panel 1977–96	VAR model using ln(AFDC caseloads) and unemployment rates as co-determined. (State fixed effects also included.)		One-point rise in unemployment leads to • 3.5% in AFDC-Basic • 20% rise in AFDC-UP over an 18-month period
Council of Economic Advisers (1997)	Annual state panel 1976–96	ln(AFDC caseloads)/total population	Unemployment rates Program (waivers and AFDC benefits) State effects Year effects State year trends	Estimated caseload change due to economic factors: • 24–31% in 1989–93 • 31–45% in 1993–96 4.1% estimated change in AFDC caseloads due to 1-pt. increase in unemployment. –5.2% change due to waivers.

(continued)

Table 1 (continued)

Study	Data	Dependent variable	Included variables	Results on key variables
Levine & Whitmore (1998)	Same as CEA study	Same as CEA study	Same as CEA study, with more detailed data on waivers	Economic effects of same size as CEA study. Waiver states have almost twice the caseload reduction, but no difference in unemployment rates.
Ziliak, Figlio, Davis, & Connolly (1998)	Annual state panel 1987–96	Same as CEA study	Unemployment rates Waiver data State effects Year effects	4.1% estimated change in AFDC caseloads due to 1-pt. increase in unemployment. −9.1% change due to waivers.
	Monthly state panel 1987–96	Same as CEA study	Same as above	No separate estimates of economic effects alone. In 26 states with the largest caseload reduction, 78% of change due to economic *and* seasonal factors, 1993–96.

of time limits, expanded work requirements, expanded earnings disregards, strengthened sanctions, and family caps (limiting AFDC benefits to women who have additional children while receiving AFDC).[5]

Most of these waivers were approved in 1994 or later; following the 1996 legislation, many states with major waivers developed TANF-funded programs that were similar to their waiver programs. States without waivers often looked to the states with waivers for ideas about how to restructure their programs. This suggests that estimates of the impact of these waivers on caseload changes might provide a minimal estimate of the expected effect of welfare reform. We return to this issue below.

As Table 1 demonstrates, the research using annual panel data by state and year produces reasonably consistent results. A 1-point increase in the unemployment rate appears to produce about a 4 percent increase in the AFDC caseload share, while the implementation of a waiver program produced a 5–10 percent decline in caseload share. The economic cycle variables appear to explain about one quarter to one-third of the total caseload change in the early 1990s. In contrast, Ziliak et al. utilized monthly data on caseloads and unemployment rates and found far larger effects for the macroeconomy and smaller effects for program variables. It is difficult to make direct comparisons between their monthly data results and the other studies; this is one reason we estimate both annual and monthly models below. The difference appears to be primarily due to the difference in specifications and in how the results are reported.[6]

The general conclusion from this research is that a host of variables appeared to influence caseload changes through the mid 1990s. While the macroeconomy was important, there is evidence that program changes also had a substantial impact, particularly in states which implemented early waivers. The size and the interpretation of the effect of waiver implementation remain controversial. The increase in caseloads in the early 1990s is only poorly explained in these equations; neither the macroeconomy nor program changes justify the increase that occurred.

WHY FOOD STAMP CASELOADS ARE ALSO INTERESTING

So far as we know, there has been no equivalent analysis of food stamp caseloads to date. This is perhaps surprising, since food stamps have historically been as large a program as AFDC in terms of total expenditures. From a budget perspective, large changes in food stamp caseloads are nearly as costly as large changes in AFDC caseloads, although the states do not bear the cost of food stamps.[7]

Food stamps have historically served a broader population than AFDC and have been available to all low-income persons regardless of family composition, including the elderly as well as younger childless individuals and couples. Hence, a substantial share of the food stamp population does not receive AFDC.[8] On the other hand, most AFDC recipients are food stamp recipients. This share of the food stamp caseload should move in very similar ways to the AFDC caseload,[9] but other food stamp recipients may be less affected by program changes directed at the single-parent AFDC population and may respond differently to changes in the economic environment as well. Some of these other food stamp recipients are elderly and may be quite unresponsive to macroeconomic fluctuations, while others are single individuals or childless couples who might respond more strongly to changes in economic opportunities than single mothers.

The Food Stamp program also experienced major program changes in the mid 1990s. A one-time reduction in food stamp eligibility occurred as a result of the 1996 legislation, when most immigrants were removed from the rolls.[10] In addition, for many areas of the country, childless individuals or families were time-limited in their receipt of food stamps. For most single-parent families—the group that historically received both AFDC and food stamps—little changed in the Food Stamp program, but food stamp receipt has historically been closely linked to AFDC receipt, and the major changes in AFDC/TANF programs will affect food stamp eligibility. For instance, if welfare-to-work programs move most people into intermittent or very-low-wage jobs, they are likely to retain their food stamp eligibility. On the other hand, if these programs move families out of poverty, then food stamp caseloads will fall with TANF caseloads.

As Figure 1 illustrated, food stamp caseloads and AFDC/TANF caseloads have moved in similar ways. This is somewhat surprising. One might have expected the economic expansion that started in 1991 would have affected food stamp caseloads sooner than AFDC. Similarly, because food stamp eligibility was not as affected by waivers and state reform efforts in the mid 1990s, one might not have expected ongoing food stamp caseload declines once food stamp eligibility changes were implemented in 1997.

The close historical correlation between food stamp and AFDC caseload changes suggests that the behavioral and program changes driving AFDC recipiency also affect food stamp recipiency. In this case, the biggest uncertainty in the future evolution of the food stamp program may be whether the transformation from AFDC to TANF will fundamentally change who does or doesn't use food stamps. Historically, AFDC recipients were categorically eligible for food stamps and most states had combined eligibility determination procedures. With the implementation of time limits and restricted eligibility in many state TANF-funded programs, the number of food stamp eligibles who also receive TANF is likely to fall. Whether or not this expected reduction in the TANF-eligible food stamp population results in a fall in food stamp caseloads depends on whether individuals know about their continuing food stamp eligibility.[11] Whether food stamp receipt will remain as closely linked to TANF receipt as it was to AFDC receipt remains to be seen.

ESTIMATES OF THE DETERMINANTS OF BOTH AFDC/TANF AND FOOD STAMP CASELOADS

In this section, we provide comparative estimates of the determinants of both AFDC and food stamp caseloads based on annual panel data. Table 2 presents a set of regression estimates of the determinants of AFDC total caseloads based on three different specifications (columns 1 to 3) and compares these with caseload determinants for several food stamp caseload specifications (columns 4 to 6). Annual panel data on caseloads by state and year are used from 1980 through 1996.

Table 2 Estimates of the Determinants of Public Assistance Caseloads[a]

	Col. 1 Total AFDC cases[b]	2 Total AFDC cases[c]	3 Total AFDC cases[d]	4 Food stamp cases[e]	5 Residual food stamp cases[f]	6 Food stamp cases[g]
Unemployment rate	-0.004 (0.006)	0.015** (0.006)	0.008* (0.005)	0.015** (0.005)	0.015 (0.009)	0.007* (0.004)
Unemployment rate$_{-1}$	0.021** (0.009)	0.022** (0.007)	0.020** (0.005)	0.019** (0.006)	0.021* (0.012)	0.007 (0.005)
Unemployment rate$_{-2}$	0.047** (0.006)	0.023** (0.005)	0.019** (0.004)	0.033** (0.005)	0.049** (0.009)	0.021** (0.004)
ln(median wage)	—	-0.644** (0.137)	-0.297* (0.134)	-0.557** (0.121)	-0.550** (0.234)	-0.229** (0.100)
ln(20th wage percentile)	—	-0.115 (0.106)	-0.130 (0.095)	-0.103 (0.093)	-0.247 (0.180)	-0.044 (0.076)
Percent black	—	0.291 (0.871)	3.034* (1.496)	1.704** (0.765)	2.377* (1.482)	1.555** (0.624)
Percent single female heads	—	-0.495 (0.526)	-0.302 (0.428)	1.254** (0.462)	3.697** (0.894)	1.505** (0.377)
Percent nonmarital births	—	1.392** (0.255)	1.025** (0.295)	1.084** (0.224)	0.870* (0.435)	0.375* (0.187)
Years of education	—	-0.140** (0.040)	0.078* (0.045)	-0.117** (0.035)	0.063 (0.068)	-0.046 (0.029)
Percent elderly	—	-1.204** (0.459)	0.565 (0.424)	-0.866* (0.403)	-0.084 (0.781)	-0.253 (0.330)

	(1)	(2)	(3)	(4)	(5)	(6)
Percent immigrants$_{-1}$ (×100)	—	−0.017 (0.025)	0.015 (0.019)	0.019 (0.022)	0.094* (0.042)	0.027 (0.018)
Percent immigrants$_{-2}$ (×100)	—	0.020 (0.027)	−0.024 (0.021)	0.027 (0.023)	−0.025 (0.045)	0.017 (0.019)
Party of Governor (1=Republican)	—	−0.050** (0.008)	−0.042** (0.007)	−0.064** (0.007)	−0.089** (0.014)	−0.039** (0.006)
Both state Senate & House Democratic	—	−0.004 (0.013)	−0.014 (0.011)	−0.004 (0.011)	−0.017 (0.022)	−0.002 (0.009)
Both state Senate & House Republican	—	−0.042** (0.017)	−0.010 (0.014)	−0.031* (0.015)	−0.003 (0.028)	−0.010 (0.012)
AFDC-UP program (1=yes)	—	0.163** (0.015)	0.128** (0.016)	0.068** (0.013)	−0.022 (0.025)	−0.015 (0.011)
ln(maximum AFDC benefit level)	0.542** (0.071)	0.532** (0.061)	0.203** (0.062)	−0.068 (0.054)	−0.413** (0.104)	−0.339** (0.046)
Any major waiver	−0.104** (0.023)	−0.072** (0.020)	−0.040** (0.018)	−0.032* (0.017)	0.061* (0.033)	0.005 (0.014)
AFDC caseloads	—	—	—	—	—	0.509** (0.026)
State effects	Yes	Yes	Yes	Yes	Yes	Yes
Year effects	Yes	Yes	Yes	Yes	Yes	Yes
State time trends	No	No	Yes	No	No	No
Number of obs.	850	850	850	850	850	850

(continued)

Table 2 (continued)

[a] Dependent variable is ln(caseloads/total population). All regressions based on data for 49 states and D.C. from 1980–96. (Data on food stamps in Vermont are not available for this time period. For consistency we drop this state in the AFDC estimates as well.) Standard errors in parentheses. ** indicates significance at the 1 percent level; * at the 5 percent level.

[b] Specification includes unemployment rate + program variables + state and year effects.

[c] Specification is that of Col. 1 + control variables (see pp. 62–63).

[d] Specification is that of Col. 2 + state specific time trends.

[e] Specification is that of Col. 2.

[f] Dependent variable is residual food stamp cases, which equals food stamp caseloads minus estimated AFDC recipients who also receive food stamps (see p. 64).

[g] Specification is Col. 4 + AFDC caseload control.

The dependent variable is the ln(share of caseloads), with caseloads in each state and year divided by total state population.

The models in Table 2 include fixed effects for each state and for each year. This allows each state to have a different constant level of caseloads and controls for any omitted variables in the specification that might be largely constant within states over time. This specification essentially allows the coefficients to be interpreted as the effect of changes in the independent variables over time within a state on a state's caseload. We discuss below the impact of also including state-specific time trends in these models.

The first column presents a specification similar to that used by the CEA (1997), which is quite sparse and includes only unemployment rates and a few program variables. The results are estimated over a longer time period and include 1996, for which data were not available when the CEA report was produced. The second and third columns use a much richer specification, originally utilized by Blank (1997b). The independent variables include four sets of variables.[12] First, a set of economic-related variables are included. The unemployment rate (current, lagged one year, and lagged two years) is probably the best state-specific measure of economic cyclicality. In addition, we have calculated the natural logarithms of median wages and of the 20th quintile of the wage distribution.[13]

Second, a set of state demographic variables are included, consisting of percent elderly, percent black, percent single-female headed families, percent non-marital births, average years of education, and percent immigrant. The immigrant share is defined as the number of newly admitted immigrants in a state divided by the state's total population. The immigrant share is lagged by one and two years to allow time for increases in immigration to affect public assistance caseloads. Third, a set of political variables are included, based on the political affiliation of the governor, whether both state legislative houses are Republican, and whether both state legislative houses are Democratic.

Finally, we include program-related variables. AFDC benefit levels measure the maximum cash support available to a four-person family in the state. A dummy variable for the presence of an AFDC-UP program is included where appropriate. We also include a variable for the share of the year in which a state has a major program waiver approved for implementation in the post-1991 period.[14] As noted above, these waivers allowed states to implement major variations to the AFDC program and were precursors to the TANF-funded programs that flourished after welfare reform.

The coefficients in columns 1 through 3 provide an indication of how AFDC caseloads respond to these variables, particularly the economic and program variables. Column 1 shows results for a model that includes only unemployment rates and program variables, i.e., those variables which often receive the most attention from policymakers. Although the estimating period and the specification are slightly different, the results are very similar to those reported by the CEA (1997). Unemployment has a strong relationship to caseloads, although much of this effect occurs only over time. Three years after a 1-point rise in the unemployment rate, caseloads will have risen by 6.4 percent. Program variables also have strong effects. States that raise their AFDC maximum benefits levels experience a rise in caseloads; states that implemented waivers experienced a decline in caseloads, all else equal.

As earlier researchers indicated, interpreting this waiver coefficient is difficult. These effects are almost surely more than just the direct program effects of the waivers; they probably also include "demonstration effects," whereby individuals who were actually unaffected by the waivers nonetheless changed their behavior because of the strong message states were trying to send that they were going to "get tough" on welfare recipients. Evidence of this is in Blank (1997b), who showed that states with waivers actually saw significant declines in their caseload in the year before the waiver was granted.

Even with state fixed effects included, one might worry that the model in column 1 excludes a large number of variables that might reasonably affect caseloads within a state over time. Column 2 provides a much richer specification. The most striking result in column 2 is that the impact of unemployment and of program variables is quite similar, even when a very rich set of other control variables is included in the model. Although the timing of the unemployment effect is somewhat different in column 2, a 1-point rise in unemployment results in a 6.0 percent rise in caseloads over a three-year period, very similar to column 1. The coefficients on AFDC benefit levels and waivers are virtually identical between the two columns; this is true even though the additional variables in column 2 are collectively quite important in explaining caseload changes over time.

Changes in median wages, in non-marital birth rates, in years of education, and in percent elderly are all important in determining state caseload changes. With regard to state political variables, Republican governors appear to negatively affect AFDC caseloads. There is an additional negative effect on AFDC caseloads if both state legislative branches are controlled by Republicans. The magnitude and significance of these political effects indicate that even prior to TANF, states could affect caseloads, probably through their organization of public assistance offices and the messages which case workers were instructed to deliver to clients. But these variables must be largely uncorrelated with the unemployment and program variables in column 1, since their inclusion has little affect on those coefficients.

Column 3 includes state-specific time trends, in addition to state and year effects. On the one hand, this controls more fully for omitted variables within states that might be trending up or down over time. On the other hand, the effect of the included variables that are validly correlated with caseload changes may be reduced by the inclusion of state-specific time trends if those variables also trend up or down gradually over time. Our own preference is for the specification in column 2, which does not include these state-specific time trends that we think may overcontrol for omitted variables, but the results in column 3 provide a comparison for those who prefer to include state-specific trends.

Column 3 indicates that including controls for state-specific time trends reduces the magnitude of most coefficients, as expected. Yet, almost all of the same variables are significant in columns 2 and 3, and the general conclusions about what drives caseload changes over time within states would be similar regardless of the specification. In column 3, a 1-percentage-point rise in unemployment results in a 4.7 percent increase in caseloads over a three-year period. We interpret column 3 as indicating that state-specific time trends do not change most of the larger conclusions about the determinants of caseloads.

Because we prefer the specification in column 2, we use that specification in analyzing the food stamp data in columns 4 through 6. We have repeated the food stamp regressions with state-specific time trends included, and the results are similar to those seen in comparing columns 2 and 3 (data not shown).

Column 4 estimates total food stamp caseloads using a specification identical to column 2. Ideally, given the very diverse populations on food stamps, one would like to look at single-parent food stamp recipients separately from other recipients, just as one might separate AFDC-Basic and AFDC-UP recipients. Unfortunately, there are no data available which provide regular information on food stamp receipt by family composition by state. Hence, we try two different approaches in order to separate the AFDC population from the rest of the food stamp recipients.

First, we attempt to net out the AFDC population from food stamp caseloads. In each year, we know nationally how many AFDC recipients also receive food stamps.[15] We take this share and multiply it by the number of AFDC recipients in each state and subtract this from the food stamp caseloads. This should leave us with a dependent variable that provides an estimate of non-AFDC food stamp recipients, which we refer to as "residual food stamp cases." This number is used as the dependent variable in column 5. Note that this dependent variable is measured with error; in general, measurement error in the dependent variable will not bias the estimates, but it will increase the standard errors.

Our second effort to net out the effect of AFDC is seen in column 6, where we include AFDC caseloads as a control variable in the regression for total food stamp caseloads. Since food stamp and AFDC recipiency are often jointly determined, there are some endogeneity problems with this approach. Thus, we prefer the estimates in column 5, but we provide the estimates in column 6 as a comparison.

Begin by comparing the determinants of food stamp caseloads in column 4 to the AFDC caseload estimates in columns 1 through 3. Food stamps are more responsive to the unemployment rate than AFDC. A 1-point rise in the unemployment rate will increase the food stamp caseload by 6.8 percent over a three-year period.[16] Like AFDC, food stamp caseloads are also responsive to median wage levels in the state. Food stamps also appear to be more responsive to demographic factors than AFDC. The percent black, the percent single female heads of household, and the percent of nonmarital births significantly increase food stamp caseloads, while years of education and the percent elderly decrease food stamp caseloads.

The political variables have very similar effects on both AFDC and food stamp caseloads. This is unexpected, since there are no avenues by which states can directly affect food stamp eligibility and payment rules through state legislation or regulations. However, to the extent that AFDC and food stamp recipiency are jointly determined, discouraging AFDC participation may also discourage food stamp participation. This historical evidence of a tight link between food stamp caseloads and variables that can only affect food stamps through AFDC receipt is consistent with more recent stories which suggest that current food stamp caseloads are being affected by women leaving the TANF program.

AFDC benefit levels are not highly correlated with food stamp caseloads, although the presence of an AFDC-UP program does cause higher food stamp caseloads, perhaps because it provides easy access to food stamps for the AFDC-UP population. The implementation of waivers appears to have a negative effect on food stamps, although smaller than their effect on AFDC. This result further suggests that food stamp participation is linked to AFDC utilization, since few of these waivers involved changes to food stamp rules, *per se*. Food stamp recipients may also experience some of the same demonstration effects as AFDC recipients, hearing the message about "getting tough" on welfare recipients without clearly distinguishing that it does not apply to the Food Stamp program.

Comparing columns 4 and 5, column 5 provides an (admittedly imprecise) measure of food stamp usage among non-AFDC recipients. We see somewhat stronger responsiveness to unemployment in column 5. A 1-point rise in unemployment results in an 8.5 percent rise in residual food stamp caseloads over three years. The coefficients on wages and on demographic effects are generally similar to those for total food stamp caseloads.

The determinants of residual food stamp usage show strong policy responsiveness. The presence of a major waiver increases the non-AFDC food stamp population, while the increases in the level of AFDC benefits decrease the non-AFDC food stamp population. The sign of the effect of a major waiver and AFDC benefit levels on residual food stamp caseloads is consistent with the hypothesis that the people who are pushed off AFDC because of waiver implementation or falling real benefit levels remain in low-wage employment, thus, retaining their food stamp eligibility. Hence, higher AFDC benefits result in fewer non-AFDC food stamp cases, and waivers (which reduce the AFDC caseload) result in more non-AFDC food stamp cases.

There are some difficulties in the interpretation of column 6, which includes AFDC caseloads as an independent variable explaining food stamp caseloads, because of the endogeneity between AFDC caseloads and food stamp caseloads. AFDC caseloads are highly correlated with food stamp caseloads, and once AFDC caseloads are included in the food stamp regression, other variables generally become much less significant.

In general, the results in Table 2 demonstrate that food stamp caseloads have been quite closely tied to AFDC caseloads, and AFDC program variables affect food stamp receipt. The determinants of food stamp caseloads appear quite similar to the determinants of AFDC caseloads, although food stamp caseloads are somewhat more cyclical and more affected by a range of demographic characteristics.

HOW WELL DO THESE ESTIMATES EXPLAIN BOTH THE RISE AND FALL OF CASELOADS?

The sharp rise and fall in caseloads in the 1990s raises the question of how well these estimates are explaining this pattern. At some level, it would be very surprising if they fully explained these changes; such dramatic changes in program utilization are rarely well explained by smoothly changing economic or demographic variables.

Figure 2 provides a sense of how (in)effectively the rise and fall in caseloads is explained by the control variables in Table 2. The figure shows the value of the year fixed effects from 1985 through 1996 (with 1985 normalized to 0) for AFDC and food stamp caseload shares (columns 2 and 4 in Table 2). These fixed effects measure the unexplained caseload level in that year (relative to 1985), after the effects of the included variables on caseloads are taken into account. If the regressions fully explain all the variation in the data, the year effects should be zero in all years. If, however, there is a rise or fall in the dependent variable over time which the included variables do not account for, then the year effects will rise or fall.

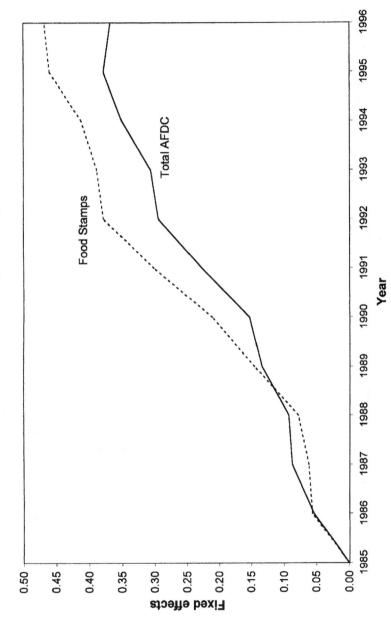

Figure 2 Year Fixed Effects from the Total AFDC and Food Stamp Share Regressions (1985 normalized to 0)

Figure 2 suggests that there was a significant unexplained increase in both AFDC and food stamp caseloads during much of the period from 1985 to 1996. Interestingly, as Blank (1997b) indicated, this unexplained increase starts around 1985, although the actual caseload data is flat from 1985 to 1990. This increase in the year fixed effects after 1985 suggests that the included variables predict that caseloads should have fallen between 1985 and 1990; instead they remained constant. From 1985 to 1989 unemployment fell, median wages rose, and AFDC benefits declined. All of these should have led to a decline in caseloads during these years, which did not occur. A mild recession in 1990 and 1991 was followed by an economic expansion and changes in the political and policy environment that (by 1994) should have produced much lower caseloads than were realized.[17]

Table 3 provides additional information on how well (or how poorly) these regressions predict actual caseload changes over these years. Columns 1 through 3 provide information on actual and predicted changes based on the annual panel data models for AFDC cases, food stamp cases, and residual food stamp cases. The table focuses on three periods:1990–94, when caseloads were rising rapidly; 1994–96, the period for which we have a complete set of control variables and when caseloads began to fall; and 1994–98, the entire recent period of caseload decline (for which we have only limited information on other variables.)

Between 1990 and 1994, the ln of AFDC-Total caseload share rose by 0.18 points (row 1, column 1), but our regression forecasts that it should have fallen by 0.02 points (row 2). In short, over this time period, the model has no predictive power at all; none of the caseload increase is explained. This does not mean that none of the variables have predictive power, however. Changes in unemployment alone would have predicted 50.5 percent of the actual caseload rise (row 3), but these changes were offset by strong predicted falls due to movements in demographic and program variables. Although only a few states implemented waivers during this time period, these waivers by themselves would have caused a 13 percent decline in caseloads (row 4).

In contrast, the food stamp caseload share prediction (column 2) for 1990 and 1994 at least moves in the same direction as the actual caseload, but far under-predicts the actual rise that occurs. The regression predicts a 0.10-point increase, when in reality a 0.30-point

Table 3 Predicted versus Actual Changes in Public Assistance Caseloads, and Share Explained by Economic Factors[a]

	Models from annual panel data			Models from monthly panel data			
				24 lags, no lagged dependent variable		12 lags, with lagged dependent variable	
	1 AFDC-Total[b] caseload share	2 Food stamp caseload share	3 Residual food stamp caseload share	4 AFDC-Total caseload share	5 Food stamp caseload share	6 AFDC-Total caseload share	7 Food stamp caseload share
Years							
1990–94							
Actual change	0.175	0.300	0.397	0.252	0.362	0.252	0.362
Predicted change	−0.020	0.100	0.297	0.036	0.068	0.083	0.078
% of actual predicted by:							
Unemployment alone	50.5	34.3	34.9	19.8	20.3	36.5	22.4
Waivers alone	−13.1	−3.4	4.9	−5.3	−1.5	−3.8	−0.8
1994–96							
Actual change	−0.149	−0.084	−0.078	−0.113	−0.029	−0.113	−0.029
Predicted change	−0.165	−0.139	−0.109	−0.080	−0.083	−0.053	−0.044
% of actual predicted by							
Unemployment alone	47.4	95.9	136.1	39.2	226.1	20.9	122.1
Waivers alone	21.5	16.9	−34.7	31.3	57.8	25.8	26.8

(continued)

Table 3 (continued)

| | Models from annual panel data | | Models from monthly panel data | | | |
			24 lags, no lagged dependent variable		12 lags, with lagged dependent variable	
1994–June 98						
Actual change	-0.621	-0.350	-0.611	-0.269	-0.611	-0.269
Predicted change	NA	NA	-0.535	-0.340	-0.386	-0.249
% of actual predicted by						
Unemployment alone	18.7	37.6	12.2	41.3	8.0	26.7
Waivers and welfare reform dummy variable	NA	NA	75.4	84.8	55.2	65.7

[a] The actual and predicted change in each column are based on the ln(caseload share of the total population).
[b] For 1994–98 rows, this column is AFDC/TANF caseload share.

increase occurs. This suggests that two-thirds of the food stamp case-load increases between these years is unexplained by the model. Changes in the unemployment rates alone would have predicted 34 percent of the increase that actually occurred. Changes in residual food stamp caseloads are better explained by this model (recall that they are more affected by demographic and economic factors). Only 25 percent (0.10/0.397) of the rise in residual food stamp caseloads is unexplained.

The model does not do quite so badly for the 1994–96 period when caseloads begin to decline. For both food stamps and AFDC, the regression predicts a larger decline than actually occurred. For AFDC, the regression predicts a 0.17-point decline in the caseload share; the actual decline was 0.15 points. Changes in the unemployment rate explain just under half of this decline. For food stamps, changes in unemployment explained 96 percent of the decline in total caseloads and predict a substantially larger decline for residual food stamps than actually occurred. The implementation of waivers in a growing num-ber of states explain another 21 percent (17 percent) of the decline in AFDC (food stamps). This suggests that information on unemploy-ment and waivers would explain 69 percent (112 percent) of the total decline in AFDC (food stamp) cases.

At the bottom of Table 3 we include information on TANF case-loads and explore the decline in caseloads through mid 1998. Because we lack information on many of the explanatory variables in the annual data model for 1998, we cannot predict an aggregate 1998 caseload number; however, we do have actual information on unemployment, which we can use to predict the share of caseload change due to unem-ployment alone.[18] The AFDC/TANF caseload share fell 0.62 points from 1994 through mid 1998, with particularly steep declines post-1996. The unemployment rate alone explained 19 percent of this decline, and 38 percent of the decline in food stamps. This suggests that the most recent and rapid decline in TANF and food stamp case-loads is only partially explained by economic factors.

The results in Table 3 indicate three things. First, changes in case-loads in the 1990s are only poorly explained by these regressions. None of the increase in AFDC and only a small share of the increase in food stamps in the early 1990s is predicted by these models. Second, if unemployment alone was used to predict caseload change, it would explain about half of the increase in caseloads in the early 1990s, but only about 20 percent of the decline in caseloads in the mid 1990s. The inability of economic factors to explain the dramatic fall in caseloads after 1994 suggests that other factors have influenced participation in TANF-funded programs in recent years. This is consistent with the argument that welfare reform has caused changes in behavior among potential welfare recipients (more leave early or never enter) or is limiting the rolls (keeping people off or removing current recipients) through tighter sanctioning and eligibility requirements. Third, food stamp changes are better predicted by these models than AFDC changes. This is particularly true for residual food stamp cases where participation in food stamps is not tied to the AFDC program. Like AFDC, however, the majority of the change in total food stamp caseloads is unexplained by economic factors through most of the recent time period.

CROSS-CHECKING THESE ESTIMATES WITH MONTHLY DATA

In this section, we use monthly data to examine the responsiveness of AFDC/TANF and food stamp caseloads to the monthly state unemployment rate, early implementation of waivers, and program changes associated with the 1996 welfare reform legislation. These estimates serve two purposes. First, they provide an important robustness check of our estimates using annual caseload data.[19] Secondly, use of the monthly data allows us to analyze the caseload data after 1996. A major drawback of utilizing the annual panel data is that many of the dependent variables are only available through 1996, although the caseload data is available through June 1998 for AFDC/TANF and for food stamps.

With monthly data, we are forced to use a much sparser specification: the only variable available monthly by state is the unemployment rate. This lack of data limits our ability to interpret the results. For instance, if states with more rapidly plummeting unemployment rates are also states that move faster and push harder on welfare reform, then we will pick up some program effects with the unemployment variable.

Hence, these regressions provide an alternative estimate of the extent to which employment changes are driving caseloads, but it is probably a somewhat less reliable estimate than we were able to derive in Table 2 with annual data. On the other hand, the addition of other variables to the model in Table 2 (compare columns 1 and 2) appeared to have only minor effects on the unemployment coefficients, and we take this as evidence that a sparser specification with monthly data may produce reasonably reliable results.

In addition to the unemployment rate, we include the waiver dummy variables described above, which "turn on" in states in the month when a waiver is approved for implementation,[20] and a dummy variable for welfare reform, which equals 1 in all months after December 1996. This latter variable will pick up any shift in the constant (in the models described below, this represents a shift in the rate of change in caseloads) after the passage of the welfare reform legislation in late 1996. The coefficient on this dummy variable will describe the average unexplained caseload change in states post-1996 after controlling for unemployment and a host of state and month fixed effects.

There are several difficulties in dealing with the monthly caseload data: the data is highly seasonal; seasonal patterns vary significantly across states; and the data has a strong trend. Because each state's data is very different in terms of seasonal patterns and trend, it is difficult to estimate traditional panel data models. What is needed to obtain accurate estimates from the monthly caseload data is an estimation procedure that accounts for the different patterns of seasonality and trending between states, while throwing away as little information as possible. Figure 3 shows the monthly caseload data from three states: Alaska, California, and New York. The diversity of the monthly caseload data in terms of trend and seasonal patterns is apparent. The data from Alaska is highly seasonal and exhibits a strong upward trend over the sample range; the data from California exhibits a strong upward trend but is not very seasonal; and the data from New York exhibits neither a strong seasonal pattern nor an upward trend.

The usual way of dealing with seasonality in aggregate monthly data is to include month fixed effects in the set of regressors. Because the seasonal patterns in the caseload data are not consistent across states, this approach is not ideal. With one set of monthly dummy variables each state's caseloads will be adjusted with respect to the average

Figure 3 AFDC/TANF Caseloads from Three States

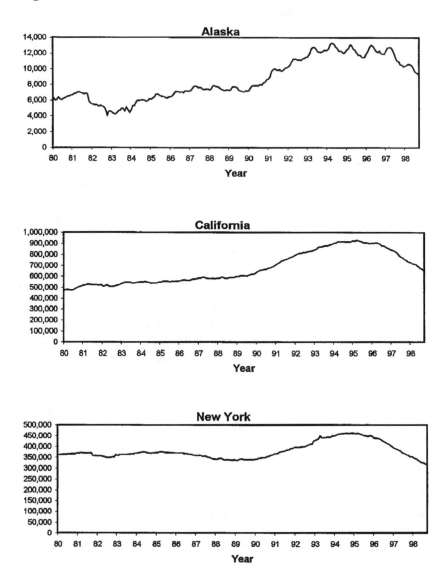

state's seasonal pattern. This sort of adjustment is not a problem for states in which seasonal fluctuations are close to the average, but it is a problem for states in which the seasonal patterns are very different from the average. Take, for example, a state without a seasonal pattern in the caseload data (like New York in Figure 3). With one set of monthly dummy variables for all states, this state's caseloads will be adjusted up in months where the average state caseloads are low relative to the omitted month and will be adjusted down in months where the average state caseloads are high relative to the omitted month. The net effect of this seasonal adjustment for a state without a seasonal pattern is to add meaningless seasonal variability to the data.

An alternative approach to dealing with seasonality in the monthly caseload data is to estimate models with state-specific month effects. Dealing with the problem of seasonality in this manner requires estimating 612 (51×12) separate state-month effects, but it avoids the problem of incorrectly assigning the same month effects to all of the states despite their differing seasonal patterns. It should be noted that state fixed effects are a linear combination of state-month effects, thus the inclusion of state-specific month effects implies that the resulting estimator will be directly comparable to the specifications in Table 2.

There are several plausible approaches to dealing with the trend in the monthly caseload data. The simplest approach to dealing with the problem of strongly trending caseload data (i.e., nonstationarity) is to estimate a model with period fixed effects (i.e., a separate fixed effect for each month of data). This is the approach taken with the annual data in the Table 2 regressions. The potential drawback of this approach is that the combination of period fixed effects and state fixed effects is perfectly collinear with state-month effects if there are more than 12 years of data. This perfect collinearity means that if state and period fixed effects are included in the set of regressors, state-month effects cannot be. Since the inclusion of state-month effects is important for reasons described above, dealing with the problem of nonstationarity through the inclusion of period fixed effects is not ideal. Indeed, state-month effects provide a more flexible specification and constrain the data less than period fixed effects.

Another approach to this problem is to estimate models with state-specific time trends. Since much of the pattern in monthly state caseload data is composed of a strong upward trend and seasonal components, detrending the caseload data may throw out too much variability in the data. This is similar to our argument against including state-specific time trends in Table 2.

We adopt a third approach to address the problem of trending dependent variables, by estimating all models in first-difference form. While this is not a perfect way to deal with the problem of non-stationary monthly caseload data, it is probably the best choice given the constraint that the data from all of the states must be treated in a like manner. This approach does seem to produce stationary time series for most of the states and is probably better than the alternatives of detrending or estimating a model with period fixed effects.[21]

In order to assess the sensitivity of the results to choice of specification we estimate models with and without a lagged dependent variable and investigate the effects of different lag lengths within each model. Assume that ln caseloads in state i during period t are generated by the process

Eq. 1 $$\ln(c_{i,t}) = \sum_{j=0}^{q} \left[\beta_j u_{i,t-j} + \gamma_j w_{i,t-j} + \eta_j r_{i,t-j} \right]$$
$$+ \sum_{k=1}^{12} sm_{i,k} + \varepsilon_{i,t}$$

where

q = lag length
$u_{i,t}$ = the state monthly unemployment rate
$w_{i,t}$ = a binary variable indicating whether a state has a waiver in effect
$r_{i,t}$ = the welfare reform binary variable that equals 1 after January of 1997
$sm_{i,k}$ = the month effect associated with state i during month k
$\varepsilon_{i,t}$ = a random, mean zero error term.

Taking first differences and rearranging terms yields the following

Eq. 2 $\ln(c_{i,t}) = \beta \Delta u_{i,t-q} + \gamma \Delta w_{i,t-q} + \eta r_{i,t-q}$

$$+ \sum_{j=0}^{q} \left[\beta_j (\Delta u_{i,t-j} - \Delta u_{i,t-q}) \right.$$

$$+ \gamma_j (\Delta w_{i,t-j} - \Delta w_{i,t-q})$$

$$\left. + \eta_j (\Delta r_{i,t-j} - \Delta r_{i,t-q}) \right] + \sum_{k=1}^{12} \Delta sm_{i,k} + \Delta \varepsilon_{i,t}$$

where $\beta = \sum_{j=0}^{q} \beta_j$, $\gamma = \sum_{j=0}^{q} \gamma_j$, and $\eta = \sum_{j=0}^{q} \eta_j$. Note that β, γ, and η represent the long-run effects of the unemployment rate, waivers, and the recent welfare reform legislation on caseloads. Also note that this model allows for exogenous caseload growth as long as $\sum_{k=1}^{12} \Delta sm_{i,k}$ is greater than zero. This offers some control for steady caseload growth due to changes in omitted variables such as demographic or political factors.

The first two columns of Table 4 present the estimates of the long-run effects of the unemployment rate, waiver implementation, and welfare reform on AFDC/TANF caseloads (part A) and food stamp caseloads (part B) with the lag length (q) set to 12 and 24 months, respectively.[22] The estimates of the long-run effect of unemployment from the monthly model with the lag length set to 24 months are remarkably similar to the estimates from the annual data. The estimates from the model with 24 monthly lags indicate that a one-point rise in the state unemployment rate will cause a 4 percent increase in AFDC/TANF caseloads. This estimate of the impact of the unemployment rate on AFDC caseloads is close to the 6 percent increase in caseloads associated with a one-point increase in the unemployment rate estimated using the annual data model.[23] For food stamp caseloads, the monthly model with 24 monthly lags and the annual data model both imply that the long-run effect of a one-point increase in the state unemployment rate is about a 6 percent increase in caseloads.

Table 4   Estimates of the Long-Run Determinants of AFDC/TANF and Food Stamp Caseloads by Model Specification

	No lagged dependent variable		With lagged dependent variable	
Long-run effect of	12 lags	24 lags	12 lags	24 lags
A. Dependent variable: ln(total AFDC/TANF caseloads)				
Employment ($\Sigma\beta_j$)	0.026**	0.040**	0.035	0.046
Waivers ($\Sigma\gamma_j$)	–0.079**	–0.138**	–0.107	–0.193
Welfare reform[a] ($\Sigma\eta_j$)	–0.277**	–0.347**	–0.362	–0.421
B. Dependent variable: ln(total food stamp caseloads)				
Employment ($\Sigma\beta_j$)	0.041**	0.061**	0.048	0.055
Waivers ($\Sigma\gamma_j$)	–0.025	–0.075**	–0.035	–0.117
Welfare reform[a] ($\Sigma\eta_j$)	–0.137**	–0.166**	–0.177	–0.199

[a] Dummy variable equal to 1 from first quarter 1997 onward.
** indicates significance at the 1 percent level.

The estimated long-run effect of waivers implied by the monthly data model with a lag length of 24 months is almost twice as high as the estimate generated with the annual data models. This result is not surprising considering that many of the waivers were not implemented until 1995 and 1996. If caseloads take time to adjust to the implementation of a waiver, the full effect of the waivers will not be realized until after 1996. Because the annual data only runs through 1996, it is doubtful that the specifications using annual data will pick up the full effect of the waiver.

The estimated effect of welfare reform (the post-96 dummy variable) is very large in this model, although interpreting this coefficient in any programmatic way is difficult. The model suggests that caseloads were 28 to 35 percent lower following the 1996 welfare reform legislation, all else equal. It is not possible to conclude anything about how much of this effect is due to program eligibility changes, behavior changes by clients and caseworkers, or other factors occurring at the same time. At best, this provides a maximal estimate of the impact of welfare reform on caseloads over this time period.

One assumption of the distributed lag models estimated in Table 4 is that the adjustment period to shocks in unemployment or implementation of waivers is limited to the length of the lag in the model. It is useful to see how the estimated long-run effects change when this restriction is lifted. The restriction that the adjustment period is limited to the lag length can be lifted by allowing for lagged values of the dependent variable to enter into the right-hand side of eq. 1. Modifying eq. 1 to include lagged values of the dependent variable yields the following equation:

Eq. 3

$$\ln(c_{i,t}) = \sum_{j=1}^{q} \ln(c_{i,t-j})$$

$$+ \sum_{j=q}^{q} \left[\beta_j u_{i,t-j} + \gamma_j w_{i,t-j} + \eta_l r_{i,t-j} \right]$$

$$+ \sum_{k=1}^{12} sm_{i,k} + \varepsilon_{i,t}$$

Taking first differences and rearranging terms,

Eq. 4

$$\Delta \ln\left(C_{i,t} \right) - \Delta \ln\left(C_{i,t-q} \right) = -\alpha \cdot \Delta \ln\left(C_{i,t-q} \right) + \beta \Delta u_{i,t-q}$$

$$+ \gamma \Delta w_{i,t-q} + \eta \Delta r_{i,t-q}$$

$$+ \sum_{j=0}^{q} \begin{bmatrix} \beta_j \left(\Delta u_{i,t-j} - \Delta u_{i,t-q} \right) \\ + \gamma_j \left(\Delta w_{i,t-j} \right) - \Delta w_{i,t-q} \\ + \eta_j \left(\Delta r_{i,t-j} - \Delta r_{i,t-q} \right) \end{bmatrix}$$

$$+ \sum_{k=1}^{12} \Delta sm_{i,k} + \Delta \varepsilon_{i,t}$$

where $\alpha = 1 - \sum_{j-1}^{q} \alpha_j, \beta = \sum_{j-0}^{q} \beta_j, \gamma = \sum_{j=0}^{q} \gamma_j$, and $\eta = \sum_{j=0}^{q} \eta_j$.

The long-run effects of the state unemployment rate, implementation of waivers, and the recent welfare reform legislation on caseloads are given by β/α, γ/α, and η/α.

Columns 3 and 4 of Table 4 present the estimated long-run effects of the unemployment rate, waivers, and welfare reform on AFDC/TANF and food stamp caseloads for lag lengths of 12 and 24 months in models with a lagged dependent variable. These estimates are quite similar to the estimates in columns 1 and 2, which are without the lagged dependent variable. The models that allow for lags of 12 months imply slightly lower estimates of long-run effects of the unemployment rate, waivers, and welfare reform than the models that allow lags of 24 months. While the estimated effects of the state unemployment rate from the model with 12 lags are lower than those estimated from the annual data, the estimated effect of the state unemployment rate from the model that allows for 24 lags are very close to the estimates from the annual data. As in columns 1 and 2, with an additional two and one-half years of data the estimated long run effects of waiver implementation are higher than those implied by the annual data.

Columns 4 though 7 in Table 3 present the predicted versus actual changes from the monthly data.[24] Columns 4 and 5 show the estimates for AFDC/TANF and for food stamps based on the model with 24 lags and no lagged dependent variable; columns 6 and 7 provide the same figures for the model with 12 lags and a lagged dependent variable. There is no good way to determine which of these models and what lag length to use. We show these two specifications to provide a range of estimates. The fact that both of these models produce relatively similar results suggests that the results are robust to these specification choices.

As with the annual data, the models which utilize the monthly data do not do a satisfactory job of predicting the changes in caseloads between 1990–94, 1994–96 and 1994–98. The models without lagged dependent variables account for 14 percent of the growth in log AFDC/TANF caseloads between 1990 and 1994 and about 19 percent of the growth in log food stamp caseloads over the same time period. The models which allow for lagged values of the dependent variables do a better job of accounting for the growth in both AFDC/TANF and food stamp caseloads between 1990 and 1994, explaining 33 percent and 22 percent of the increases in AFDC/TANF and food stamp cases, respectively. The fact that the monthly data models do a better job than the annual data models in predicting the caseload increases between 1990 and 1994 is due to the absence of a full set of demographic, economic, and program factors in the monthly specifications; as discussed above, many of these variables suggest caseloads should be declining over this period, not rising.[25] While the monthly models do a better job than the annual models of predicting the change in both AFDC/TANF and food stamp caseloads between 1990 and 1994, they imply a smaller percentage of the increase in caseloads can be attributed to changes in economic factors.[26]

Our greatest interest is in how the monthly models handle the caseload decline between 1994-98, a period over which we could not effectively make predictions from the annual models because many of the included variables were unavailable past 1996. The monthly models predict a high share of the fall in caseloads between 1994 and 1998. These "predictive" models include, however, the dummy variable for welfare reform post 1996. A better measure of the predictive power of the monthly models is the share of the caseload decline that would have been forecast by the changes in unemployment alone. For 1994–98, unemployment changes would have forecast between 8 and 12 percent of the AFDC/TANF caseload decline and between 27 and 41 percent of the food stamp decline. These figures are reasonably consistent with the prediction from the annual data.

The results in Table 3 for both monthly and annual panel data suggest that economic factors explain only a small share of the changes in AFDC/TANF and food stamp caseloads, (although the models do a somewhat better job of explaining food stamp caseload changes than AFDC/TANF caseload changes). This is true both for the rise in caseloads from 1990–94 and for the fall in caseloads from 1994–98.

The results presented in Table 4 show only a small subset of possible specifications available for obtaining estimates of the effect of employment and program changes on caseloads using monthly data. Because the models presented in Table 4 deal with the problems of seasonality and trending in what we think is the most reasonable way, they provide what is—in our opinion—the best approach to estimating these relationships. It is, however, important to note that alternative specifications provide different estimates of the impact of employment and program changes on AFDC/TANF and food stamp caseloads. In particular, Ziliak and Figlio (1999) come to very different conclusions about the relative impact of employment and waiver implementation on AFDC caseloads using monthly data and estimate much smaller effects of waivers.

Their preferred model for estimating monthly AFDC caseloads differs from the models estimated in this section in several ways. First, their specification does not contain any lags of the waiver variable. Instead, they include a contemporaneous waiver effect as well as a binary variable which, in a first-differenced model, is equal to 1 for all months between waiver approval and waiver implementation in their set of exogenous variables. Secondly, their model incorporates a slightly different lag structure.[27] Thirdly, they estimate their models with state fixed effects and month fixed effects, while we employ state-month effects. Fourth, they include a national quadratic trend to adjust for long-run changes in national factors such as the expansion of the Earned Income Tax Credit or shifting demographic and political factors. This section would be incomplete without a few comments about which of the differences between these models are responsible for the differences in results.

We do not have data on the time between waiver approval and waiver implementation, so we can not directly test the importance of including this variable. We can, however, perform an ad hoc analysis of this issue. If all states have the same time between waiver approval and waiver implementation, then the combination of a contemporaneous waiver effect along with this implementation lag variable is equivalent to restricting the lagged waiver coefficients in our specifications, where the waiver lag length is the number of months between waiver approval and waiver implementation. For example, suppose all states that approved a waiver for implementation waited 18 months before they actually implemented that waiver. Then, in a first-difference model of monthly caseloads, having a contemporaneous waiver effect, and a waiver implementation lag is the same as having a contemporaneous waiver effect and 18 lags of the waiver effect, with the coefficient on all 18 of the lags constrained to be the same. In the case where all states implement waivers at the same speed, we can test how important Ziliak and Figlio's restriction on the lagged waiver effects are in explaining the differences between their results and the results presented in this paper. It turns out the restrictions implied by their approach under the scenario where all states are the same do not make a measurable difference in assessing the long-run effects of the unemployment rate and waivers on AFDC caseloads.

How much of the difference between the results in Ziliak and Figlio is attributable to differing lag structures? The answer seems to be not very much. Estimating specifications equivalent to theirs but with our lag structure leads to surprisingly similar results. We do estimate slightly higher long-run effects of unemployment and waiver implementation, but the differences are small. Surprisingly, another difference that does not matter very much is the treatment of seasonality. Whether state fixed effects and month fixed effects or state-month effects are used makes very little difference in the estimated long-run effects of the unemployment rate and waiver implementation in the first-differenced caseload models.

The major factor in explaining the differences between Ziliak and Figlio's results and ours is that they include a quadratic time trend in their specifications, while we do not. When we include the quadratic time trend in our specifications, the long-run effect of unemployment remains virtually unchanged while the long-run effect of waiver implementation decreases by over half. This result is robust across all of the Table 4 specifications. What inferences are drawn about the magnitude of the effect of waiver implementation on caseloads hinges on whether you believe including a quadratic trend in models like the ones described in this section is appropriate.

We argue against including quadratic time trends in these specifications. For most states, the trend in the monthly caseload data is removed by first-differencing. After seasonally adjusting this differenced monthly caseload data, we believe that most (if not all) of the remaining variability in the data is meaningful and we should let it identify the parameters of interest. A simple look at Figure 1 will indicate why a quadratic term is highly significant, but this movement is exactly what we want to explain with the dependent variables. In our view including a quadratic time trend over adjusts the data and misestimates the actual effects of program changes over time.

CONCLUSION

This paper investigates the determinants of caseloads for both the AFDC and Food Stamp program, with particular attention to the role played by the macroeconomy. The results suggest that recent changes in caseloads appear to be due to a multitude of factors, many of them not readily measurable even with a very rich specification including economic, demographic, political, and policy-related variables. Although many of these factors are clearly correlated with caseload changes within states over time, they do not explain the recent trends well. The fact that the sharp increase in caseloads in the early 1990s is poorly explained by either our annual or monthly data models suggests that the on-going rapid drop in caseloads in the mid to late 1990s is also likely to be largely unexplained by these models.

At best, the ongoing decline in unemployment rates can explain about 8 to 19 percent of the AFDC caseload declines since 1994 and about 28 to 44 percent of the food stamp caseload declines. Based on our best estimates from historical data, the expected effect of any future one-point increase in unemployment will be to increase TANF caseloads by 4 to 6 percent and food stamp caseloads by 6 to 7 percent. These estimates indicate that any future recession will surely raise caseloads, but is unlikely to bring them back to their mid 1990s level, all else equal.

This suggests that the recent caseload decline must be largely due to factors other than the strong economy. A minimal estimate of the affect of welfare reform is to forecast that welfare reform was the equivalent of implementing waivers in all states. Based on annual data, this approach indicates that welfare reform explains 8 percent (6 percent) of the caseload decline in AFDC/TANF (food stamp) caseloads from 1994–98. In reality, however, many states have implemented TANF programs that were quite different and more extensive than waivers (most notably, TANF programs typically affect a larger share of the recipient population than did many waiver programs.) A maximal effect of welfare reform from 1996–98 is the unexplained decline in caseloads, along with any ongoing effects of state waivers. Using this estimate from monthly data, welfare reform can explain up to 75 percent of the AFDC caseload decline and up to 85 percent of the food stamp caseload decline. Of course, these estimates ascribe all unexplained effects post-1996 to welfare reform and probably overestimate the effect.

The wide range between these minimum and maximum estimates indicates the need for further research to look more closely at behavioral changes in take-up, as well as state-specific changes in eligibility that might be driving these dramatic changes in caseloads. These results are certainly consistent with a story whereby potential welfare recipients are strongly influenced by a host of less-measurable factors (including their own sense of the "acceptability" of utilizing public assistance) when deciding whether or not to participate in public assistance.

The food stamp caseload has historically moved in very similar ways to the AFDC caseload. Given that many AFDC recipients also receive food stamps, the correlation in historical patterns of AFDC and foods stamp caseloads is not surprising. More surprising is the observation that food stamp caseloads appear to be influenced by political and program variables that should have no direct effects on the food stamp program but which do affect AFDC receipt. This tight historical correlation between food stamps and AFDC receipt raises major questions about the effect of current welfare reform on food stamp usage. It remains to be seen whether food stamp caseloads continue to fall along with TANF caseloads, or whether these two programs begin to diverge, as food stamp usage remains relatively high among low-wage working families even as many of these families leave TANF-funded services. Residual food stamps, those food stamps not received by AFDC/TANF-eligible households, are more cyclical than overall food stamps and their levels appear to be better explained by economic and demographic variables than are overall food stamp caseloads.

From a research perspective, we are just beginning to acquire the data necessary to begin to understand the impact of the recent welfare reform. Future work on caseload changes might involve more detailed coding of state-specific program changes, allowing us to identify the effect of specific program interventions on caseload changes. As more data becomes available, the inclusion of a richer set of control variables in the post-1996 period will allow us to better separate out the impact of welfare reform from the impact of other changing political and demographic factors. Finally, as data on household income, labor force behavior, and family composition become available for the post-1996 period, this can be used to identify behavioral changes and differentiate how much of the recent caseload decline is due to reductions in public assistance participation among eligibles as opposed to changes in eligibility.

Notes

Wallace received support from the office of the Assistant Secretary for Planning and Evaluation, Department of Health and Human Services, for work on this paper. This paper reflects only the views of the authors

1. Many of these changes are still underway. The New Fiscal Federalism project of the Urban Institute indicates many of the state-specific changes on their Web site at <http://newfederalism.urban.org>. Gais and Nathan (1999) provide a recent description of the nature of these state changes, while Blank (1997a) described these changes in a broader context.

2. Food stamp and TANF data are currently only available through June 1998. We use the average caseload in the first six months as the 1998 observation.

3. For instance, see Congressional Budget Office (1993) or Gabe (1992). Blank (1997b) included citations to a number of earlier studies.

4. Monthly cash benefits from AFDC were primarily available to single-parent families (known as the AFDC-Basic program), but a small number of two-parent families also received AFDC (known as the AFDC-UP program, "UP" for unemployed parents). Blank (1997b) demonstrated that the AFDC-UP program caseloads have a very different set of determinants than the AFDC-Basic program, and that the program is much more responsive to cyclical indicators. In addition, the changes in AFDC-UP caseloads over the 1990s are more readily explained by available data than are the changes in AFDC-Basic.

5. The CEA (1997) study put a great deal of effort into coding the point at which major state waivers were approved, with the assistance of those within the Department of Health and Human Services who approved the waivers. Blank (1997b) and Levine and Whitmore (1998) use this coding; Ziliak et al. (1998) used somewhat different coding.

6. Ziliak et al. reported the combined effect of the economic variables and their seasonal factors; it would be interesting to know the effects of the cyclical variables alone. The present paper presents a comparison of monthly versus annual data estimates and finds little difference in results.

7. In 1996, the average annual cost of food stamps was $1072 per person, while average annual cost of AFDC per person was $1865 (U.S. House of Representatives, 1998, Tables 7–11, 15–4, and 15–8). Both numbers include administrative costs as well as benefits paid. Historically, the Federal government has paid virtually all food stamp costs but split AFDC costs with the states through a matching

grant formula. Under TANF, the Federal payment share is substantial, but it is fixed by the block grant amount.

8. In 1996, an estimated 61 percent of food stamp households did not receive AFDC benefits.

9. Surprisingly, although virtually all AFDC recipients are eligible for food stamps, not all choose to receive them. Blank and Ruggles (1996) estimated that among single mothers eligible for both AFDC and food stamps only 54 percent received assistance from both programs; 11 percent reported receiving AFDC but not food stamps. The remainder did not participate in the AFDC program, despite their estimated eligibility.

10. Some of these changes were reversed in 1998.

11. Recent anecdotal stories suggest that, at least in some cases, when families end their TANF services, they are not being given information or encouragement to remain on food stamps.

12. Data sources and more detailed descriptions of these variables are available in Blank (1997b).

13. This data is based on the Outgoing Rotation Group data from the Current Population Survey, which provides a large enough sample to estimate annual numbers by state.

14. These waiver variables equal the share of the year they were in effect in the year in which they were approved and then equal 1 in all following years. In 1996, we turn "on" the waiver variable in September for all states, indicating the passage of the 1996 welfare reform act.

15. This is based on an annual calculation in the CPS. We actually calculate this number separately for New York, California, and the rest of the United States. These two states have a large enough representation in the CPS to allow state-specific estimates.

16 The impact of unemployment on food stamp caseloads is even stronger if we use a sparser specification as in column 1.

17. Blank (1997b) also indicated that about 40 percent of the AFDC caseload increase between 1990 and 1994 is due to a rise in child-only cases, where children collect benefits but the adult caretaker is not eligible. She discussed this change at length. We do not focus on that issue here, largely because we want to compare aggregate AFDC and food stamp caseload trends.

18. In addition, we use projected population information for the total population. All other variables are maintained at the 1996 levels.

19. These estimates also provide further information on the claim in Ziliak et al. that the monthly panel data provides different answers than the annual panel data.

20. Once a waiver dummy variable is set to 1 within a state, it stays on for the remainder of the time period, even after the implementation of welfare reform. This allows states that received early waivers to show different caseload changes than states that did not and is consistent with the fact that the welfare reform legislation allowed states to continue their waiver programs.

21. The monthly data from some states is not characterized by a strong trend. Examples of states where ln(caseloads) looks to be stationary prior to differencing include Alabama, Illinois, Maine, Maryland, Massachusetts, Pennsylvania, South Carolina, South Dakota, and Wisconsin.
22. In the context of the distributed lag models in columns 1 and 2 of Table 4, the term "long run" refers to the length of the lag.
23. To see this, compare the coefficients on unemployment and waivers in Table 4 with the sum of the three unemployment rate coefficients in columns 2 and 4 of Table 2.
24. Note that the estimates in Table 3 for the monthly models are not entirely comparable to the estimates from the annual data models. This inconsistency is due to fact that all of the calculations for the annual data are computed in terms of the log caseload share while the calculations using the monthly data are computed in terms of log caseloads. The other major difference is that the regressions used to generate the figures for the annual data are weighted by the state total population, while the regressions used to generate the monthly data are not weighted.
25 The annual data models actually predict a decrease in AFDC/TANF caseload share between 1990–94, largely because of changes in demographic factors, political factors, and AFDC benefit levels.
26 In the context of the annual models, economic factors include unemployment rates, log median wages, and the log of the 20th percentile of wages, while in the monthly models the economic factors are the unemployment rates.
27. They estimate a autoregressive distributed lag model with three lags of the dependent variable and six lags of the unemployment rate.

References

Blank, Rebecca M. 1997a. *It Takes A Nation: A New Agenda for Fighting Poverty.* Princeton, N.J.: Princeton University Press.

Blank, Rebecca M. 1997b. *What Causes Public Assistance Caseloads to Grow?* NBER working paper 6343, National Bureau of Economic Research, Cambridge, Massachusetts, December.

Blank, Rebecca M., and Patricia Ruggles. 1996. "When Do Women Use AFDC and Food Stamps? The Dynamics of Eligibility vs. Participation." *Journal of Human Resources* 31(1): 57–89.

Congressional Budget Office. 1993. "Forecasting AFDC Caseloads, with an Emphasis on Economic Factors." CBO Staff Memorandum, Washington, D.C.: CBO. July.

Council of Economic Advisers. 1997. *Technical Report: Explaining the Decline in Welfare Receipt, 1993–1996.* A report by the Council of Economic Advisers, Washington, D.C. April.

Gabe, Thomas. 1992. *Demographic Trends Affecting Aid to Families with Dependent Children (AFDC) Caseload Growth.* CRS Report for Congress. Washington, D.C.: The Congressional Research Service, December.

Gais, Thomas, and Richard P. Nathan. 1999. *Implementing the Personal Responsibility Act of 1996: A First Look.* Albany, N.Y.: Nelson A. Rockefeller Institute of Government.

Levine, Phillip B., and Diane M. Whitmore. 1998. "The Impact of Welfare Reform on the AFDC Caseload." *Proceedings of the National Tax Association's Ninetieth (1997) Annual Conference*, Washington, D.C.: National Tax Association, pp. 24–33.

U.S. House of Representatives, Committee on Ways and Means. 1998. *1998 Green Book.* Washington, D.C.: Government Printing Office. May.

Ziliak, James P., David N. Figlio, Elizabeth E. Davis, and Laura S. Connolly. 1998. "Accounting for the Decline in AFDC Caseloads: Welfare Reform or Economic Growth?" Unpublished paper, University of Oregon at Eugene.

Ziliak, James P., and David N. Figlio. 1999. "Welfare Reform, the Business Cycle, and the Decline in AFDC Caseloads." In this volume, pp. 17–48.

The Effect of Pre-PRWORA Waivers on AFDC Caseloads and Female Earnings, Income, and Labor Force Behavior

Robert A. Moffitt
Johns Hopkins University

The passage of the Personal Responsibility and Work Opportunity Reconciliation Act (PRWORA) in September 1996 has led to increased interest in the effects of welfare reform on caseloads and on individual and family well-being. A number of evaluation efforts of PRWORA are underway around the country, but these will not be issuing findings for some time. In the meantime, some attention has been directed toward analyzing the effects of pre-PRWORA waiver activity, which by definition ended in 1996. While there have been some evaluation reports of specific waiver demonstrations during this period, another approach to evaluation is to conduct a cross-state econometric analysis, using the pre-1996 variation in waiver activity among states to estimate the effect of waivers on various outcomes. That is the approach discussed in this paper.

The most widely circulated study taking this approach is the report of the Council of Economic Advisers (1997), hereafter called the CEA report. The CEA report used aggregate state-level AFDC caseload data as the outcome and the state unemployment rate and state waiver activity as independent variables. Using data from 1976 to 1996, the CEA report found that waivers significantly reduced the caseload. However, the report also found that the decline in the unemployment rate had a large effect, greater in magnitude than that of waivers. The findings of the report indicated that the unemployment-rate decline explained from 31 percent to 44 percent of the caseload decline between 1993 and 1996 (depending on the model), while the increase in waiver activity explained between 14 and 30 percent.

There has been considerable discussion of the CEA report's methodology and findings (Martini and Wiseman 1997; Ziliak et al. 1997), as well as an update and extension of the report (Levine and Whitmore, forthcoming).[1] A number of issues have been raised: whether other policy developments such as those in Medicaid or the Earned Income Tax Credit (EITC) could have been alternative or additional contributors to caseload decline; the coding of the waiver activity in the states and the difference between official waiver start dates and genuine implementation dates; whether waivers were endogenous and introduced with a higher probability in states whose caseloads were going to decline for other reasons; and modeling issues such as the inclusion of the lagged dependent variable, the length of lags used, whether monthly or annual data are preferred, estimating in levels vs. first differences, and many other issues. Another issue is the question of whether the waiver activity was significant enough in the states to have plausibly generated the size of effect estimated in the CEA report, and exactly what the waiver variables were proxying—a specific policy, or a more general set of policies which, together, might have had an effect.

Most of these issues will not be joined here, with the exception of the business cycle; its contribution to caseload growth is subjected to sensitivity testing in the last section below. Aside from this one departure from the CEA specification, the bulk of the paper takes the CEA methodology as given and studies the implications of applying that methodology, with all its strengths and weaknesses and all the uncertainty surrounding it, to micro data from the Current Population Survey (CPS).

Microdata should have an important role to play in econometric evaluations of welfare reform. Aggregate data at the state level necessarily gloss over the differences within a state's population and do not permit analysis of the groups most likely to be affected by welfare reform. Not only should individual data on the most-likely-affected groups permit a more precise estimation of the effect of the welfare; they should also aid in the detection of spurious effects that might have been estimated at the aggregate level (because if effects are detected in the microdata even for groups that are credibly unaffected by the reform, this suggests that the aggregate estimate might be spuriously picking up some more-general trend). In addition, while aggregate data are available on the AFDC caseload, none are available for individual and family outcomes of interest like earnings, family income, and labor force behavior. Consequently, the CPS can contribute to the study of welfare reform to outcomes other than the caseload.

The study reported on here applies the CEA methodology to CPS microdata. The major distinction made with the microdata is between women of higher and lesser education levels, because education is the best single proxy for labor market skill and hence for outside opportunities off welfare. It is the best single scale of how well-off a welfare recipient is, in general. The analysis here finds that the CEA methodology implies that more-educated and less-educated women are affected in different ways by welfare reform. For the least-educated women, welfare reform decreases AFDC participation and increases annual hours of work and annual weeks of work, but it has no statistically significant effects on earnings, wages, or family income. For somewhat more-educated women, on the other hand, welfare reform increases earnings as well as hours of work. The findings of the paper demonstrate that a recognition of the diversity and heterogeneity of the population, as well as the differences in their response to welfare reform, is critical to understanding the effects of that reform.

The CEA methodology requires that the effect of the business cycle on caseload and other outcomes be estimated in order that the effects of welfare reform be estimated, for the latter are estimated after implicitly netting out the caseload trends that would have occurred from the unemployment rate decline resulted even in the absence of those reforms. There were only two significant recessions between 1977 and 1995, and they had different effects on the caseload. Moreover, cross-state variation in the unemployment rate has had different effects over time. The analysis here shows that the caseload has become more cyclically sensitive over time; hence forecasting what the effects of the decline in the unemployment rate would have been in the absence of the waiver activity could be argued to be best conducted with the most recent data possible, namely, data in the late 1980s. The results here show that when the most recent business cycle is used to estimate the model, all aggregate caseload effects of waivers disappear, as do the positive effects on earnings of more-educated women. More analysis is needed to resolve this issue.

REPLICATING THE CEA REPORT FINDINGS

The CEA report used annual data from 1976 to 1996 on 1) average annual monthly AFDC caseloads per capita, 2) average annual monthly unemployment rates, and 3) waiver activity within each year (see below), all at the state level.[2] The analysis considers the relative influences on the caseload of the unemployment rate and of waivers. The waivers were coded from Department of Health and Human Services (DHHS) information on the approval dates for AFDC waivers; dummy variables indicate whether the state had any waiver in effect in the year in question (thus the dummy variable goes from 0 to 1 and stays at 1 for as long as the waiver is in force).[3] Additional dummy variables were constructed that indicate whether waivers were in effect for particular policies—JOBS exemptions, JOBS sanctions, family caps, time limits, and other specific types of reforms. Only waivers since 1993 were coded, on the grounds that waivers before then did not affect a sufficient fraction of the caseload. Waivers were also coded only if the waiver activity was statewide; of the 43 waivers in effect in the final year, only 35 were in this category.[4]

Figure 1 shows the trends from 1976 to 1996 in the aggregate AFDC caseload, the unemployment rate, and waiver activity. The AFDC caseload was fairly stable until 1989, when it began to grow significantly. The growth peaked in 1993 and declined thereafter.[5] The unemployment rate has also gone through considerable gyrations during two recessions occurring over the period. The caseload and unemployment cycles have a rough positive correlation in the late 1970s and after 1988, but not from 1979 to 1987. The CEA report ascribes the latter to the influence of the Omnibus Budget Reconciliation Act (OBRA), which had a caseload-depressing effect, although this seems an inadequate explanation for the long length of the lack of relationship. In any event, the methodology used to estimate waiver effects, as shown below, does not make use of this aggregate time-series correlation (or lack of it) because state-level data, not aggregate data, are used.

The third curve in Figure 1 shows the fraction of states with statewide waivers and hence demonstrates the rise of waiver activity after 1991. The figure makes clear that the separation of the effects on the caseload of waivers (on the one hand) and the declining unemployment

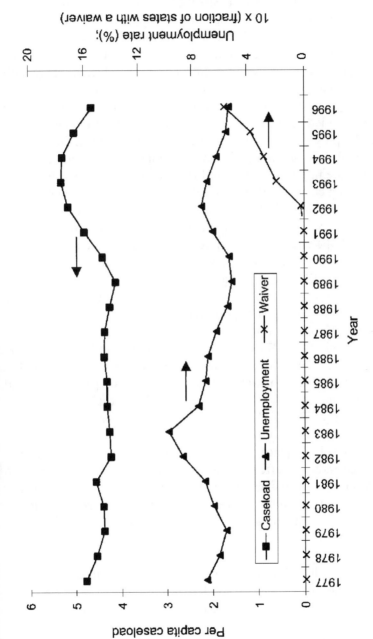

Figure 1 Trends in AFDC Recipiency and Other Variables

rate (on the other) must necessarily be a major challenge, given that they both changed course around the same time (1992) and given that they continued changing in the same direction thereafter.

The models estimated in the CEA report use the natural logarithm of the per capita caseload as the dependent variable, and they include year dummies, state dummies, and, in most cases, state dummies multiplied by a year variable (i.e., a time trend) as independent variables. Also included in the equations are variables for the unemployment rate, the presence of a welfare waiver, and the state AFDC guarantee. With both year dummies and state dummies included, the coefficients on the unemployment rate and the waiver variables represent the effects of a change in their respective variables on the deviation from a state-specific trend in the per capita caseload. As noted above, therefore, the analysis does not make use of the relationship between the caseload, the unemployment rate, and waivers at the aggregate level, but rather the relationship between these variables at the state level, and in first-difference, or change, form (i.e., the relationship between year-to-year changes in waivers, changes in unemployment rates, and changes in caseloads across different states).[6,7]

The March Current Population Survey can be brought into the analysis only for 1977 and after, for only starting in 1977 were all individual states identified (see below). Thus the year 1976 is deleted from the analysis of administrative data as well, for comparability. In addition, the analysis below deletes the year 1996 because it is close to the enactment of PRWORA.[8] Some caution is reasonable under these circumstances, given that the heightened welfare reform activity at the federal level just prior to that enactment could have influenced state caseload-reducing efforts. However, as will be shown momentarily, while some of the tangential findings of the CEA report are sensitive to the inclusion of this year, the main ones are not. Nevertheless, the 1996 year is still excluded from the main analyses to ensure that no ambiguities will arise in the interpretation of the findings in this respect.

It is worth noting that the caseload modeling strategy of the CEA report, like many caseload modeling approaches, captures both the entry and exit effects of welfare reform on the caseload. Unlike many studies of waivers, which determine the rate at which families who are initially on the welfare rolls leave them following the enactment of a waiver, studying the caseload as a whole implies that the effects of a waiver on entry are also captured. A decline in entry rates can lower the caseload just as an increase in exit rates can, and hence the caseload can fall for either reason. Thus, the caseload modeling approach has a distinct advantage over welfare "leaver" studies and other waiver evaluations, which take as their study populations only families initially on welfare.[9]

Replication of CEA Results

Columns 1–4 of Table 1 estimate models whose specification (that is, dependent and independent variables) are exactly the same as those in the CEA report.[10] As in the CEA report, the dependent variable equals the natural logarithm of a ratio whose numerator is the size of the AFDC caseload (taken from administrative data) and whose denominator is the state population. The independent variables are as defined previously. The major difference in the regressions reported in Table 1 and those appearing in the CEA report is that the Table 1 regressions exclude the years 1976 and 1996.[11]

The basic specification ("Spec. 1") allows for effects of the current and lagged unemployment rate and an overall waiver dummy. The lagged unemployment rate and waiver coefficients are significant, as in the CEA report, and similar in magnitude. The coefficients in the CEA report for this specification imply that the unemployment rate explains 45 percent of the decline in the per capita caseload between 1993 and 1996 and that the waiver variable explains 13 percent (Council of Economic Advisers (1997), Table 3). The corresponding coefficients in Table 1 imply contribution percents of 47 and 15, respectively.[12]

The results for specifications 2, 3, and 4 are, however, rather different than those in the CEA report, at least for the waiver variable coefficients. Specification 2 shows a barely significant coefficient on a waiver for work requirement time limits and a more significant effect of waivers for a family cap, whereas the CEA results showed neither of these to be significant; only JOBS sanctions effects were significant in the CEA report. This change is entirely the result of excluding year 1996, when several states added new waivers. The sensitivity of these coefficients to the years included and excluded is unfortunate and compounds the already existing suspicion that the separate effects of the

Table 1 Aggregate State-Level Caseload Regressions, 1977–1995[a]

Variable	ln(Caseload per capita)				ln(AFDC participation rate)[b]	
	Spec. 1	2	3	4	Unweighted	Weighted
Unemployment rate	0.031	0.010	0.037	0.062	-0.512	-0.866
	(0.435)	(0.43)	(0.435)	(0.435)	(1.127)	(1.167)
Lagged unemployment rate	4.334*	4.323*	4.329*	4.316*	4.672*	4.780*
	(0.424)	(0.424)	(0.424)	(0.424)	(1.098)	(1.143)
Any waiver	-5.751*	–	-2.694	-0.280	-15.047*	-17.68*
	(2.600)		(3.475)	(4.185)	(6.735)	(6.981)
JOBS sanctions	–	-2.043	-5.740	-2.705	–	–
		(5.641)	(4.305)	(5.249)		
JOBS exemptions	–	5.733	–	–	–	–
		(4.695)				
Termination time limits	–	-6.790	–	–	–	–
		(7.000)				
Work requirement time limits	–	-9.211*	–	–	–	–
		(5.600)				
Family cap	–	-10.580*	–	–	–	–
		(4.751)				
Earnings disregard	–	-4.569	–	–	–	–
		(4.318)				
Lead of any waiver	–	–	–	-3.203	–	–
				(3.638)		

Lead of JOBS sanction waiver	–	–	–	-4.083	–	–
				(4.207)		
ln(Max AFDC benefit for family of 3)	14.352*	12.831*	14.345*	14.123*	4.148	1.948
	(5.286)	(5.335)	(5.283)	(5.276)	(13.691)	(14.230)

[a] All coefficients and standard errors have been multiplied by 100; * indicates significance at the 10% level. Standard errors are in parentheses. All regressions include state dummies, year dummies, and interactions of state dummies with year trend variable. All regressions are unweighted by state population.
[b] CPS data.

individual waivers are not being correctly picked up by these variables. The results for specification 3 show significant effects for neither the any-waiver variable nor the JOBS-sanctions variable, the latter of which was significant in the CEA report; again, the exclusion of 1996 is responsible for this result. Specification 4 was tested in the CEA report to determine whether there was an advance response to waivers, by including a one-year lead variable for both the any-waiver and sanctions variables.[13] The CEA report found significantly negative effects of both, whereas neither is significant in Table 1; again, the exclusion of 1996 is the reason for the difference.[14]

Given that specifications 2–4 test tangential hypotheses and that the simple specification in column 1 is robust to inclusion of different years—and because the exclusion of 1996 is a conservative strategy, as argued above—the rest of the analysis in this paper will use specification 1.[15]

EXTENDING THE MODEL TO THE CPS

The Current Population Survey is a relatively large monthly household survey which is representative of the U.S. population. For most of the analysis we use only the March survey in each year, which gathers information on AFDC receipt, employment and labor force behavior, and annual earnings and income at both the family and individual level. Identifiers for all states are available beginning in 1977, and we therefore use the March CPS files from 1977 to 1995. The means of all the CPS variables used in the analysis are shown in Appendix Table 1 (p. 118).

We begin by replicating the CEA results just reported to the closest degree they can be, using information in the CPS. Rather than administrative counts of AFDC recipients in each year, we use the number of women aged 16–54 reporting AFDC receipt in each state. In addition, rather than dividing by total population, we divide by the number of women aged 16–54. Since women in this age range are the primary population group from which AFDC recipients are drawn, this should provide a more precise measure of the rate of receipt than that out of the entire population.[16] With the dependent variable defined in this way for each state in each year 1977–1995, we can use for regressors the exact same set used in the CEA analysis: state and year dummies and state-level variables for waiver activity, the unemployment rate, and the state benefit level.[17]

The right-most two columns in Table 1 show estimates using specification 1. The dependent variable is the natural logarithm of the AFDC participation rate in the state and year in question, as defined above. One column shows the results when the simple unweighted mean is used, and the second column shows the results when weighted least squares is applied, using as weights the ratio of the mean administratively defined caseload per capita in the state to the mean CPS-defined AFDC participation rate in the state, the weights are normalized to one. These weights adjust for the sampling error in the CPS which arises from small sample size by raising each of the CPS means to its proper population proportion as represented in the administrative data. The small samples in some states in some years is the main obstacle to using the CPS for state-specific policy analysis in general, and the use of weights in this way reduces the impact of that problem.[18]

As the results show, the CPS generates remarkably similar estimates for the effects of the state unemployment rate on the caseload as those which use administrative caseload data. The effects of waiver policy are also highly significant, and considerably larger in magnitude than in the equations using the administrative caseload data. Thus the CPS is clearly consistent with the finding of significant waiver effects on caseloads.[19]

Disaggregating and Using Other Outcomes with the CPS

As noted in the introduction, the CPS data afford the opportunity of examining effects of waivers on subcomponents of the caseload and on the within-state population, thereby permitting a more disaggregate analysis than is allowed with state-level administrative data. For simplicity, only two demographic dimensions are examined here, education and age. Education is classified into four categories: less than 12 years of schooling, 12 exactly, 13–15, and 16 or more years. Age is classified into four categories: 16–25, 26–34, 35–44, and 45–54. Within each state and each year, these four education and age categories are used to form 16 age-education cells, for each of which a mean

AFDC participation rate is calculated.[20] The resulting sample has 15,504 observations (51 states, 19 years, 16 demographic groups per state and year). The AFDC participation-rate models already estimated can be reestimated on this larger sample, using the same state-level regressors as used in the previous analysis. However, age and education effects can now also be allowed, and waiver effects can be estimated separately for different age and education groups as well. Some of the age-education cells in some states have very few observations, so we shall conduct sensitivity analysis to the exclusion of small cells.[21]

There is relatively little formal evidence upon which to generate hypotheses regarding the differential effect of waiver policies by age and education. The strongest dimension upon which generally accepted knowledge of waiver policies can be applied is education, for education is generally regarded as the best proxy for labor market skill and hence potential earnings off the welfare rolls. All available evidence, which is admittedly anecdotal, suggests that the caseload-reducing effects of waiver policy have had their greatest impact on those women on the rolls who were in a better position, i.e., the better educated. There is widespread agreement that those with greater labor market opportunities have been disproportionately represented among those leaving the rolls, thereby increasingly leaving the welfare caseload composed of the worse-off cases, those with the fewest outside opportunities.

However, much of this consensus is based upon the presumed effects of the decline in the unemployment rate, which is almost surely likely to have drawn off the rolls those with higher labor market skills. The effects of welfare reform are to some extent more ambiguous. While it should be presumed that the increased emphasis on work (which is the central feature of most welfare reform programs) would be most easily accommodated by those with more labor market skill, it is simultaneously the case that those with less labor market skill may be less able or willing to comply with work requirements while on the rolls and hence may be more likely to be sanctioned or otherwise leave because of an inability to cope with the requirements. Evidence on this issue is thus far lacking.

A second potential of the CPS is to permit the examination of outcomes other than AFDC participation. For this purpose, we construct, for each of the age-education cells in each state in each year, the means of annual weeks worked, annual hours worked, and real annual earnings of the woman in question, and also real family income of the family in which she resides.[22] Welfare reform and waiver activity may, on the one hand, improve these outcomes if such policies are successful in stimulating former welfare recipients to improve their labor market position, while they may, on the other hand, leave women worse off if they are not able to do so.

The problem of small samples in some of the age-education cells in some states will be addressed in two ways. First, some of the equations will be estimated only on state-demographic cells with more than some minimum number of observations. Second, equations will also be estimated using the outgoing rotation group (ORG) data from the CPS. Every month, about one-quarter of the CPS sample is asked questions about weekly earnings. Taking the samples of individuals asked these questions over all 12 months in a year yields a sample that is approximately three times the size of the single-month March CPS. Models identical to those estimated with the March CPS can be estimated with these data, thereby implicitly gauging the importance of sample size to the results.

Results

Table 2 presents results of models for the AFDC participation rate using the March CPS data. Because about a quarter of all the education-age cells have a zero participation rate, the absolute level of the participation rate is used rather than its logarithm. The first column of Table 2 shows an aggregate-state level regression for comparability. The results indicate that the signs and significance levels of the coefficients are similar to those in the last column of Table 1, implying that the waivers reduced the fraction of women aged 16–54 who were on AFDC by about 0.8 of a percentage point. The second and third columns use the within-state education-age demographic cell data. The first "No interactions" column simply includes education and age dummies but continues to estimate an average, state-level welfare effect. The coefficients on the education and age dummies are usually significant and in the expected direction, with higher education groups having a lower probability of being on AFDC and with participation rates

Table 2 CPS AFDC Participation Rate Regressions[a]

		Demographic cell data[c]	
Variable	State-level aggregates[b]	No interactions	Interactions
Unemployment rate	−0.002	−0.003*	−0.003*
	(0.001)	(0.001)	(0.001)
Lagged unemployment rate	0.002*	0.006*	0.006*
	(0.001)	(0.001)	(0.001)
Any waiver	−0.008*	−0.010*	–
	(0.003)	(0.004)	
Education 12 yr.	–	−0.058*	−0.058*
		(0.007)	(0.007)
Education 13–15 yr.	–	−0.061*	−0.061*
		(0.007)	(0.007)
Education 16+ yr.	–	−0.065*	−0.065*
		(0.007)	(0.007)
Age 26–34	–	0.034*	0.034*
		(0.002)	(0.001)
Age 35–44	–	0.001	0.001
		(0.001)	(0.001)
Age 45–54	–	−0.024*	−0.023*
		(0.001)	(0.001)
Waiver × (Education<12)	–	–	−0.017*
			(0.006)
Waiver × (Education=12)	–	–	−0.009
			(0.006)
Waiver × (Education 13–15)	–	–	−0.007
			(0.006)
Waiver × (Education 16+)	–	–	−0.008
			(0.006)

[a] The dependent variable is the AFDC participation rate. All regressions are estimated on years 1977–1995. The omitted education category is "less than 12 years" and the omitted age category is "16–25 years old." All regressions use administrative CPS weights. Standard errors are in parentheses; *denotes significance at the 10% level.

[b] Other variables included in this regression include the AFDC maximum benefit, year dummies, state dummies, and state × trend variables.

[c] Other variables included in these regressions are all those in the "state-level aggregates" specification plus interactions between the education dummies and year dummies and interactions between the education dummies and the current and lagged unemployment rate.

highest among women aged 26–34. The waiver coefficient is significant and of approximately the same magnitude as that in the state-level regression, indirectly indicating that the education and age compositions of waiver and nonwaiver states were not very different.

The more important results are those in the right-most column, which gives separate waiver effects by education category. The results indicate that the largest effects of waivers on AFDC participation rates occurred among women with less than 12 years of education, for whom waivers reduced participation by 1.7 percentage points; (recall that the base is all women in this education category). This is in accord with expectations, for the impact of welfare reform should be expected to occur among the most disadvantaged and most welfare-prone. It also suggests that the state-level results are not spuriously picking up effects that were occurring across the education distribution, thus providing some support for the credibility of those results.[23]

Table 3 shows the results for the other outcomes taken from the CPS, when state aggregates are used as well as with the demographic cell data are used. All of the estimated effects at the state level are insignificant except for annual earnings, which is significantly positive and implies that waivers increased earnings by $274 per year.[24] The results are somewhat different when the results are disaggregated by education group, however. Both the weeks worked and annual hours worked of those with the least education increased from waivers, but neither their annual earnings nor weekly earnings increased. The aggregate annual earnings effects occurred instead among those with 12 years of education only. For that group, there was a significant increase in hours of work, although of somewhat smaller magnitude than that for the least educated group.

These findings, therefore, suggest that waivers had a major impact on very low-skilled women by reducing their rates of participation in AFDC (through both entry and exit, presumably) and increasing their labor force attachment and levels of connection to the workforce (again, possibly through non-entry as well as exit). However, there was little effect on their annual or weekly earnings, indirectly indicating that the wage rates of the jobs they obtained were very low. Somewhat more educated women—those with 12 years of education, to be exact—whose participation rates also fell, experienced both increases in workforce attachment as well as increases in earnings. This sug-

Table 3 Effect of Waiver Policies on Female Labor Force and Income[a]

Variable	Annual weeks worked		Annual hours worked		Annual earnings		Weekly earnings		Annual family income	
	State aggregates[b]	Demog. cells[c]	State aggregates	Demog. cells	State aggregates	Demog. cells	State aggregates	Demog. cells	State aggregates	Demog. cells
Any waiver	0.303	–	15.3	–	274.3*	–	3.4	–	392.7	–
	(0.270)		(11.7)		(161.8)		(2.4)		(474.0)	
Waiver ×	–	1.536*	–	67.6*	–	87.8	–	1.61	–	-239.7
(Educ<12)		(0.573)		(25.1)		(318.6)		(4.32)		(909.3)
Waiver ×	–	0.545	–	41.0*	–	560.0*	–	6.27	–	568.7
(Educ=12)		(0.573)		(25.1)		(318.6)		(4.32)		(909.3)
Waiver ×	–	0.504	–	11.7	–	441.4	–	4.38	–	869.7
(Educ13–15)		(0.573)		(25.1)		(318.5)		(4.32)		(909.3)
Waiver ×	–	0.176	–	0.6	–	154.7	–	1.29	–	-898.4
(Educ 16+)		(0.308)		(25.1)		(318.7)		(4.32)		(909.3)

[a] All regressions are unweighted. All data are from the March CPS (1977–1995) except for real weekly earnings, which is from the CPS ORG (1970–1995). Standard errors are in parentheses; * denotes significance at the 10% level.
[b] The other variables included in the "State aggregates" regressions are those in column 1 of Table 1.
[c] Other variables in "Demog. cell" regressions are those in the regressions reported in the last two columns of Table 2.

gests that it was the better-educated, presumably more-skilled, women who did better off the rolls and were able to better replace their lost welfare benefits with earnings.

The final column in the table shows the effects on family income, where the findings indicate no significant effects for any education group. Indirectly, therefore, this implies that the least educated women must have replaced their welfare benefits from some other source, either through income from others in the family or from other government programs. This bears more investigation in the future.

The standard errors on many of the coefficients in Table 3 are relatively high and suggest that small sample sizes in the CPS may be weakening the results. The results for weekly earnings (which come from the much larger ORG data set) are, however, no more significant than the March CPS coefficients and, in fact, generally less so. Of course, the less significant coefficients in the ORG data could be a reflection of a lack of increase in wage rates as a result of waivers; the positive effects on annual earnings of the 12-years-of-education group could be entirely a result of their increases in hours worked. Table 4 reports results when small cell sizes are excluded from the regressions, as an additional check on this aspect of the findings. Virtually all results in the table are of the same general magnitude as those in Tables 2 and 3, with the exception that welfare participation and annual earnings effects are stronger for those with 13–15 years of education, a moderately implausible result (at least in the magnitude implied by the coefficients). The ORG data, when restricted to even larger cell sizes than those in the CPS, however, reveals significantly positive effects on weekly earnings of those with 12 and those with 13–15 years of education. These effects corroborate the March CPS results for annual earnings to some extent and increase our confidence in those findings.

BUSINESS CYCLE SENSITIVITY

The separation of waiver effects from business cycle (i.e., unemployment) effects on caseloads and other outcomes implicitly requires a judgement on what the course of those outcomes would have been in the absence of the decline in the unemployment rate that accompanied

Table 4 Effect of Waiver Policies on Participation Rate, Labor Force, and Income: Excluding Small Cells[a]

Variable	Participation rate	Weeks worked	Hours worked	Annual earnings	Family income	Weekly earnings	
						20+ Observ.	50+ Observ.
Waiver × (Educ <12)	-0.015*	1.269*	63.9*	-150.6	-772.3	1.87	-5.91
	(0.006)	(0.602)	(26.2)	(331.9)	(976.3)	(4.52)	(4.93)
Waiver × (Educ=12)	-0.007	0.365	36.6*	505.1*	-727.7	6.31	8.09*
	(0.005)	(0.476)	(20.7)	(262.6)	(772.4)	(4.26)	(3.90)
Waiver × (Educ13–15)	-0.009*	0.377	14.5	498.6*	907.8	4.40	6.89*
	(0.005)	(0.476)	(20.7)	(262.6)	(772.5)	(4.26)	(3.90)
Waiver × (Educ 16+)	-0.009	-0.049	-10.9	-87.1	104.1	-0.54	1.08
	(0.006)	(0.532)	(23.1)	(293.1)	(862.3)	(4.30)	(4.24)

[a] All other variables in regressions are identical to those in the last column of Table 2. All regressions impose a minimum of 20 observations per cell except the last column, which imposes a minimum of 50 observations per cell. Standard errors are in parentheses; the * denotes significance at the 10% level.

the growth of waiver activity. Waiver effects are necessarily estimated from the implicit residual change in the caseload and other outcomes after the effect of the unemployment rate has been netted out. Although there is some variation in unemployment rates in each state after waivers are introduced, the unemployment rate effect for waiver states is largely determined from the data on the cyclical relationship over the years prior to 1992. For the estimates of waiver effects to be correct, therefore, it must be the case that the cyclical relationship between unemployment rates and caseload and other outcomes be the same in 1992 and after as it was before 1992. While there is a sense in which this can never be known with certainty, for we will never know what would have happened over the 1992–1995 period if waiver activity had not increased, we can determine what the historical experience of the cyclical relationship was and can make estimates of waiver effects conditional upon assumptions about whether that historical experience was maintained over the 1992–1995 period.

The regression specifications reported thus far implicitly make such an assumption, by assuming that the average unemployment rate relationship over the 1977–1991 period, estimated in the same way that waiver effects are estimated—namely, from the relationship between year-to-year changes in caseload and other outcomes and year-to-year changes in the unemployment rate across different states—would have persisted over the 1992–1995 period. One issue is whether the 1977–1991 period is long enough to have estimated that relationship reliably, for there were only two major recessions at the national level during those years. On the other hand, there was considerable cross-state variation in the magnitude of those recessions, and this reduces this problem to some extent. Another issue is whether the cyclical relationships were stable over the 1977–1991 period itself. This issue is more easily addressed with the data at hand, for one can simply estimate different cyclical sensitivities for different periods.

Table 5 shows results of models which test whether cyclical effects have been stable and, if not, whether estimated waiver effects are sensitive to them. The regressions reported are comparable to those in Table 1 and are run at the state level using the administratively defined AFDC caseload variable used in the CEA report. Thus, these regressions return to the CEA data and aggregate caseload model. "1977–92 Observations" include only pre-waiver observations

Table 5 Aggregate State-Level Caseload Regressions: Sensitivity to Nonconstant Cyclical Effects[a]

Variable	1977–92 Observations	1981–95 Observations	1987–95 Observations
Unemployment rate	–	–0.745*	0.031
		(0.458)	(0.421)
Lagged unemployment rate	–	4.500*	2.220*
		(0.443)	(0.450)
Any waiver	–	–1.653	3.744*
		(2.498)	(1.825)
Unemployment rate 1977–1980	–1.571*	–	–
	(0.591)		
Unemployment rate 1981–1986	2.364*	–	–
	(0.297)		
Unemployment rate 1987–1992	3.885*	–	–
	(0.446)		

[a] All coefficients are multiplied by 100. Population weights are not used. The dependent variable is ln(AFDC per capita caseload) and the specification of regressions is identical to that in Table 1, column 1. Standard errors are shown in parentheses; the * indicates significance at the 10% level.

and allows the unemployment-rate coefficient to vary with three distinct time periods (based on Figure 1): 1977–1980, before the early 1980s recession and recovery; 1981–1986, which includes one full cycle; and 1987–1992, which covers the slight decline and rise of unemployment in the late 1980s and early 1990s, the second cycle in the pre-waiver data. As the results show, the cyclical sensitivity of the caseload has risen drastically over time. In the late 1970s, the caseload was, oddly, procyclical, and during the 1980s and through 1992 it was countercyclical but increasing in sensitivity.[25]

Given this instability, a natural hypothesis is that cyclical sensitivity during the post-1992 period, the period of interest, would have been, in the absence of PRWORA, closest to the cyclical sensitivity exhibited in the pre-1992 period closest to it in calendar time, namely, the period in the late 1980s and early 1990s. The right-most two columns in Table 5 show the estimates of waiver effects when, respectively, the 1977–1980 observations are deleted and the 1977–1986 observations are deleted, thus gradually deleting more of the more historically distant observations from 1992. As the table shows, the waiver coefficients lose significance when pre-1981 observations are excluded, and they even become significant and positive when the pre-1987 observations are included. This should not be surprising given the results in column 1, for since the more recent periods have greater cyclical sensitivity, excluding the more distant years results in a larger expected post-1992 caseload decline from the unemployment rate alone. Hence the role of waivers in explaining caseload decline is correspondingly reduced.

Table 6 shows the results of estimating the CPS-based models on the 1987+ period only. The results in this case are, interestingly, very similar to those reported earlier, with the notable exception of a lack of significant increase in annual earnings for those with 12 years of education. The disaggregation thus appears to be important here, for the reduced impact of waivers on the caseload reported in Table 5 appear to be masking continued declines among the least-educated women. On the other hand, these results suggest that the positive earnings impacts reported earlier may be sensitive to the implicit cyclical assumption, for Table 6 has the implication that there were, in the population, no significant increases in earnings or wages for any group despite reductions in caseloads and increases in hours worked and weeks worked. This is a somewhat different conclusion than was reached previously.

It is worth emphasizing that it cannot be known with certainty that the most recent recession prior to the waiver activity is the best for forecasting cyclical effects after 1992. Indeed, the true cyclical sensitivity post-1992 could be different than that exhibited in any historical experience in the years of these data. One could argue that the best way to proceed is to average over the cycles that are available in the data, on the assumption that the post-1992 period should be expected, on average, to be like all those in the past, not the most recent one. Some other source of information needs to be brought to bear on this issue to make further progress.

Table 6 Effect of Waiver Policies on Participation Rate, Labor Force, and Income: 1987–1995 Years[a]

Variable	Participation rate	Weeks worked	Hours worked	Annual earnings	Family income	Weekly earnings
Waiver × (Educ<12)	-0.017*	1.437*	58.0*	-295.1	-948.7	-1.02
	(0.008)	(0.632)	(27.7)	(369.9)	(1097.9)	(4.86)
Waiver × (Educ=12)	-0.010	0.410	29.1	153.8	-195.3	3.57
	(0.008)	(0.632)	(27.7)	(369.9)	(1097.9)	(4.86)
Waiver × (Educ13–15)	-0.008*	0.441	2.3	60.4	171.2	1.90
	(0.008)	(0.632)	(27.7)	(369.9)	(1097.9)	(4.86)
Waiver × (Educ 16+)	-0.009	0.107	-9.2	-231.1	-1573.8	-0.91
	(0.008)	(0.632)	(27.7)	(369.9)	(1098.0)	(4.86)

[a] All other variables in the regressions are identical to the last column of Table 2. Standard errors are in parentheses; * denotes significance at the 10% level.

CONCLUSIONS

A recent report of the Council of Economic Advisers (1997) examined the effect of pre-PRWORA waiver activity in the early 1990s on the AFDC caseload and found that waivers made a substantial contribution to the reduction in the AFDC caseload although less than that of the declining unemployment rate. The CEA study used an aggregate state-level caseload model estimated over the period 1976–1996. This paper uses the CEA methodology but applies it to microdata from the Current Population Survey, where information is available on labor force activity, earnings, and income, as well as on demographic characteristics such as age, sex, and education. The results from the CPS data show that less educated women had gains in labor force attachment in the form of increased weeks worked and hours of work as a result of waivers, but no statistically significant increases in earnings or wages. The only statistically significant earnings or wage increases occurred among better-educated women, generally those with at least 12 years of education. The latter result is, however, somewhat sensitive to which historical recession is used to forecast the effect of the business cycle. The findings of the paper demonstrate that a recognition of the diversity and heterogeneity of the population, and the differences in their response to welfare reform, is critical to understanding the effects of that reform.

Notes

A previous version of this paper was presented at the ASSA meetings in New York in January 1999. The author thanks Phillip Levine for providing the data used in the CEA Report and for helpful discussions and comments, and Gary Burtless and Sheldon Danziger for additional comments. Cristian deRitis provided able research assistance.

1. See Blank (1997) and Stapleton, Livermore, and Tucker (1997) for other caseload models, but these two papers focused more on the origins of the increase in the caseload in the late 1980s and early 1990s than on its later decline.
2. Thus, with 51 states for 21 years, a total of 1071 observations were used in the estimation. All caseload, unemployment, and waiver data are on a fiscal year basis. Thus the variables for year t are calculated as averages of the months from October of year $(t-1)$ to September of year t.

3. In the year in which the waiver first appears, the variable is coded as the fraction of the year that the waiver was in effect.

4. An appendix in the CEA report shows the exact waiver dates and provides more discussion of the nature of the different types of waivers

5. The caseload has continued to decline markedly since 1995.

6. The CEA model does not include some of the main variables posited in the economic model of welfare participation to affect the takeup decision—for example, potential wage rates and exogenous nonlabor income. The implicit assumption is that these variables do not vary in their trends in waiver and nonwaiver states.

7. The major danger in this method is that those states who adopted waivers may have had different changes in their caseloads than nonwaiver states even in the absence of adopting a waiver. For example, Appendix Table 1, which reports caseloads for waiver and nonwaiver states, shows that waiver states had higher caseloads. If those caseloads were higher in the pre-waiver period, then they may have declined even in the absence of waivers. We will not address these types of specification issues but will maintain the CEA model throughout.

8. As noted in a prior footnote, all data are in fiscal year form, so the 1996 data end in September 1996. Thus, the amount of actual overlap is trivial.

9. See Moffitt (1996) for a discussion of entry effects in the context of education and training programs for welfare recipients.

10. To be precise, these models appear in columns 3–6 of Table 2, in Council of Economic Advisers (1997).

11. The Table 1 regressions do not use state population weights, unlike those in the CEA report. However, this difference is responsible for only a small portion of the difference in results. Estimates using population weights and the years 1976–1996 exactly replicate the results in Table 2 of the CEA report.

12. A specification was also estimated which replaced the waiver dummy by dummy variables for the number of years since the waiver was approved in order to test whether the effects were growing, declining, or constant. The coefficients revealed a growing effect (i.e., a more negative coefficient) with each passing year.

13. The coefficients on the lead variables are open to multiple interpretation. One interpretation, that preferred by the CEA report, interprets the coefficients as representing advance, or anticipatory, behavior on the part of the states, given the publicity surrounding the submission of waiver requests to the federal government. An alternative interpretation is that the coefficients of the lead variables are measuring endogenous policy responses, with causality running from a declining caseload to a later waiver introduction. The latter interpretation is the basis, in fact, for econometric tests for unobserved heterogeneity in panel data which use the inclusion of a future value of the dependent variable as a regressor. On the assumption that future variables cannot be true causal influences on contemporaneous outcomes, the coefficients can be interpreted as measuring persistent unobserved individual effects. See Heckman (1981) and Heckman and Borjas (1980). Without further analysis, these and other interpretations cannot be distinguished.

14. The lead variables also present a special problem if the year 1996 is included because in that case their use requires an assumption of what would have happened in 1997 had PRWORA not passed. The CEA report coded the lead variables in 1996 as equal to their 1996 values, under the assumption that states did not expect further waiver activity in 1997. Excluding 1996 allows us to avoid having to make an assumption about expectations in that year.

15. The CEA report (Table 2) also included two simpler specifications, one without the lagged unemployment rate and one without state × trend variables. Estimation of those models on the 1977–1995 data also show, as in the CEA report, significant effects of the any-waiver variable.

16. It could be argued that an even more precise population on which to measure AFDC receipt is the population of female heads of family. However, there is some evidence that female headship itself responds to AFDC policy. Therefore, as a conservative strategy to avoid missing some of the policy effects, we examine only women as a whole.

17. Appendix Table 1 shows the means of the CPS participation rates. The sample sizes in the CPS are an issue whenever the data are used for state-level analysis. The minimum number of observations for any state (averaged over the number of observations in each of the 1977–1995 years for that state) is 387. The average is 847. These samples are adequate for the state-level analysis reported in Table 1.

18. Using WLS with weights of this kind is an application of the weighted maximum likelihood methods developed in choice-based sampling, most particularly that of Manski and Lerman (1977). The Manski-Lerman estimator was developed for a case in which a binary outcome equation is to be estimated (e.g., transportation mode choice, denoted as y) where the data are composed of two samples, one composed of individuals with $y = 1$ and one composed of individuals with $y = 0$, but not from a random sample and hence not in correct population proportions. Manski and Lerman showed that reweighting the sample to blow it up to population proportions results in consistent estimates of the coefficients. For studies from a related literature, that concerning the use of aggregate totals and outside data in microdata equation estimation, see Imbens and Lancaster (1994) and Imbens and Hellerstein (1999).

19. These results are somewhat sensitive to the treatment of the retrospective nature of the CPS welfare receipt questions, which ask the respondent for such information for the prior calendar year. The CEA data pertain to the fiscal year, so it is not possible to align the CPS data to the CEA time frame. The results shown in Table 1 align the CEA fiscal year with the year of the March survey date; the results are, for reasons we cannot discern, weaker when the CEA fiscal year is aligned with the CPS year prior to the March survey date.

20. Thus, the analysis here still uses grouped data, even if using 16 times as many groups as used in the aggregate state-level analysis. It may be reasonably asked if it would not be preferable to use the individual micro data rather than the means of the 16 cells in each state and year. The answer is that a micro regression with 16 dummies for the age-education cells would have no advantage over using the

group means of those 16 cells except for efficiency. Efficiency gains could be had because the standard errors of the means could be used in the estimation. Of course, the use of variables in addition to age and education could result in a more meaningful extension of what we have done here, but that extension could also be conducted either with group means over more variables, or at the micro data level. In the limit, if every micro observation has a unique set of regressors, a microdata regression is equivalent to a grouped regression because each individual represents a single "group."

21. Small cell sizes are not a problem if the waiver variable is kept at the state level and not interacted with age and education. In that case, using age-education means instead of aggregate state means can only increase efficiency. However, when the waiver effect is allowed to be different for some of the 16 cells, as it will be here, these effects will be less precisely estimated than the average effect at the state aggregate level because the effective sample size going into each waiver coefficient is smaller. The average cell size taken over the 51 states at this disaggregated level is 55 and ranges from 1 to 564. We will continue to reduce these efficiency losses by weighting the observations by the state-level administrative weights, however.

22. Zeros are included for all the variables.

23. On the other hand, the waiver coefficients for the four education categories are not statistically significant from one another because the standard errors are relatively large. It should also be noted that the coefficients in these regressions on the variables which interact 1) education level and the unemployment rate and 2) education level and year dummies are significant and are needed as controls, for the waiver coefficients change when they are not included (not shown in Table 2). The unemployment effects are consistently less negative for more educated women, for example.

24. These and all other dollar figures in the paper are in real 1992 dollars.

25. It is worth emphasizing that these estimates are based upon cross-state variation in unemployment changes. Since unemployment rates change quite differently from state to state, there is considerable variation in the data even in periods when the overall unemployment rate is not changing very much.

References

Blank, R. 1997. *What Causes Public Assistance Caseloads to Grow?* NBER working paper 6343, National Bureau of Economic Research, Cambridge, Massachusetts.

Council of Economic Advisers. 1997. *Explaining the Decline in Welfare Receipt, 1993–1996.* Washington, D.C., May.

Heckman, J. 1981. "Heterogeneity and State Dependence." In *Studies in Labor Markets*, S. Rosen, ed. Chicago: University of Chicago Press, pp. 91–139.

Heckman, J., and G. Borjas. 1980. "Does Unemployment Cause Future Unemployment? Definitions, Questions, and Answers from a Continuous Time Model of Heterogeneity and State Dependence." *Economica* 47(August): 247–283.

Imbens, G., and J. Hellerstein. 1999. "Imposing Moment Restrictions from Auxiliary Data by Weighting." *Review of Economics and Statistics* 81(February): 1–14.

Imbens, G., and T. Lancaster. 1994. "Combining Macro and Micro Data in Microeconometric Models." *Review of Economic Studies* 61: 655–680.

Levine, P., and D. Whitmore. Forthcoming. "The Impact of Welfare Reform on the AFDC Caseload." *National Tax Journal*.

Manski, C., and S. Lerman. 1977. "The Estimation of Choice Probabilities from Choice-Based Samples." *Econometrica* 45: 1977–1988.

Martini, A., and M. Wiseman. 1997. *Explaining the Recent Decline in Welfare Caseloads: Is The Council of Economic Advisers Right?* Washington, D.C.: Urban Institute.

Moffitt, R. 1996. "The Effect of Employment and Training Programs on Entry and Exit from the Welfare Caseload." *Journal of Policy Analysis and Management* 15(Winter): 32–50.

Stapleton, D., G. Livermore, and A. Tucker. 1997. *Determinants of AFDC Caseload Growth.* Washington, D.C.: U.S. Department of Health and Human Services.

Ziliak, J.P,, D.N. Figlio, E.E. Davis, and L.S. Connolly. 1997. *Accounting for the Decline in AFDC Caseloads: Welfare Reform or Economic Growth?* Discussion paper 1151–97, Institute for Research on Poverty, Madison, Wisconsin.

Appendix Table 1 Means of the Outcome Variables in the CPS[a]

Variable	All states	Early waiver states[b]	Late waiver states[b]	No waiver states[b]
ln(Caseload per capita)[c]	4.18	4.70	4.11	4.08
	(1.61)	(1.71)	(1.16)	(1.86)
CPS AFDC	0.049	0.053	0.048	0.049
participation rate	(0.013)	(0.015)	(0.010)	(0.015)
Real annual earnings	9.907	9.905	10.168	9.727
(thousands)	(1.743)	(1.082)	(1.580)	(2.005)
Annual weeks worked	30.8	30.7	31.6	30.3
	(2.5)	(1.9)	(1.9)	(2.9)
Annual hours worked	1.115	1.088	1.143	1.102
(thousands)	(0.091)	(0.068)	(0.586)	(0.110)
Real family income	30.025	40.671	40.000	39.907
(thousands)	(4.822)	(4.408)	(5.778)	(4.050)
Real weekly earnings	201.8	202.8	206.3	198.3
(CPS-ORG)	(35.3)	(24.3)	(32.9)	(39.9)

[a] Standard errors in parentheses. Sample consists of all women aged 16–54.

[b] "Early waiver states" are those with waivers in 1992 or 1993; "late waiver states" are those with waivers in 1994 or 1995; and "no waiver states" are those which never had a waiver approved by the end of 1995.

[c] This variable is taken from the administrative data rather than the CPS. Included for comparison with CPS participation rate.

Examining the Effect of Industry Trends and Structure on Welfare Caseloads

Timothy J. Bartik
Randall W. Eberts
W.E. Upjohn Institute for Employment Research

Welfare caseloads have dropped dramatically in recent years, prompting many policymakers to declare an end to welfare as we have known it. The recent decline in caseloads has occurred concurrently with two distinct events. First, most states have restructured their welfare programs to place greater emphasis on getting welfare recipients into jobs. Second, the economy has exhibited strong employment growth with historically low unemployment rates throughout this period, providing unprecedented opportunities for welfare recipients to find employment. Determining the relative importance of these two effects in explaining past changes in welfare caseloads is essential in assessing future caseload trends.

Two recent studies, one by the Council of Economic Advisers (1997) and the other by Ziliak et al. (1997), have found that economic conditions dominate in explaining caseload reductions, but they differ widely in the estimated size of the effect. The Council of Economic Advisers (CEA) attributes 40 percent of caseload decline to economic conditions measured by unemployment rates, whereas Ziliak et al. attribute 78 percent to such conditions. With economic conditions accounting for a substantial portion of the downward trend in welfare caseloads, the question confronting many policymakers is what might happen to the number of welfare cases when the inevitable downturn in the economy occurs. This question has far-reaching ramifications not only for those who turn to welfare programs for income support, but also for the financing of state and federal welfare programs, for the funding of other programs that have benefitted from the reduction in welfare expenditures, and for the remaining income maintenance programs such as unemployment insurance and disability insurance.

Several studies have addressed the effect of business cycles on welfare caseloads. The approaches taken by these studies range from national time-series analyses to state-level pooled cross-section, time-series studies. Some micro-level studies of individual welfare recipients, while not directly addressing the effect of business cycles on caseloads, are pertinent to this issue as well. Our proposed study relates most closely to four recent analyses of the effect of economic conditions on welfare caseloads by Blank (1997), Council of Economic Advisers (1997), Ziliak et al. (1997), and the Lewin Group (1997). The Lewin Group study is representative of the general methodology employed to estimate this relationship and to simulate the effects of various scenarios of business cycle trends on caseloads. Specifically, they regress the number of cases (and other measures of program participation) on demographic, programmatic, and economic variables. By using pooled cross-section, time-series data, they control more fully for state and time effects than is possible with only time-series data or cross-sectional data. They find that changes in the unemployment rate have substantial effects on program participation and that these effects are more persistent than previously found.

Although these studies show the relationship between welfare caseloads and economic conditions, models such as these, which use unemployment rates as the only measure of economic conditions, have been unable to explain the dramatic reduction in caseloads in recent years. Nor has this genre of models been able to explain the large run-up in caseloads during the latter part of the 1980s, when the economic conditions were quite robust.

The purpose of this paper is to extend the current models to include additional measures of labor market conditions that may affect the variation in welfare caseloads. We believe the unemployment rate by itself may be a woefully incomplete measure of economic conditions affecting potential welfare recipients. The measures we develop are intended to reflect the availability of attractive jobs to welfare recipients. The paper is exploratory, in that the variables we develop have not previously been used to model welfare caseloads. Some of these variables have been used in the regional economics literature, but not as much in labor economics; others are newly developed for this paper. These variables are all meant to measure aspects of the structure of local labor demand that might affect welfare recipients, and all can reasonably be viewed as exogenous to the welfare caseload and to the labor supply behavior of potential welfare recipients. For example, we eschew variables that simply measure the economic status of potential welfare recipients, such as the unemployment rate of female household heads with lower levels of education. The economic status of potential welfare recipients is clearly endogenous (in that it will be determined by unobserved welfare policies that affect welfare caseloads), and the economic status of potential welfare recipients is clearly affected by labor supply behavior as much as labor demand. Our focus is on labor demand factors affecting welfare caseloads.[1]

In one set of models, we attempt to explain welfare caseloads at the state level by not only unemployment, but also state employment growth and three measures of the industrial mix of the state. State employment growth has been shown in the regional economics literature to have powerful effects on labor market outcomes, particularly for less-skilled groups (Bartik 1991, 1996; Blanchard and Katz 1992). Local employment growth may also affect exit rates from welfare (Hoynes 1997). One of the industrial mix measures, the average wage premium implied by the area's industry mix, has also been found in the regional economics literature to affect labor market outcomes (Bartik 1993a, 1996). Finally, we include two other industrial-mix measures, one that measures the extent to which the state's industries are likely to hire only those with high school degrees, and the other measuring how likely the state's industries are to hire welfare recipients. These measures are new, but they have some logical relationship to whether welfare recipients are likely to find jobs.

In another set of models, at the metropolitan level, we go beyond net employment growth to examine how welfare caseloads are related to gross job flows. Studies such as Davis and Haltiwanger (1992) have shown that the gross flows of employment change capture the dynamics of labor markets better than aggregate measures (such as net employment change or unemployment rates). It may be the case that welfare recipients in labor markets with high job turnover have a difficult time finding and retaining jobs. Using a unique data set that contains estimates of the components of employment change at the metropolitan level, we examine the effects of gross job flows and its components on welfare caseloads for metropolitan areas during the early 1990s.

Our finding from both sets of models is that welfare caseloads are explained not only by unemployment but also by many other aspects of the structure of local labor demand. At the national level, we are able to explain the run-up in caseloads during the later 1980s as largely due to decreasing demand for less-skilled workers. On the other hand, the recent reductions in welfare caseloads cannot be explained by our labor-demand indicators and are most plausibly explained by a variety of welfare policies; this supports previous results using unemployment only. However, with an expanded set of labor-demand indicators, the conclusion that welfare reform policies are lowering caseloads is strengthened. For prediction purposes, our results suggest an expanded set of economic variables that might improve prediction, whether at a national, state, or local level. Our results also suggest some policies that might help to lower welfare caseloads, including measures to reduce the extent of job destruction or job instability in the labor market and measures to improve the educational credentials of welfare recipients.

EXTENSION OF STATE-LEVEL ESTIMATES

Most studies, including those of Blank (1997), Council of Economic Advisers (1997), Ziliak et al. (1997), and the Lewin Group (1997), use the total unemployment rate (TUR) to characterize labor market conditions. The TUR is intended to reflect the job vacancies for low-skilled workers. However, the TUR has been a poor predictor of the number of cases during certain time periods. Consider Michigan's experience. If the TUR accurately reflected the job opportunities for low-skilled workers, one would have expected the rapid rundown in the state's total unemployment rate during the 1980s to be accompanied by a significant decline in AFDC cases. As illustrated in Figure 1, the caseloads remained stubbornly high during this period. Only after Michigan's AFDC waiver went into effect (August 1992) did the number of cases start to follow the decline in the unemployment rate, which had already been falling for two years prior to the waiver.

As shown in Table 1, a simple model (Model A) of the monthly change in the logarithm of cases regressed on unemployment rates of various lags shows that the unemployment rate does little to explain the differences in caseloads. However, a dummy variable denoting the

Figure 1 Michigan's AFDC Caseload and Unemployment Rate, 1980–98

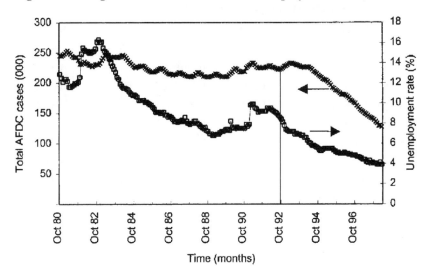

month in which Michigan was granted a waiver is statistically significant as related to AFDC caseloads. The waiver affects the intercept of
the regression but does not affect the slope at any of the lags (Model
B). This brief exercise is presented only to illustrate that, at least for
the state of Michigan, additional macroeconomic variables must be
introduced in order to explain caseload reduction.

Model Specification: Additional Variables
Reflecting Job Opportunities for Low-Skilled Workers

We add to the typical welfare model, estimated using pooled data
on states, several variables that will more fully reflect the labor demand
conditions facing potential welfare recipients. Our first labor-demand
variable is the employment growth rate of the state. A higher state
employment growth rate presumably implies more job vacancies, as
well as fewer jobs being lost through business closings and contractions. It is arguable that job vacancies and job loss may be at least as
important in determining welfare caseload growth as the percentage of
the labor force that happens to be unemployed at a point in time.

Table 1 Estimates of the Effect of Unemployment Rates on AFDC Caseloads, Michigan, Monthly 1980–1998

Model	Model A		Model B	
	Coeff.	S. E.	Coeff.	S. E.
Constant	−0.0120***[a]	0.0019	−0.00007	0.0027
Unemployment rate	0.00168	0.0023	0.0011	0.0021
Unemployment rate (t–1)	0.00109	0.0036	0.0013	0.0034
Unemployment rate (t–2)	0.00084	0.0036	0.0016	0.0034
Unemployment rate (t–3)	−0.00511	0.0036	−0.0063*	0.0034
Unemployment rate (t–4)	0.00028	0.0036	0.0017	0.0034
Unemployment rate (t–5)	0.00140	0.0036	−0.0001	0.0033
Unemployment rate (t–6)	0.00085	0.0022	0.0006	0.0033
Waiver × UR			0.0065	0.0097
Waiver × UR (t–1)			−0.0030	0.0128
Waiver × UR (t–2)			−0.0127	0.0141
Waiver × UR (t–3)			0.0097	0.0143
Waiver × UR (t–4)			−0.0103	0.0142
Waiver × UR (t–5)			0.0224	0.0138
Waiver × UR (t–6)			−0.0078	0.0098
Waiver			−0.0359***	0.0057
R^2	0.098		0.335	

Source: State of Michigan, Department of Social Services, Family Independence
Agency, selected years.
[a] *** = statistical significance at the 0.01 confidence level.
   * = statistical significance at the 0.10 confidence level.

In regional economics research, local employment growth has frequently been used to explain labor market outcomes of individuals in
local labor markets (Bartik 1991; Blanchard and Katz 1992). This
research suggests that local employment growth can plausibly be
viewed as exogenous shocks to local labor demand in the short run and
medium run, based on using instrumental variables that attempt to
measure shifts in national demand for an area's export industries.[2]

The second local labor-demand variable we add is the average
wage premium implied by the area's industrial mix. We use the wage
premiums estimated by Krueger and Summers (1988) for each of 40

industries at the national level. The wage premium represents estimated industry effects from regressing wages (including fringe benefits) on worker characteristics, occupation dummies, and dummies for each industry. The resulting industry effects reflect the level of compensation that a worker in a specific industry receives that is different from what the market would dictate based on personal characteristics, including education and experience.[3] These industry wage premiums, which do not vary over time, are multiplied for each state/year by the proportion of employment in each SIC two-digit industry, and this product is then summed over all industries for that state/year cell to get the "average wage premium" variable that we use. Although the estimated wage premiums are taken from a particular year, Krueger and Summers (1988) and Katz and Summers (1989) suggest that these premiums are remarkably stable over time. If the wage premium entices welfare recipients into the labor force by exceeding their reservation wage, then states with higher wage premiums would be expected to have fewer welfare cases per capita. On the other hand, if a higher wage premium entices more higher-skilled workers into the labor force as well, and employers use these premiums to be more selective about hiring and retaining workers, then the premium might damage job prospects for lower-skilled workers and thus increase welfare cases.

The average wage premium (or similar variables measuring whether an area has a high proportion of "good" jobs) has frequently been used to explain labor market outcomes in regional economics research. A number of studies have used the percentage of employment in manufacturing (or some set of manufacturing industries) to explain local labor market outcomes (Borjas and Ramey 1994; Bound and Holzer 1993; Juhn 1994; Karoly and Klerman 1994). Research by Bartik (1996) suggested that the average wage premium variable dominates manufacturing-related variables in explaining labor market outcomes. All these studies show significant effects of some aspect of job quality on local labor market outcomes. Most of the studies suggest that local job quality has progressive effects, for example, helping less-educated workers more than more-educated workers (Borjas and Ramey 1994; Bartik 1993a, Bound and Holzer 1993), and blacks more than whites (Bound and Holzer 1993; Bartik 1993a). However, Bartik (1996) found that the wage premium variable tends to help more middle-income groups rather than low- or high-income groups. Several studies have found that the wage premium or other local job-quality variables tend to affect labor market outcomes for women as much as for men (Karoly and Klerman 1994; Bartik 1993a, 1996), which suggests that these variables will be relevant to welfare caseloads.

The other two measures of local labor demand are also based on the mix of industries in the state. Specifically, we include one variable measuring the educational requirements implied by the state's industry mix; the other variable is the percentage of welfare recipients employed implied by the state's industry mix. These two industry-mix variables do not have extensive previous use in research, but they do seem logically related to labor demand for potential welfare recipients.

For the educational requirements variable, we calculated—for the nation as a whole and for each year separately—the percentage of employees in each two-digit industry that were high school graduates, using data from the March CPS from March 1983 to March 1997. These data were then combined with data from each state and year on the proportion of employment in each two-digit industry in order to calculate a variable measuring the proportion of employees in each state/year cell that would be high school graduates if each industry hired in a pattern similar to that of its national counterpart for that year. We regard this variable as a rough measure of the extent to which a state's demand is skewed by industrial composition toward more highly educated workers. This variable for a state will increase relative to that for other states if the state's industrial composition becomes more concentrated than the national average in industries that have a high percentage of employees with a high school education. Because the characteristics of industries for this variable are measured separately for each year, this variable will also increase relative to that of other states if a state's industrial mix stays the same, but that mix happens to show a greater-than-average gain in percentage of employees with a high school education. The hypothesis is that welfare recipients may qualify for fewer jobs in states that have a higher-than-average concentration of jobs requiring high school degrees. As a result, we would expect this variable to be positively correlated with caseloads.

The second variable was measured in a similar manner: the percentage of welfare recipients employed in each two-digit industry at the national level was calculated using March CPS data, but for this variable we used only March 1996 data to define industry characteristics for all years. As will be seen later, we want to determine if our variables can explain recent national trends in caseloads, and we do not want them to be spuriously correlated with national trends in welfare caseloads. The March 1996 percentage employed who are welfare recipients in each industry was multiplied times the state's proportion of employment in that year in each respective two-digit industry to create a weighted variable for each state/year cell. This weighted variable tells us what proportion of employees would be welfare recipients in each state/year cell if each industry in that state and year had employed welfare recipients in the same proportion that its national counterpart did in 1996. Our first intuition was that this variable should be negatively correlated with caseloads, because one might expect that states whose industries tend to employ welfare recipients would be easier labor markets for welfare recipients to obtain jobs in. A second explanation, and one that comports with the results, is that industries that hire a great many welfare recipients may also be the same industries with high turnover rates and other characteristics that *create* more welfare recipients, thus increasing welfare caseloads.

One obvious alternative to our industry-mix variables is simply including variables for the proportion of state employment in each of the two-digit industries used in constructing these industry-mix measures. We rejected this alternative because of our expectation, based on previous research projects, that such estimation would lead to hopeless problems with multicollinearity.[4] Even if multicollinearity were not a problem, there would be some serious problems with trying to interpret the large numbers of resulting coefficients on individual industries. Using these industry-mix variables at least provides a manageable number of coefficients and some idea about what the underlying variables are measuring.

Descriptive Statistics

To get a better sense of the nature of these local labor-demand variables, we report a variety of descriptive statistics. Table 2 reports, for each of the three industry-mix variables, the "top six" and "bottom six" industries in the calculations used to generate these indices. The pattern is what one would expect. The education variable tends to be high for various white-collar-dominated industries and low for various low-

Table 2 Top and Bottom Six Industries for the Three Industry-Mix Variables[a] (%)

High-school-graduates variable		Welfare-recipients variable		Wage-premium variable	
Top six industries:					
Banking and other finance	98.1	Private household services	3.78	Petroleum products	61.9
Communications	96.4	Leather and leather products	3.56	Tobacco manufactures	52.7
Other professional services	96.3	Miscellaneous manufacturing	2.92	Public utilities	33.6
Public administration	96.3	Social services	2.65	Communications	29.3
Professional and photo equipment and watches	95.8	Personal services, excluding private household services	2.27	Railroad	26.8
Educational services	95.1	Retail trade	2.13	Transportation equipment	26.7
Bottom six industries:					
Lumber and wood products	69.8	Not specified metal industries	0.0	Retail trade, other than eating and drinking places	−18.6
Textile mill products	69.1	Aircraft and parts	0.0	Personal services, excluding private household services	−19.4
Leather and leather products	66.7	Other transportation equipment	0.0	Education services	−21.6
Agriculture	63.4	Tobacco manufactures	0.0	Eating and drinking places	−21.9
Apparel and other textile products	62.4	Petroleum and coal products	0.0	Social services	−33.0
Private household services	48.4	Forestry and fisheries	0.0	Private household services	−51.7

[a] The high-school-graduates variable is the percentage of the industry's employees with a high school degree as of 1996 (taken from the March 1997 CPS). The welfare-recipient variable is the percentage of the industry's employees who also received welfare the previous year (taken from the March 1996 CPS). The wage-premium number for each industry is actually 100 times the differential of each industry from the all-industry average for ln(wage).

skill manufacturing and service industries and agriculture. The welfare-employment variable is high for various service-oriented industries and lower-skill manufacturing. The wage-premium variables are high for some high-wage manufacturing and other heavy industries, as well as more unionized industries, and lower for service-oriented industries.

Table 3 presents the means and standard deviations for all five of the local-labor-demand variables. Because the eventual estimation includes a complete set of state and year dummies, it is the variation in these variables after controlling for unobserved state and year effects that is really crucial. Therefore, we also report the standard deviation of the residuals from regressing these variables on a set of state and year dummies. As the table shows, the standard deviations of the three industry-mix variables are dramatically reduced after controlling for state and year effects, meaning that these variables show some pronounced national time trends and persistent patterns of variation across states.

Table 4 presents the correlation of the five labor-demand variables, again after controlling for state and year effects. Although many of the correlations are statistically significant and of moderately large size, considerable independent variation in these five variables remains. For example, the largest absolute value of any correlation in the table is 0.554. The R^2 in regressing a variable on another variable will be the square of its correlation. Hence, the largest amount of variance that one variable explains of another is $(0.554)^2$, or 0.307, less than one-third.

The pattern of correlations is as one might expect. Employment growth and unemployment are strongly negatively correlated, although considerable independent variation remains; i.e., there are states in which unemployment remains low even though employment growth declines. The welfare variable is negatively correlated, as one would expect, with the high-school-graduates variable and the wage-premium variable. States that have an increasing proportion of industries that employ welfare recipients also tend to have an increasing proportion of industries that pay poorly and have lower educational requirements. However, the variables are not close to perfectly correlated. Finally, the wage-premium variable is positively correlated with employment growth and negatively correlated with the unemployment rate. This is

Table 3 Means and Standard Deviations of the Five Local-Labor-Demand Variables[a]

Variable	Mean	Standard deviation	Adjusted standard deviation
Unemployment rate (%)	6.85	2.03	1.08
Employment growth (%)	1.89	1.89	1.19
High school graduates (%)	84.43	2.25	0.23
Welfare recipient (%)	0.95	0.04	0.01
Wage premium (%)	−1.35	1.26	0.25

[a] All means and standard deviations are weighted by the 1996 population of the state. Means and standard deviations are calculated based on data for 51 states (including D.C.) and 15 years (1982–96). The adjusted standard deviation is the weighted standard deviation of the residual from a preliminary regression of the variable on year and state dummies. This preliminary regression was also weighted.

Table 4 Correlations for the Five Local-Labor-Demand Variables[a]

Variable	Employment-growth variable	High-school-graduates variable	Wage-premium variable	Welfare-recipients variable
Unemployment rate	−0.538 (0.0001)	0.091 (0.0114)	−0.364 (0.0001)	0.032 (0.3837)
Employment growth		−0.112 (0.0019)	0.153 (0.0001)	−0.003 (0.8990)
High school graduates			0.283 (0.0001)	−0.525 (0.0001)
Wage premium				−0.554 (0.0001)

[a] These are weighted correlations using 1996 population weights for all states. Correlations are for residuals from weighted regression of each of five variables on year and state dummies. Underlying observations are for 51 states (including D.C.) and 15 years (1982–96). The number in parentheses is the probability of correlation of this size occurring by chance if the true correlation was zero.

consistent with previous research that found, using causality tests, that trends in employment growth and the wage-premium variable at the local level tend to mutually cause each other (Bartik 1993a). This pattern of mutual causation is sensible. A state which gains higher-wage industries will tend to experience some growth in labor demand from higher personal income. A state which experiences tightening labor markets may find it easier to attract higher-wage-premium industries, which may be less sensitive to the wage rate paid for labor.

Table 5 explores the spatial pattern of these local demand variables, showing, for 1996, the six states with the highest and lowest values of each. Unemployment tends to be low in rural states but high in a diverse group of states having probably quite diverse economic problems. Employment growth tends to be high in some western and southern states, and low in the diverse group. The spatial pattern of these two variables is far from perfectly matched; for example, California was fourth in unemployment in 1996 even though it was twelfth in employment growth. The high-school-graduates variable tends to be high in northeastern states with many white-collar industries and low in southern and western states. The wage-premium variable is high in heavily unionized, manufacturing-dominated states and low in states with a great deal of retail trade and service businesses. The welfare variable varies high and low in a diverse collection of states that are difficult to generalize about.

Figure 2 shows the national time trends in these labor-demand variables. The unemployment rate and employment growth (Fig. 2A) have the pattern one would expect, with employment growth trends seeming to lead unemployment rate trends slightly. The three industry-mix variables (Figs. 2B–D) show pronounced national time trends. The wage-premium variable has dramatically declined over time as higher-paying manufacturing industries have declined. The high-school-graduate variable has increased as the proportion of educated workers employed has increased in many industries. The welfare-employment variable has increased as service-oriented industries have increased. Some additional work (not reported here) shows that the increase in the high-school-graduate variable is totally due to changes in the educational composition of individual industries and not to changes in industry mix in favor of higher-education industries. If the

Table 5 States with Highest and Lowest Values of Local-Labor-Demand Variables in 1996 (%)

Rank	Unemployment variable	Employment-growth variable	High-school-graduates variable	Wage-premium variable[a]	Welfare-recipients variable
Top six states:					
1	Washington D.C. 8.7	Nevada 6.19	Washington D.C. 91.76	Indiana -0.23	Nevada 1.25
2	West Virginia 7.6	Utah 4.58	New York 88.18	Michigan -0.32	Rhode Island 1.06
3	Arkansas 7.5	Arizona 4.54	Massachusetts 87.97	Delaware -0.64	Florida 1.05
4	California 7.5	Oregon 3.40	Connecticut 87.83	Ohio -0.64	Montana 1.05
5	New Mexico 6.7	Colorado 3.06	New Jersey 87.82	Illinois -0.80	Maine 1.03
6	Louisiana 6.6	Georgia 3.01	Maryland 87.73	Kansas -0.92	New Hampshire 1.03
Bottom six states:					
46	Wisconsin 3.6	New Mexico 0.85	Mississippi 85.79	Maine -3.53	Indiana 0.94
47	Iowa 3.3	New York 0.77	Idaho 85.78	Florida -3.84	Connecticut 0.93
48	Utah 3.2	Arkansas 0.67	Arizona 85.70	Montana -4.34	Washington 0.93

49	North Dakota 3.0	Rhode island 0.50	North Carolina 85.53	Washington D.C. -4.55	Kansas 0.91
50	South Dakota 2.9	Hawaii -0.07	South Carolina 85.48	Hawaii -5.65	Arkansas 0.89
51	Nebraska 2.8	Washington D.C. -2.51	Nevada 84.77	Nevada -5.86	Washington D.C. 0.73

[a] The wage-premium variable is 100 × (ln wage differential) for state predicted by its industrial mix. This number is negative for all states in 1996 because the original wage premiums were calculated so that weighted national average was zero in 1984, and the industry mix has shifted towards lower-wage industries since then.

Figure 2 National Time Trends in Five Labor Demand Variables

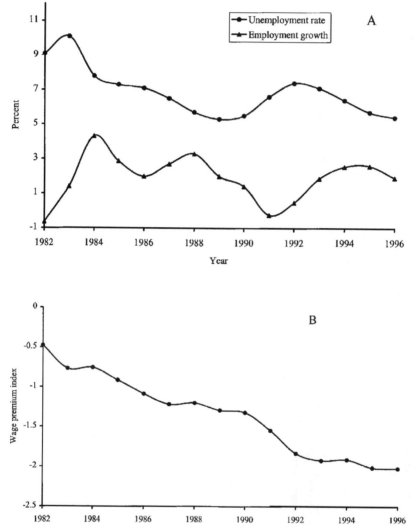

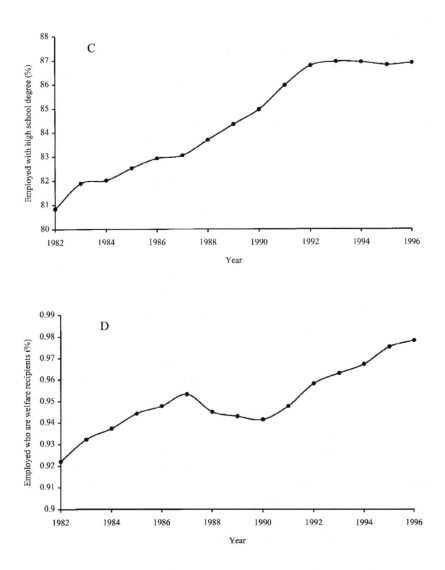

Note: All national averages are calculated using 1996 population weighted for each state. The three industry mix variables all predict a particular variable based on mix of industries and some industry characteristic.

same industry variables are used for all years in calculating the high-school-graduate variable, the national time line is flat.

RESULTS

Our models are extensions of those used by Blank (1997) and the Council of Economic Advisers (1997). The data used are pooled time-series, cross-section data at the annual level for all 50 states (plus the District of Columbia), for 1984 to 1996. The dependent variable in our preferred models is the natural logarithm of AFDC cases per capita in each state/year cell. All regressions include a complete set of dummy variables for states and years in order to control for unobserved fixed state characteristics and for unobserved national trends that might affect caseloads.[5] The specifications include various combinations of the five economic characteristics discussed above. In addition, the preferred specifications include the logarithm of the AFDC benefit level and whether or not the state has by that year received a waiver for welfare experimentation from the federal government.[6] The specifications differ in the dynamic specification describing the time pattern by which state economic characteristics affect welfare caseloads.

We began by estimating specifications that matched, as closely as possible given our data, the empirical models used by the CEA, Blank, and some of the annual models used by Ziliak et al. (These results are not fully reported here, but are available upon request.) Specifically, we tried to match the specifications used by the CEA (their Table 2, column 1), Blank (her Table 2, column 1), and Ziliak et al. (their Table 4, column 4). For Blank's model, this involved switching the denominator of the dependent variable from total state population to the number of female household heads, with other relatives present, ages 16–44, with less than 16 years of education. It turns out that the choice of denominators does not significantly affect the coefficients on the economic variables that we focus on, so the remainder of this paper continues to focus on welfare caseloads per capita. In general, we were able to replicate their results fairly closely for the economic variable we have in common—the unemployment rate—despite some inevitable differences in the precise data used.

Our detailed presentation stresses three models. The first model (Table 6, Model I) is similar to those of the CEA and of Blank in simply having the level of the ln(caseloads per capita) as a dependent variable, without allowing for any lagged effects of caseloads. All five economic characteristics are included. In deciding on an optimal lag structure, we first tested from zero to two lags in unemployment in a model with only unemployment as a state economic characteristic. The optimal lag length in unemployment was then chosen based on the Akaike Information Criterion (AIC). We then added employment growth to this optimal model and tested from zero to two lags in employment growth, choosing the optimal lag length in employment growth based on the AIC. Finally, we added the three industry-mix variables to the regressors and tested the optimal lag length (from zero to two lags) using the AIC while restricting these three variables to the same lag length. We include lags in all the local-labor-demand variables to allow for the possibility that wages, labor force participation rates, and other labor market outcomes that affect welfare caseloads will take some time to respond to labor demand shocks, and that this response may change over time as the local labor market adjusts.[7]

Our second model adds the lagged level of the ln(caseloads per capita) as a regressor, inspired by Ziliak et al.'s findings that state welfare caseloads appear to be quite persistent from year to year. We also find great persistence, with a coefficient on the lagged dependent variable of 0.913 (standard error = 0.014; see Table 6, Model II). This second model uses the same sequential testing procedure to separately determine the optimal lag length for each of the economic-characteristics variables.

Finally, our third model drops the lagged dependent variable and uses the change in the ln(caseloads per capita) as a dependent variable. As noted by Ziliak et al., the coefficient close to 1 on the lagged caseload-dependent variable suggests the possibility that the caseload variable is nonstationary. Research by Nickell (1981) suggested that coefficients on the lagged dependent variable in panels with short time series and fixed cross-sectional effects may be biased towards zero, so it is possible that the true coefficient on the lagged caseload variable is 1. Again, the optimal lag length for the economic-characteristics variables in this "changes" model is determined by sequential testing of various lag lengths. Despite the possibility that the caseload variable is nonstationary, we regard this possibility as theoretically implausible, because it implies that caseloads per capita are a random walk, with any

Table 6 Models of the Effect of Economic Variables on AFDC Caseloads[a]

Independent variable	Model I: Dep. var. = ln(caseloads/population)	Model II: Dep. var. = ln(caseloads/population)	Model III: Dep. var. = change in ln(caseloads/population)
Lagged dependent variable	–	0.9129*** (0.0136)	–
Unemployment rate:			
Current	0.0218*** (0.0082)	0.0018 (0.0029)	–0.0001 (0.0030)
Lag 1	–0.0003 (0.0093)	0.0075*** (0.0026)	0.0005 (0.0034)
Lag 2	0.0431*** (0.0067)	–	0.0040* (0.0024)
Log of maximum AFDC benefit	0.5099*** (0.0842)	0.2005*** (0.0295)	0.1794*** (0.0302)
Any statewide waiver	–0.0945*** (0.0188)	0.0066 (0.0068)	0.0161** (0.0069)
Employment growth[b]			
Current	1.2660*** (0.4806)	–0.2228 (0.1721)	–0.3988** (0.1766)
Lag 1	–	–0.5646*** (0.1736)	–0.7475*** (0.1802)
Lag 2	–	–0.3400** (0.1401)	0.4040*** (0.1454)
High school graduates[c]			
Current	–0.0707 (0.0442)	0.0269* (0.0155)	0.0187 (0.0160)
Lag 1	0.0359 (0.0495)	0.0249 (0.0174)	0.0270 (0.0180)
Lag 2	0.0235 (0.0392)	–0.0269** (0.0137)	–0.0346** (0.0142)
State wage premium[d]			
Current	0.1086 (0.0687)	–0.0114 (0.00241)	–0.0265 (0.0248)
Lag 1	–0.0311 (0.0877)	–0.0508 (0.0328)	0.0582* (0.0339)
Lag 2	–0.1037* (0.0558)	0.0615*** (0.0217)	0.0910*** (0.0225)

Independent variable	Model I: Dep. var. = ln(caseloads/ population)	Model II: Dep. var. = ln(caseloads/ population)	Model III: Dep. var. = change in ln(caseloads/ population
Welfare recipients[e]			
Current	2.6822**	0.7886*	0.5108
	(1.3279)	(0.4684)	(0.4826)
Lag 1	1.1941	–0.5080	–0.7093
	(1.7426)	(0.6470)	(0.6675)
Lag 2	0.4381	0.2957	0.4345
	(1.2418)	(0.4641)	(0.4815)
Adjusted R^2	0.9300	0.9915	0.7489
Sample size	663	663	663

Significance level: *** = 1%; ** = 5%; * = 10%.

[a] Standard errors are in parentheses. All regressions use pooled time-series cross-section data of observations on state/year cells, with data on the dependent variable for all years from 1984 to 1996 (because of the two lags in some variables, data for 1982 and 1983 are also used), and for all 50 states plus the District of Columbia. All regressions are weighted by 1996 values for state population. All regressions, in addition to including variables for which coefficients are reported in the table, include complete sets of state dummies and year dummies to control for unobserved state or national influences on welfare receipt rates. F-tests reveal that for each group of current and lagged variables for a particular state economic climate variable (e.g., unemployment), the group is statistically significant at the 5 percent level in all cases except the unemployment variable for Model III and the welfare variable for Model III.

[b] Change in log of employment.

[c] Percentage of employees that would be high school graduates based on industry mix.

[d] Calculated as differential of average ln(wage) based on industry mix.

[e] Percentage of employees that would be welfare recipients based on industry mix.

random factor that happens to push caseloads up or down persisting indefinitely into the future. It seems more plausible that caseloads are merely highly sluggish in adjusting to shocks and that the true coefficient on lagged coefficients is less than 1. Hence, we regard model II as the most intuitively plausible of the three models.

We wish to note several features of these models that already are apparent in this Table 6. First, it is clear that much more than unemployment in a state's economic environment matters to caseloads. Employment growth and the three industrial-mix variables also appear to be highly statistically significant in explaining state caseloads, and this occurs holding constant any fixed state characteristics and national trends. Second, lags matter a great deal in explaining caseloads, with the lagged value of state economic characteristics in many cases mattering more than current characteristics. Third, in the case of employment growth, controlling for lagged caseloads makes a major difference in the estimated effects of this variable. Without such control, employment growth is estimated to have positive effects on caseloads, whereas controlling for lagged caseloads, employment growth has negative effects. One explanation for this pattern of results is that states which in the past have had recessions and employment declines, and as a result have had high caseloads, may tend on average to have higher employment growth as they recover from the downturn. The omission of lagged caseloads may bias the coefficient on employment growth because higher employment growth may proxy for poor growth and high caseloads in the past, and past caseloads tend to persist.

Table 7 shows simulations of the effects of state economic variables, reporting the estimated effects of a 1 percent change in the economic variable four years after the shock, which helps make the effects more comparable between the static and the more dynamic specifications. The standard deviations shown in the column heads are those for each variable after controlling for state and year effects, that is, the standard deviation of the residual from regressing that state's economic characteristics on state and year dummies. This number gives some sense of how much each economic variable varies independently over time for different states. Both unemployment and employment growth show a similar percentage variation, while the high-school-graduate and wage-premium variables vary only one-fifth as much, and the welfare variable varies one-hundredth as much.

In addition to reporting results for the state economic characteristics in our models I, II, and III, we report effects of unemployment in identical models that only include unemployment as a state economic characteristic. We also report effects of unemployment in three models similar to those estimated by the CEA (1997), Blank (1997), and Ziliak et al. (1997). The CEA model mainly differs from our Model I with just unemployment in not including lags in the unemployment rate. The Blank model mainly differs in having a different dependent variable, the logarithm of caseloads per female-headed household with relatives present. The Ziliak model uses as a dependent variable the "change" in ln(caseloads per capita), as in our model III, but also first differences all the other right-side variables, including the unemployment rate.

The simulation results in Table 7 also show a great sensitivity to the exact dynamic specification. For example, the effects of employment growth and the state economic characteristics vary greatly from Model I through Model III. Even if only the unemployment rate is included, the exact dynamics of the specification make a great deal of difference. Including lagged unemployment rates increases the estimated effects of unemployment on caseloads, as is evident from comparing a CEA-type model (no lags in unemployment) to Model I with unemployment only. In addition, the Ziliak type of model, which first-differences all variables, shows a very small effect of unemployment, perhaps because in this model all effects of unemployment must occur immediately and the changes in the unemployment rate variable on the right side cannot proxy for past lags in the level of unemployment.

In our preferred model (Model II), the effects of unemployment are considerably reduced (by more than half) when one adds employment growth and the three industrial-mix effects to the specification. A permanent shock to employment growth of 1 percent has effects similar to a permanent shock to the unemployment rate of 1 percent, and the variation in these variables over time and states is fairly similar. A one-standard-deviation change in the high school graduates variable or in the welfare recipient variable also yields roughly similar effects in magnitude to the employment-growth or unemployment-rate effects, while the effects of the wage premium are considerably smaller and are statistically insignificant. The point estimates suggest, as one would expect, that faster employment growth lowers welfare rolls. A shift in industrial mix toward industries that tend to employ high school graduates increases welfare rolls, while the point estimates suggest that an increase in high-wage-premium industries in an area tends to reduce welfare rolls. These effects are as expected.

A surprising finding is that a shift in the industrial mix toward industries that tend to employ welfare recipients is estimated to increase welfare rolls. This finding appears to be somewhat sensitive to the specification. As mentioned above, perhaps this finding can be explained if industries that employ welfare recipients are also those that tend to have less-stable jobs, which might contribute to increasing welfare rolls. Welfare rolls might function as a type of substitute for

Table 7 Simulated Effects of State Economic Variables on Caseloads[a]

Model	Unemployment (s.d. = 1.00)	Employment-growth variable (s.d. = 1.33)	High-school-graduates variable (s.d. = 0.22)	Wage-premium variable (s.d. = 0.27)	Welfare-recipient variable (s.d. = 0.01)
Full model I	0.0646 (12.93)	0.0127 (2.63)	0.1301 (5.85)	-0.0263 (1.09)	4.3143 (7.23)
Full model II	0.0337 (3.73)	-0.0390 (4.32)	0.1242 (3.46)	-0.0596 (1.41)	2.2924 (2.61)
Full model III	0.0136 (1.28)	-0.0620 (5.91)	0.0710 (2.18)	-0.0925 (-1.72)	1.0205 (0.95)
Model I w/only unemployment	0.0622 (14.40)				
Model II w/only unemployment	0.0793 (13.95)				
Model III w/only unemployment	0.0865 (11.59)				
Levine-Whitmore type of model	0.0421 (9.23) [orig = 0.0473]				
Blank type of model	0.0548 (9.98) [orig = 0.038]				
Ziliak et al. type of model	0.0080 (2.80) [orig = 0.0066]				

unemployment insurance for some of these industries. We explore the effect of gross job flows on welfare caseloads in the next section.

A key policy issue is the effects of national or local recessions on welfare caseloads. Because our preferred specification, with other local-labor-demand variables, estimates a smaller coefficient on unemployment, does our preferred specification imply that a recession with high unemployment has less effect than is believed by other researchers? Our answer is that the effect of a recession depends upon whether increases in unemployment are accompanied by similar changes in other local-demand variables, as have typically occurred in the past. One could argue that the specifications with only unemployment as a local-demand variable already show the effects of unemployment, with other local-labor-demand variables allowed to endogenously adjust along with unemployment in whatever pattern of correlation has characterized their past joint behavior. In other words, one could view the specifications with only unemployment as a local-demand variable as a "reduced form" of the fuller specification.

To explore this point further, we estimated several auxiliary regressions in which each of the four labor-demand variables (other than unemployment) are regressed on unemployment and a complete set of state and year dummies. These auxiliary regressions are used, along with the specification with five labor-demand variables and a lagged dependent variable that we call "Full Model II," to simulate the effect on welfare caseloads after four years of a one-point rise in the unemployment rate. As can be seen in Table 8, the effects of unemployment in this multiequation simulation approximate that of Model II with only unemployment included. We then experiment with dropping each one of the four auxiliary regressions, one at a time, from the multiequation simulation. Dropping an auxiliary regression from the simulation implies that we are holding that variable constant (not allowing it to change as it does on average when unemployment goes up). As the table makes clear, it is largely the employment growth variable that is generating the smaller coefficient on unemployment in Full Model II.

Therefore, the correct answer to the effects of unemployment on caseloads is that the results of previous authors are fine as long as employment growth increases (as it has in the past) when unemployment goes up. However, if the nation's (or a state's) unemployment were to go up without the usual slowing of employment growth, then

Table 8 Simulated Effects of a 1% Increase in Unemployment on ln(caseload per capita)[a]

Model	Effect on ln(caseload per capita)
Full Model II (from Table 7)	0.0337
	(3.73)
Model II with only unemployment (from Table 7)	0.0793
	(13.95)
Full Model II, with auxiliary regressions	0.0649
	(10.02)
Employment growth held constant	0.0424
	(4.52)
High school graduates held constant	0.0618
	(9.78)
Wage premium held constant	0.0601
	(8.15)
Welfare recipients held constant	0.0637
	(10.01)

[a] Numbers in parentheses are pseudo t-statistics from 1000 Monte Carlo repetitions of simulations. There are four auxiliary regressions, regressing the four local-demand variables (other than unemployment) on unemployment and year and state dummies. Full model II with auxiliary regressions uses these four additional equations to simulate effect of 1% increase in unemployment, with the four other demand variables allowed to change. Remaining models drop one of four auxiliary equations, thus implicitly holding that variable constant.

the effects of that unemployment rise on welfare caseloads will be smaller than some researchers have predicted. Conversely, if the nation or a state were to experience slower employment growth without a rise in unemployment, our model would predict a possibly significant rise in welfare caseloads. For example, one could imagine a state with economic problems that lead to slow employment growth or employment declines but with sufficient out-migration and labor force dropouts that unemployment does not increase.

One key issue is whether the models estimated here, with additional labor-demand variables, can explain the national trends in caseloads in the 1980s and 1990s. We explore this issue in two ways. First, we consider the year dummies estimated by the model (Figure 3).

**Figure 3 Year Dummies from Various Models Explaining
ln(caseload per capita)**

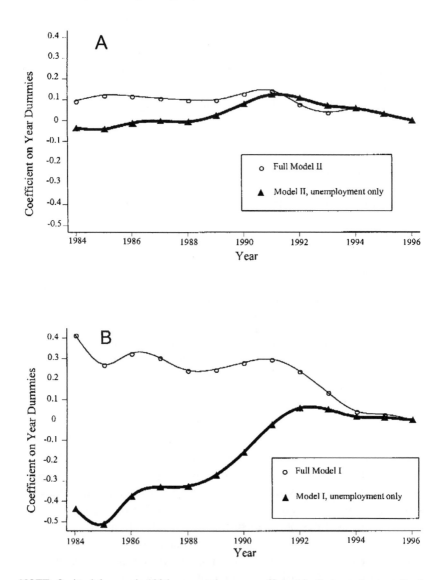

NOTE: Omitted dummy is 1996, so year dummy coefficient in that year is normalized
to zero.

(The 1996 dummy is the omitted dummy, so all year effects are relative to what occurs nationally on average in 1996). Figure 3A compares our preferred model, Full Model II, with an alternative model, Model II with only unemployment as a labor-demand variable. Analyzing the year dummies here is complicated because these models include a lagged dependent variable; hence, if a year dummy is high relative to another year's dummy, this will push up caseloads in subsequent years as well. In any event, this graph indicates that with only unemployment as a labor-demand variable, caseloads were pushed up by national year trends throughout the 1980s and early 1990s. With the other local-labor-demand variables, the year dummies have a fairly consistent effect throughout the 1980s, followed by some decline in the early to mid 1990s. Figure 3B shows that for the models without a lagged dependent variable (Full Model I and Model I with only unemployment) there is a more dramatic contrast. Model I with just unemployment shows a huge, unexplained run-up in caseloads in the 1980s and early 1990s, whereas the full Model I shows, if anything, some unexplained decline in caseloads, particularly in the early 1990s.

Analyzing how different variables contribute to these national trends is complicated in our preferred specification, Full Model II, because of a lagged dependent variable. With such a variable, caseloads at any point in time can be considered as a function of caseloads at any lagged past point in time and of trends in between that past time and the present in other variables (including the year dummies). It happens that in 1984 and 1989, caseloads per capita were virtually the same; so in this case the rise in caseloads over some subsequent period is totally a function of all the other variables in the model. Table 9 uses this fortunate coincidence to consider whether the model can explain the rise in caseloads that occurred in the 1990s. Previous research by Blank (1997) suggested that economic variables cannot explain the rise in caseloads that occurred during this period. As Table 9, Panel A shows, caseloads per capita rose in "ln percentage points" by 25.4 percent from 1989 to 1994. In model II, which includes only unemployment as a state economic characteristic, most of this increase is due to unexplained trends in the national time dummies over the 1989 to 1994 time period; but when other state economic characteristics are included, we actually find that unexplained time dummies show a drop in the caseload compared with what we would expect.

Table 9 Why Caseloads Increased from 1989 to 1994[a]

Panel A: Difference Between 1989 and 1994 Caseloads and Time Effects	
Difference between ln(caseloads per capita), 1994 vs. 1989	+ 0.254
Difference explained by time dummies in previous five years, model with only unemployment included as state economic characteristic	+ 0.275
Difference explained by time dummies in previous five years, model with all five state economic characteristics included	−0.096

Panel B: Breakdown of contribution of different variables to 1994 minus 1989 difference in caseloads, model with all five state economic characteristics included	
Difference in caseload five years ago	−0.004
Welfare benefits	−0.109
Waivers	0.003
Unemployment rate	−0.006
Employment growth	0.078
Industry mix: proportion of high school graduates	0.339
Industry mix: average wage premium	0.020
Industry mix: proportion of welfare recipients	0.026
Unobserved national time period effects over previous five years	−0.096
Total change in ln(caseloads) to be explained	0.254

[a] These calculations try to explain 1994 and 1989 caseloads as function of previous five year's variables, plus caseloads as of five years ago. As of five years ago (1989 for 1994, 1984 for 1989), caseloads per capita were virtually identical. These calculations simulate what happens to caseloads due to values of independent variables, allowing for lagged effects that occur due to including lags of some variables, and due to effects via lagged dependent variables. Because the model is linear, these effects should approximately add up.

Panel B breaks down how national variables explain these differences in caseload during the previous five years. Most of the increase in caseloads from 1989 to 1994 appears to be explained by the increase in the "high school graduate" industrial-mix variable. This variable increased from an average of 82.9 percent over the 1983–1989 period to an average of 85.7 percent over the 1988–1994 period, an increase of 2.8 percent.[8] The point estimates reported in Table 7 suggest that each 1 percent increase in this variable is associated with about a 0.124 change in the ln(caseloads per capita) variable, so an increase of 2.8

percent in this variable would be expected to increase the ln(caseloads per capita) by more than 0.30, or over 30 "ln percentage points."

How much should we believe this finding? It should be recognized that this finding extrapolates the effects of relatively small differences in trends among states to relatively large changes over time for the nation. As shown in Table 7, the standard deviation of this variable, controlling for state and year dummies, is only about one-fifth of 1 percent. It may be perilous to extrapolate the estimated effects of differences among states of one-fifth of 1 percent to differences in the nation of 2 percent or more. On the other hand, the estimated effect is not inherently unreasonable. Welfare rolls are only 3 or 4 percent of the labor force in the United States; a change in welfare rolls of 30 percent is not a large percentage of the U.S. labor force. Changes of 2 or 3 in the percentage of high school graduates demanded in the workforce loom very large compared with welfare-roll changes.

Gross Job Flows

In the previous section, we found an increase in caseload in areas having a high concentration of industries that employ welfare recipients. One interpretation of this result is that jobs in these industries turn over more often and provide a less-stable employment base for welfare recipients. Gross flows, the summation of job creation and job destruction, are typically used to measure job turnover. The purpose of this section is to take a closer look at the relationship between gross job flows and the number of cases to see if such information lends additional insight into the effect of labor market conditions on the welfare caseload.

Gross job flows are obtained by linking establishments longitudinally over a specific time period. The Census Bureau has embarked on a relatively new project to construct gross employment flows by linking all establishments, including the service sector, which employs a large percentage of low-skilled workers. Davis and Haltiwanger (1992) have linked manufacturing establishments using the Census Bureau's Longitudinal Data File (LRD), but manufacturing employs only a small percentage of low-skilled workers. Therefore, we requested that the Census Bureau create a special tabulation of the employment components for all metropolitan areas between 1989 and

1992. We use these data to examine the relationship between caseload and labor market conditions among metropolitan areas.

Since the employment components span only the 1989–1992 period, the analysis is basically a cross-sectional estimation. However, specification of a limited lag structure is possible, because caseload data for several years around the 1989–1992 period are available. Furthermore, specification tests of the lagged structure using state-level data reported in the previous section reveal that either first-differencing the caseloads or controlling for lagged caseloads is a plausible specification. Additional analysis reveals that caseloads at the metropolitan level are also quite stable. Rank-order correlations of the caseloads for various time differences across metropolitan areas reveal that the ordering of MSAs according to the number of caseloads is persistent over time. The correlation for caseloads one year apart is about the same as the correlation for caseloads six years apart; the correlations average between 0.90 and 0.99.

These specifications are shown in Table 10. Column A includes the change in caseloads per capita between 1990 and 1993 as a dependent variable; columns B, C, and D use the 1993 level of caseloads per capita as a dependent variable, and the 1990 level of caseloads is included as a control variable. These variables are regressed against various labor market characteristics, including gross job flows. Since gross flows are estimated for the 1989–1992 period, this variable and the net employment change variable are in essence lagged one period. As can be seen in the table, using the change in caseloads per capita between 1990 and 1993 (column A) yields similar results for the gross flows and net change variables when the lagged dependent variable specification is used (column B).

The persistence of caseloads per capita is evident in the large coefficient on the lagged dependent variable and its high statistical significance. The lagged unemployment rate variable is positive and statistically significant, while the contemporaneous unemployment variable is negative but not statistically significant. Taken together, the sum of the coefficients for these two lags are positive and statistically significant. Net employment change is relatively large and of high statistical significance. The negative coefficient suggests that areas with higher rates of net job growth have lower caseloads, as one would expect.

Table 10 The Effects of Economic Conditions on the Change in Metropolitan Caseloads, 1990–1993[a]

	A[b]	B[c]	C[c]	D[c]
ln per capita income, 1990	−0.0080**	−0.0064**	−0.0046	−0.0046
	(0.0032)	(0.0031)	(0.0030)	(0.0031)
% Poverty MSA 1990	−0.00024*	−0.00004	−0.00006	−0.00006
	(0.00013)	(0.00013)	0(.00013)	(0.00013)
Log max benefits 1990	0.00079	0.0018	0.0004	0.0004
	(0.0043)	(0.0041)	(0.0040)	(0.0040)
Log max benefits 1993	−0.00058	−0.0002	0.0014	0.0014
	(0.0046)	(0.0043)	(0.0042)	(0.0042)
Unemployment rate, 1990	0.00054**	0.00045*	0.00065**	0.00065**
	(0.00028)	(0.00026)	(0.00027)	(0.00027)
Unemployment rate, 1993	−0.00035*	−0.00017	−0.00027	−0.00027
	(0.00021)	(0.00020)	(0.0002)	(0.0003)
Gross flows, 1989–1992	0.0263***	0.0220***	0.0203**	
	(0.0043)	(0.0043)	(0.0042)	
Job creation, 1989–92				−0.0074
				(0.0058)
Job destruction, 1989–92				0.0480***
				(0.0091)
% Employment change 1989–92	−0.0286***	−0.0280***	−0.0277***	
	(0.0070)	(0.0066)	(0.0064)	
Waiver=1 (since 1992)			−0.0022**	−0.0022**
			(0.0008)	(0.0008)
Caseload per capita 1990		0.827***	0.837***	0.837***
		(0.048)	(0.0463)	(0.0463)
Intercept	0.066**	0.044	0.0264	0.0264
	(0.030)	(0.029)	(0.0291)	(0.0291)
Adj. R^2	0.282	0.890	0.896	0.896

[a] Standard errors are in parentheses. (*,**,***) denote statistical significance at the 0.10, 0.05, and 0.01 confidence levels, respectively.
[b] Dependent variable: change in caseloads per capita 1990–1993.
[c] Dependent variable: caseloads per capita, 1994.

The gross-job-flow variable is also statistically significant and is positively correlated with caseloads per capita. Thus, areas with a high degree of job turnover have a larger percentage of the population on welfare, holding constant the area's unemployment rate and its rate of net job creation. This result is consistent with the finding in the previous section that areas with more industries that employ welfare recipients will have higher caseloads (because employment in these industries is less stable). These estimates suggest that the dynamics of local labor markets that go beyond the typical measures of net employment change and unemployment rate are associated with changes in caseload. Unfortunately, longer time series of gross job flows are not available for all industries at any level of aggregation—national, state, or metropolitan. It is not possible to estimate the contribution of gross job flows to the change in caseloads from the late 1980s to the present, as we did for the industry-mix variables in the previous section.

We also entered the components of gross flows, i.e., job creation and job destruction, as separate variables in the model. Column D of Table 10 shows that job destruction has a much larger effect than job creation on welfare caseloads. The coefficient on job destruction is statistically significantly different from zero, but the coefficient on job creation is not statistically significant. Areas with higher job destruction are associated with a faster growth in caseloads per capita. Employment growth was a key variable in explaining changes in welfare caseloads in the previous section; obviously, employment growth is related to jobs created and destroyed. Our results here suggest an asymmetry in jobs created and destroyed as they relate to welfare recipients. The jobs lost in an area are those that are more likely to be held by welfare recipients, while the jobs created may be those that are less likely to be filled by welfare recipients. The asymmetry does not necessarily occur across broad sectors, with one sector experiencing primarily job gains while another experiences primarily job losses. On the contrary, most sectors experience relatively equal shares of job losses and job gains. Even manufacturing, which has suffered steady net job loss for the past two decades, experiences a large number of job gains. Rather, the asymmetry more than likely lies within the same, even narrow, sectors and is characterized by differences in accessibility and qualifications. This interpretation is supported by results from the previous section related to wage premiums and high school qualifications.

A few states were granted waivers to include a work requirement before 1993. These states included Michigan, New Jersey, Oregon, Utah, and Vermont, according to Ziliak et al. (1997). We included a dummy variable for metropolitan areas in these states. As shown in column C, the growth in caseloads per capita was somewhat slower in metropolitan areas with waivers than in metropolitan areas without waivers.

CONCLUSION

Previous studies of the macroeconomic determinants of welfare caseloads have had difficulty in explaining changes in caseloads during the last decade or so using the simple macroeconomic measure of unemployment. Because welfare recipients will typically get entry-level jobs, employment variables that are closely related to job vacancies (such as employment growth) are also important in determining welfare caseloads, as we show empirically in this study. Recognizing that welfare recipients face more substantial barriers to employment than those who typically have more education and skills, we constructed several macroeconomic variables that reflect the education requirement of industries and the predominance of low-skilled workers hired by various two-digit sectors. Estimates based on a data set of annual time-series observations aggregated to the state level suggest that these variables help in explaining welfare caseloads. More specifically, areas with higher concentrations of industries that hire welfare recipients and demand workers with higher education levels have higher caseloads. Based on a separate set of metropolitan-based estimates, we also found that gross job flows are positively correlated with welfare caseloads, with job destruction dominating the effects. While the two sets of results come from different types of estimation and for areas with different levels of aggregation, the results suggest that skill levels required of industries and the dynamics of the local labor market (which go beyond the typical measures of unemployment rate) help to explain the anomalies in changes in welfare caseloads during the past decade. The findings underscore that welfare recipients have barriers to employment that are different from the rest of the labor force, and thus variables that more closely reflect their circumstances should be considered in explaining welfare caseloads.

These findings are relevant to those attempting to predict caseloads at the national, state, or local level, in that it suggests that economic factors other than unemployment could be used to forecast welfare caseloads. In addition, the findings suggest that policies that can enhance net employment growth, reduce job volatility, and increase the educational credentials of welfare recipients may all help to reduce welfare caseloads.

Notes

The authors acknowledge the able assistance of Wei-Jang Huang, Kristine Kracker, and Phyllis Molhoek. Helpful comments on a previous version were provided by Sheldon Danziger, Joyce Zickler, and Greg Duncan. The findings and opinions of this paper are those of the authors and may not reflect the views of the Upjohn Institute, the U.S. Department of Health and Human Services, or any of the reviewers of the paper.

1. Thus, we have not implemented a suggestion by Joyce Zickler that we use the wage and unemployment rates of various groups of low-skilled workers as explanatory variables. It might be useful to include such variables in a structural model, in which such variables are treated as endogenous and other demand and supply shock variables that might affect these wage and unemployment rates are also included. Our focus here is on a simpler, reduced form specification that focuses on labor demand factors affecting welfare caseloads.

2. This is one advantage that employment growth has over the unemployment rate, which is plausibly as much due to labor supply behavior as labor demand behavior. Regional economics research shows that employment-growth shocks continue to affect labor force participation rates, wage rates, and per capita earnings in a local labor market for many years, while the effects on local unemployment rates tend to dissipate quickly (Bartik 1993b). This suggests that employment growth measures aspects of local labor demand that will not be completely captured by local unemployment rates. In addition, the effects of employment growth appear to be greater for less skilled persons than for others (Bartik 1996), suggesting that local employment growth may be particularly important in determining welfare caseloads. Hoynes (1997) suggests that local employment growth is more important in determining exit from welfare and re-entry into welfare than is the local unemployment rate. Other recent research (Ihlanfeldt and Sjoquist 1998) on the spatial mismatch hypothesis suggests that the employment growth rate in the suburbs versus the city is more important than the level of employment

in affecting the labor market outcomes of minorities, perhaps because job vacancies and job losses are particularly important to entry-level workers.

3. We extended the Krueger and Summers (1988) results for private industries to cover the government sector in a previous project that focused on the wages and employment of single mothers; the data used were data on all single mothers from the March CPS from March 1983 to March 1995. We estimated wage equations using these data, regressing the natural log of the real wage on various worker characteristics, year dummies, state dummies, and industry dummies. We included dummies for all of Krueger and Summers' two-digit private industries, plus dummies for federal employment and for state and local employment. We regressed Krueger and Summers' estimated wage premium for each private industry on the estimated wage premium we obtained from the same industry. This regression was then used to predict wage premiums for the federal sector and for state and local employment that are comparable to the private wage premium numbers generated by Krueger and Summers.

4. Bartik experimented with using unrestricted variables for the proportion of employment in each two-digit industry in the research leading to the studies reported in Bartik (1993a) and Bartik (1996). The basic problem is that nothing is significant when so many industry variables are included in the estimation.

5. State and year effects are in general strongly statistically significant. Therefore, we do not explore dropping these variables, because this might lead to omitted-variable bias.

6. We use a rather simple specification of the waiver variable, because our focus is on the effects of local-labor-demand conditions.

7. Note that the wage-premium and welfare-employment variables will vary quite a bit over time for a particular state even though the industry-specific measures used to construct these variables will not vary over time. These industry-mix variables will vary as the industry mix changes over time for a particular state. As shown in the section on descriptive statistics, even though a great deal of variation in these industry-mix variables is explained by fixed state effects and year effects, there remains much variation across time for a given state that differs from the national variation over time for the same variable.

8. For each year, the value of this variable is calculated as a weighted mean over all 50 states and D.C., using 1996 state population as weights for all years. The averages reported here are simple averages of these averages for the previous seven years, which are the years involved in these calculations given that the model includes two lags in the high-school-graduate variable.

References

Timothy J. Bartik. 1991. *Who Benefits from State and Local Economics Development Policies?* Kalamazoo, Michigan: W.E. Upjohn Institute for Employment Research.

———. 1993a. *Economic Development and Black Economic Success.* Technical Report No. 93-001, W.E. Upjohn Institute for Employment Research, Kalamazoo, Michigan.

———. 1993b. "Who Benefits from Local Job Growth: Migrants or the Original Residents?" *Regional Studies* 27: 297–311.

Bartik, Timothy J. 1996. "The Distributional Effects of Local Labor Demand and Industrial Mix: Estimates Using Individual Panel Data." *Journal of Urban Economics* 40: 150–178.

Blanchard, O.J., and L.F. Katz. 1992. "Regional Evolutions." *Brookings Papers on Economic Activity* 1: 1–75.

Blank, Rebecca M. 1997. *What Causes Public Assistance Caseloads to Grow?* NBER working paper no. 5149, National Bureau of Economic Research, Cambridge, Massachusetts.

Borjas, G.J., and V.A. Ramey. 1994. "The Relationship between Wage Inequality and International Trade." In *The Changing Distribution of Income in an Open U.S. Economy,* J.H. Bergstrand, ed. New York: North-Holland.

Bound, J., and H.J. Holzer. 1993. "Industrial Shifts, Skills Levels, and the Labor Market for White and Black Males." *Review of Economics and Statistics* 75: 387–396.

Council of Economic Advisers. 1997. *Explaining the Decline in Welfare Receipt, 1993–1996.* Technical report by the Council of Economic Advisers, Washington, D.C., April.

Davis, Steven J., and John C. Haltiwanger. 1992. "Gross Job Creation, Gross Job Destruction, and Employment Reallocation." *Quarterly Journal of Economics* 107: 819–863.

Hoynes, Hilary Williamson. 1997. "Local Labor Markets and Welfare Spells: Do Demand Conditions Matter?" University of California, Berkeley, working paper presented at the American Economics Association meetings, December.

Ihlanfeldt, Keith R., and David L. Sjoquist. 1998. "The Spatial Mismatch Hypothesis: A Review of Recent Studies and Their Implications for Welfare Reform." *Housing Policy Debate* 9(4): 849–892.

Juhn, C. 1994. *Wage Inequality and Industrial Change: Evidence from Five Decades.* NBER working paper, no. 4684, National Bureau of Economic Research, Cambridge, Massachusetts.

Karoly, L.A. and J.A. Klerman. 1994. "Using Regional Data to Reexamine the Contribution of Demographic and Sectoral Changes to Increasing U.S. Wage Inequality." In *The Changing Distribution of Income in an Open U.S. Economy,* J.H. Bergstrand, ed. New York: North-Holland.

Katz, Lawrence, and Lawrence Summers. 1989. "Industry Rents: Evidence and Implications." *Brookings Papers on Economic Activity* (Microeconomics issue): 209–290.

Krueger, Alan, and Lawrence Summers. 1988. "Efficiency Wages and Interindustry Wage Structure." *Econometrica* 56: 259–292.

Lewin Group, Inc. 1997. *Determinants of AFDC Caseload Growth.* Final report prepared for the Department of Health and Human Services, Office of the Assistant Secretary for Planning and Evaluation, July.

Nickell, Stephen. 1981. "Biases in Dynamic Models with Fixed Effects." *Econometrica* 49: 1417–1426.

Ziliak, James P., David N. Figlio, Elizabeth E. Davis and Laura S. Connolly. 1997. *Accounting for the Decline in AFDC Caseloads: Welfare Reform or Economic Growth?* Discussion paper #1151-97, Institute for Research on Poverty, University of Wisconsin-Madison, November.

Part II
How Are Recipients Faring?

Work, Earnings, and Well-Being after Welfare

What Do We Know?

Maria Cancian, Robert Haveman, Thomas Kaplan,
Daniel Meyer, and Barbara Wolfe
University of Wisconsin–Madison

The rapid reduction in Aid to Families with Dependent Children (AFDC) caseloads during its last two years and the continued decline of participation following its replacement by Temporary Assistance for Needy Families (TANF) raise the question of how families who no longer receive cash assistance are faring. What are their economic circumstances? Are they better off after leaving the program than they were as recipients? How many of the mothers are working, and how much do they earn? Do they and their families continue to rely on other, in-kind assistance programs? If so, which ones?

In this paper, we present evidence on the economic fate of single mothers who have left the welfare rolls. We summarize the results of earlier studies and then present findings from three approaches to this topic, one using national survey data, another using administrative data, and a few recent studies that use geographically targeted surveys. We conclude that reliance on administrative data provides the best option for evaluating the impacts of reform in the near future. We also recognize the limitations of these data and the need for survey data to supplement their findings.

An analysis of postwelfare economic well-being requires information on both pre-exit welfare use (to determine when a woman left welfare) and later measures of economic well-being. State administrative records have two main advantages: information on welfare use is accurate, and the data are often quite current. There are serious disadvantages, however. First, data on postwelfare economic well-being is limited. Administrative records typically do not reveal the hourly wage rates of those working, the family status of those who leave the rolls, or sources of income other than public benefits and earnings reported to public agencies. Important components of well-being, such as total child care costs, the number of children in the postwelfare family, non-public child care subsidies, and nonreported child support or earned income, are likely to be unavailable.[1]

A second approach is to use national longitudinal survey data that provide detailed information on family status, the extent of work (e.g., hours worked or weeks worked), and broader measures of economic well-being on all former recipients, including those who move across jurisdictions. However, some items of information are less accurately reported (e.g., information on welfare participation and benefits is self-reported), and the information takes longer to gather and process.

A third approach is to use a targeted survey, collecting data from a particular population that is expected to have been affected by welfare reform. This approach can gather detailed information on both the pre- and postwelfare experiences of the family. Problems with current examples of this approach include small samples that may not be representative, in addition to the information accuracy problems of surveys in general.

In the next section, we summarize some of the early studies of the economic status of women who left welfare. The two sections that follow summarize the results of the two studies of postwelfare economic patterns undertaken at the Institute for Research on Poverty, one using survey data from the National Longitudinal Survey of Youth (NLSY) (Cancian and Meyer 1998; Meyer and Cancian 1996, 1998) and the other using administrative data from Wisconsin (Cancian et al. 1998b, 1999). We then briefly summarize the methods and findings of a number of studies of postwelfare experiences in other states, comparing their findings with those of the Wisconsin study. The final section of this paper presents our conclusions.

PREVIOUS STUDIES OF POSTWELFARE ECONOMIC PROSPECTS

Previous studies have analyzed the postwelfare economic status of former welfare recipients and how a variety of factors influence both exit from recipiency and the return to welfare having once left it. Some studies (e.g., Gritz and MaCurdy 1991; Cheng 1995) have found that the average earnings of former AFDC recipients grow over time (although they remain fairly low) but others have found that hourly earnings do not increase much over time (Burtless 1995; Harris 1996). Pavetti and Acs (1997) found that only 13 percent of young women who ever received AFDC are in steady employment in a "good job" by age 26–27. Burtless (1995) and Pavetti and Acs (1997) found that many former recipients have somewhat sporadic work patterns, with a low probability of maintaining full-time, full-year work.

A few quantitative studies have analyzed broader indicators of postwelfare economic well-being. Bane and Ellwood (1983) found that nearly 40 percent of those who exited were poor in the year after exit, and a similar number were poor in the following year. Harris (1996), who examined only those who left welfare and stayed off, found that the likelihood of being poor varied substantially with the type of exit. Of those who left through marriage or cohabitation, 28 percent were poor one year after exit, compared with 46 percent of those who left through work and 75 percent of those who left for some other reason.

This research can be briefly summarized as follows: a substantial proportion of women who exited AFDC returned to the rolls, some quite quickly. Even among those who did not return, continued use of food stamps or other means-tested programs is fairly common. The hourly wage rate of the leavers was (or is likely to be) in the $5–7 range, and slow growth in wage rates is experienced. The income that these leavers obtain is generally insufficient to remove them from poverty, even if they marry. There has been little research on the actual economic well-being of the leavers, perhaps reflecting a view that dependency is a more important issue than poverty or overall well-being.

THE POSTWELFARE EXPERIENCE OF AFDC
RECIPIENTS—NATIONAL SURVEY DATA

Longitudinal survey data sets such as the NLSY identify entry and exit from the welfare rolls, and they measure a variety of aspects of the lives and living conditions of recipients during and after they have left welfare. Because the NLSY oversamples the economically disadvantaged and has many years of data, it is possible to draw sufficiently large samples for measuring long-term economic well-being following an exit from AFDC.

The NLSY includes over 5,000 women who were age 14 to 21 in 1979; in 1992, these women were 28 to 35. Hence, five years of post-exit economic status can be observed for AFDC recipients who exited by 1987, when they were 24 to 31 years old.[2] This sample (see Meyer and Cancian 1996, 1998; Cancian and Meyer 1998) includes women who enter and exit AFDC at a fairly young age (and thus have relatively young children) and is not representative of the full AFDC-reliant population.

We summarize the Cancian and Meyer findings for 984 women who exited AFDC before 1987, presenting information for the first five postwelfare calendar years for three measures of well-being: the use of means-tested benefits (AFDC and any other cash or near-cash means-tested benefit, including food stamps, Supplemental Security Income [SSI], and other public assistance); earnings and wages; and family income and poverty.[3]

Welfare Use following Exit

Many women who leave AFDC ("leavers") continue to receive some cash or near-cash means-tested benefit, but this percentage declines over time; for example, 60 percent of leavers receive a means-tested benefit in the first year, compared to 45 percent in the fifth year. Food stamps are the most common benefit, received by about half of leavers in the first year, declining to 40 percent in the fifth year. AFDC itself is less common: in each of the first five years post-exit, 28–38 percent of women returned to the program and received some AFDC benefit, with a slight trend toward decreased use between year 2 and year 5.[4]

Looking across the whole five-year period, only 21 percent of leavers never received means-tested benefits and another 17 percent received benefits in only one of the five years, but 27 percent received some benefit in each year. Examining AFDC alone, 39 percent of women never received AFDC, and 16 percent received it in only one year, but 10 percent received some AFDC income in each year.

In sum, there is substantial diversity in welfare use after leaving welfare. About 20–40 percent effectively avoid reliance on welfare benefits, and about one-half of the women continue receiving benefits of some form for several years after leaving AFDC.

Hours of Work, Wages, and Earnings following Exit

In each of the five years after exit, about two-thirds of women work. But while the proportion not working stays about the same over this period, there is an increase over time in the intensity of work effort among those who work at all. For example, the proportion working full-time, full-year increases from 13 percent in the first year following an exit to 25 percent in year 5. Over the same period. the proportion working in the lowest-intensity category (part-time, part-year) falls from 21 to 13 percent.

There is also substantial variation in an individual woman's work effort over time. Less than 5 percent of women work full-time, full-year in all 5 years, while 60 percent never work full-time, full-year. On the other hand, only 14 percent never work over the first 5 years after an exit, more than one-half work at least four of the five years, and more than one-third worked in all five years. These patterns suggest that while consistent full-time work is uncommon, so too is consistent joblessness.

Even consistent work may not suffice for self-support if wages are low. Figure 1 shows the trend of average wages in the five years after exit, as well as the quartile cutoffs. Real wages rise over the period, though not for all groups. Median wages grow from $6.36 to $6.73 between years 1 and 5 (1996 dollars), an annual rate of 1.5 percent.[5] Wages for women at the 25th percentile show virtually no change, remaining close to $5.30 throughout the period.[6] The relatively modest growth in wages for this sample is inconsistent with the suggestion that even if former welfare recipients start in low-paying jobs, they will

Figure 1 Hourly Wages in the First 5 Years after Exit

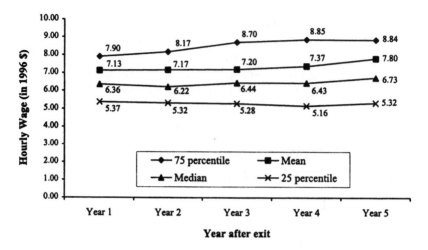

Source: Authors' calculations from the NLSY.
Note: Among workers with observed wages in each year. Unweighted sample sizes in years 1–5 are 566, 544, 539, and 538, respectively.

soon move on to jobs that pay wages that can support a family above the poverty line.

A combination of increased work effort and modest increases in hourly wages, however, results in significant growth in annual earnings over the five years. Figure 2 shows the trend in earnings among those who had earnings. Earnings grow substantially across the distribution. Median earnings among earners rise from $6,059 to $9,947 over the five-year period, and even those at the 25th percentile experience increases in own earnings from $2,276 to $3,601, or about 12 percent per year.

Income and Poverty following Exit

Among the leavers, median family income (not shown in the figures) grows from about $12,000 to $16,000–$17,000 from years 1 to 5.[7] Income increases across the distribution, with the 25th percentile increasing from about $6,500 to about $9,800.

Figure 2 Earnings among Workers in the First 5 Years after Exit

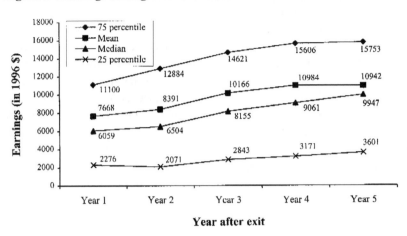

Source: Authors' calculations from the NSLY.
Note: Among workers with observed earnings in each year. Unweighted sample sizes
in years 1–5 are 580, 586, 554, 551, and 548, respectively.

Two of the main sources of family income are means-tested transfers and own earnings. While both sources are received by substantial
numbers of leavers, the pattern differs: in year 1, each source is
received by about 60 percent of the leavers; by year 5, the proportion
with earnings is still about 60 percent, while the proportion with
means-tested benefits has dropped to about 45 percent.

Income from a spouse or partner is a third important component of
family income. Spousal income is received by about 40 percent of
women in each of the five years. Income from a spouse or partner,
when available, is fairly high, with medians of about $16,000 in the
first year, rising to about $21,000 in the fifth year. Finally, child sup-
port is received by less than one-fifth of the sample, with median
annual amounts among recipients around $1,500.

These estimates make it clear that measures of income that include
only the income from a woman's own earnings and means-tested benefits may substantially understate family income, especially for those
who have a spouse or partner. This has important implications for the
interpretation of the results of the administrative data analysis discussed below.

Does the income received by the families of these leavers allow them to escape poverty? Fifty-five percent of all women are poor in the first year following an exit; by the fifth year, this has fallen to 42 percent. Especially in the early years, most of the remainder of leavers have incomes that are near the poverty level; for example, only 15 percent have income above 200 percent of the poverty line in the first year. However, by the third year after exit, 22 percent of women have incomes more than twice the poverty line. The NLSY allows us to consider both total family income and a woman's own income (not including the earnings and benefits of any spouse or partner). If we compare a woman's own income to the poverty line, a much higher proportion of women are poor: 79 percent in the first year, decreasing to 64 percent in the fifth.

When we examine family income poverty over the whole period, we find that only 19 percent are poor during *all* of the first five years. On the other hand, whereas during each of the first five years 45–59 percent are above the poverty level, only 22 percent are able to escape poverty during *all* five years. Only about 5–10 percent have own income high enough to be above the poverty line during all years.

In sum, the patterns we have described show great diversity in the economic outcomes for former recipients. Moreover, while "success" is recorded in terms of reductions in dependence on AFDC (about two-thirds of the women do not receive benefits each year), poverty-oriented measures and measures that require consistently positive outcomes over the whole period indicate less progress.

Discussion

We have also examined the factors that seem to be related to several of these measures of postwelfare economic success using multivariate statistical methods. Our results indicate that there are several paths to economic "success." Having more education and fewer children, getting and staying married, landing a "good" job and keeping it, or changing jobs several times (perhaps in order to progress) all seem to be avenues to success.

Interestingly, these statistical analyses have not found a strong effect of macroeconomic conditions on success. For example, the unemployment rate in the county of residence at the time of AFDC exit has little effect on later family income. While there is a negative relationship between unemployment rates at the time of exit and later wages, it is weak. Perhaps economic conditions are more related to whether a woman exits from AFDC and the type of exit she makes than to how she fares after leaving.[8] Alternatively, measures of overall county unemployment rates may not provide a very accurate picture of job prospects for low-skilled women (Hoynes 1996).

THE POSTWELFARE EXPERIENCE IN WISCONSIN—ADMINISTRATIVE DATA

A second research strategy is to employ administrative data on welfare recipients both while they are on the rolls and in the years after they have left. The most extensive of such studies (Cancian et al. 1998b, 1999) make use of Wisconsin administrative data to analyze the benefit use, income, and employment of women who left AFDC.

These data follow all recipients, not just a random sample. Because they are linked longitudinally, the recipients can be studied over a relatively long period of time.[9] Moreover, the data allow the postwelfare circumstances of those who leave welfare to be compared to the circumstances of those who remain recipients.

We use Wisconsin administrative data for single women with children who received AFDC-Regular benefits in July 1995. We define "leavers" as those who received no AFDC benefits for two consecutive months over the next year (from August 1995 to July 1996). The sample includes 26,047 leavers and 28,471 who stayed on AFDC.[10] We tracked those who left for a period of 15 months from the date they left and those who stayed from August 1996 to December 1997.

The state's data system provides much information on these 55,000 cases while they were receiving AFDC: the mother's age, educational level, and race; the number of children in the household and the age of the youngest child; whether or not other adults were also in the household; whether the mother or a child received SSI; the mother's AFDC status and whether or not she was an immigrant; and the county of residence. The state's unemployment insurance (UI) system provides information on the mother's quarterly earnings and employer.

Although these data provide much information on economic and social outcomes, they reflect only public assistance and covered earnings received in Wisconsin. We have no measures for individuals who moved out of state, no measures of earnings for those who remained in the state but were self-employed or in other employment not covered by UI, and no measures of a spouse or partner's earnings or other income. Furthermore, because we cannot accurately trace individuals who leave the state for all or part of the period, we cannot distinguish those who have income from benefits or earnings outside Wisconsin from those who receive no such income.[11]

Welfare Use following Exit

The use of public assistance steadily declined among all groups of leavers. Table 1 shows the use of means-tested benefits by leavers, continuous leavers (those leavers who did not return within 15 months), and stayers (those cases active in July 1995 who did not have two consecutive months without benefits in the next year). In the quarter immediately following exit, 11 percent of leavers and 14 percent of continuous leavers had ceased receiving public assistance (food stamps, Medicaid, or AFDC). Fifteen months after exit, these figures had more than doubled: about 30 percent of all leavers and 41 percent of the continuous leavers were receiving no public assistance. However, the majority of leavers continued to be enrolled in some form of public assistance over the entire period, mainly Medicaid. By definition, all stayers received some assistance in the first quarter measured (July–September 1996). Even a year later, only 7 percent received no benefits.

In general, we found that AFDC leavers who had greater human capital, fewer and older children, and who lived in an area where unemployment was lower were more likely to have ceased the receipt of public assistance than those without these advantages (see Cancian et al. 1999, Table 7).

These results are not dissimilar to those in the previous section based on the NLSY data. Those data indicated that during the first year after exit, about 60 percent of the women continued to receive some

Table 1 Percentage of Persons Not Receiving Means-Tested Benefits[a] after AFDC Exit[b]

Category	1st Quarter after exit	2nd Quarter after exit	3rd Quarter after exit	4th Quarter after exit	5th Quarter after exit
All leavers	10.8	16.1	19.1	21.6	29.7
	(N=22,726)	(N=22,079)	(N=21,791)	(N=21,604)	(N=21,151)
Continuous leavers	14.1	22.4	27.1	30.1	40.8
	(N=15,451)	(N=14,692)	(N=14,365)	(N=14,216)	(N=13,889)
All stayers[c]	–	1.3	2.9	4.5	6.6
	(N=28,471)	(N=27,980)	(N=27,463)	(N=27,094)	(N=26,701)

[a] Not receiving AFDC, food stamps, or Medicaid.
[b] The sample in each quarter includes all cases which appear in at least one administrative database during that quarter.
[c] For stayers, first quarter after exit is the third quarter of 1996.

means-tested benefit (although the NLSY analysis did not include Medicaid).

Hours of Work, Wages, and Earnings following Exit

Most women who left the AFDC rolls worked.[12] During the first year after leaving, about two-thirds of leavers worked, a figure that is nearly identical to the proportion of leavers who worked in the first year in the NLSY data.[13] Women whose youngest child was older than 12 years and women who had earnings in the two years before they left welfare were significantly more likely to work and earn. However, neither education nor the number of children had a statistically discernable impact on the probability of employment in this model (though earnings did increase with education, as discussed below). Women on SSI, women who had been sanctioned, minority women, and (surprisingly) women who had shorter welfare spells were significantly less likely to be employed.

The average county unemployment rate over the quarters during the year after exit has a marginally significant ($t = 1.8$) but quantitatively small negative effect on employment. Each 1-percentage-point increase in the local unemployment rate decreased by less than 1 percent the probability of working in the year after exiting welfare. The modest impact of the county unemployment rate parallels the results for the NLSY. As mentioned above in those results, the limited impact of unemployment may be due to the inadequacy of this measure as an indicator of local labor market conditions for this population.

About 86 percent of those leavers who were working earned more than $2,000 during the year after exit. Median annual earnings were about $7,800.[14] Women who had greater human capital (i.e., more education and prior work experience) and who were living in a county with a low unemployment rate tended to have higher earnings, as did legal immigrants and women with older children. Women who had been sanctioned, received SSI, or had a child on SSI had lower earnings.

The average county unemployment rate over the quarters during the year after exit has a statistically significant negative effect on earnings. Each 1-percentage-point increase in the local unemployment rate decreased annual earnings by about $250 in the year after exiting welfare. Again, the modest impact of the county unemployment rate may be due to its limitations as a measure of local labor market opportunities for this population.

For all leavers, in all of the socioeconomic categories, median earnings among workers increased with the length of time off welfare. For leavers working in a given quarter, earnings increased from less than $2,400 to more than $2,600 over this period, an annual growth rate of about 10.4 percent.[15] We also had information on the industry in which these women who worked found employment and hence could calculate earnings growth by industrial categories as well.[16] From the first to the fifth quarters, median earnings for leavers rose in all industrial classifications except one. Indeed, in more than half of the classifications, leavers in their fifth quarter after exit had earnings over 10 percent higher than leavers in their first quarter after exit. The only exception was leavers who were employed in temporary agencies, where fifth-quarter earnings were 12 percent lower than first-quarter earnings.

Income and Poverty following Exit

Using our administrative data, we are able to measure two concepts of income: own earnings and income, defined as the sum of own earnings, AFDC, and the cash value of food stamps. Table 2 indicates that leavers were twice as likely to have incomes above the poverty level as stayers.[17] For all groups, the percentages with income above the poverty level are not high; even those who left AFDC and did not return had only about a 27 percent probability of success in escaping poverty by this measure.[18]

Few former recipients were able to achieve an income 150 percent or more above the poverty line; even among the continuous leavers, less than 8 percent had cash incomes (including food stamps) sufficient to meet this standard. Larger families were especially unlikely to reach this level: among families with three children, only 1.9 percent of continuous leavers and 1.5 percent of all leavers reached this level.

Table 2 also shows that only about one-third of all leavers obtained the income level they received just before they left AFDC. Only among the groups with the highest postwelfare incomes (continuous leavers and those with fewer children) did more than 40 percent have income in excess of what they received immediately before leaving welfare.

Table 2 Percentage of the AFDC-Regular Caseload at Various Income Levels during Year after Exit[a]

	Income as earnings only	Income as cash income plus food stamps
All leavers (N=24,020)		
More than the poverty line	19.5	24.0
More than 150% of the poverty line	5.4	5.8
More than same measure in qtr. before exit	69.3[b]	36.0
More than maximum AFDC benefit	48.8	–
Continuous leavers[b] (N=16,325)		
More than the poverty line	25.1	27.3
More than 150% of the poverty line	7.4	7.7
More than same measure in qtr. before exit	75.9[c]	37.5
More than maximum AFDC benefit	54.6	–
All stayers (N=28,471)		
More than the poverty line	4.1	11.7
More than 150% of the poverty line	0.8	1.6
More than maximum AFDC benefit	19.0	–

[a] For stayers, the year is the 12 months from 7/96 through 6/97. This table excludes "disappearers," as defined in endnote 11.

[b] Continuous leavers are those who remained off AFDC for at least one year after exit. All reported measures are the average quarterly receipt during the year after exit calculated over the quarters in which the case appears in at least one administrative database.

[c] Calculated only for those with earnings in the quarter before exit. For example, the number in the earnings column represents the percentage of households in each category whose average quarterly earnings in the year after exit were higher than its earnings in the quarter before exit.

Summary and Comparison with NLSY

Most states have recently experienced substantial welfare caseload declines just before, and especially after, passage of the 1996 TANF legislation. The implications of these declines depend to a large degree on the ability of families who have left welfare to remain independent and move to self-sustaining employment. The Wisconsin study, while limited by the administrative data used, provides an initial indication of the economic well-being of individuals who left AFDC during the time of early work-based reforms.[19] It also provides information about the extent of employment and level of earnings, and how this evolves over the first 15 months after leaving assistance.

Compared with those who stayed on AFDC (some of whom also left the rolls in subsequent quarters), the leavers (especially the continuous leavers) were better educated, had fewer children, and were more likely to have had earnings during the two years before they left AFDC.[20] For some low-income single parents, work appears to have been fairly constant, even if not always full-time, and their earnings rose or fell in ways that made them sometimes eligible and sometimes ineligible for AFDC.[21] While employment rates remained stable among all leavers, the proportion of continuous leavers who had any earnings grew substantially over the quarters. Moreover, for all leavers, median earnings (calculated over those who worked in a given quarter) grew at a rate of about 2.5 percent per quarter.

A key question concerns the economic well-being of those who left the AFDC rolls, but as with the NLSY results reported above, there is no unambiguous answer to this question. While some of the ambiguity derives from data limitations, the picture is complex even for those success indicators (earnings and public assistance) that we measure with accuracy. A large majority of women who left AFDC worked in the first year after exit; the median annual earnings for workers were about $7,800. Those who did not return to AFDC for a 15-month period (or more) had median earnings of $9,100.

These figures conceal, however, a great deal of variation among groups of recipients. For example, women who lived in counties with an above-average rate of unemployment, who had limited education, who had been sanctioned, or who were on SSI tended to work and/or earn less than other groups of leavers. Indeed, fewer than half of the leavers achieved incomes greater than their income in the last AFDC quarter. And only about 37 percent of those with one child and who remained off the AFDC rolls—and only 17 percent of those with three children—generated incomes that exceeded the poverty line in the first year after they left welfare.

The NLSY and Wisconsin results complement each other in demonstrating the importance of women's own earnings in providing for their postwelfare well-being. In the earlier NLSY data, the average leaver with any earnings earned about $6,000–$7,000 during the first year after exit. There are reasons to anticipate that current leavers will not fare as well; in particular, current reforms may force women with fewer employment prospects to leave welfare. On the other hand, current leavers may do better, given the robust economy, pressures for job search, and the changed "welfare culture." The Wisconsin leavers had somewhat higher earnings (median about $7,800 in the first year) after leaving than did the NLSY leavers. It appears that, to a greater extent than in earlier years, most women are working and earning a nontrivial income after leaving welfare. The reasons for this increase in the level of working and earnings after leaving welfare are difficult to discern; it may be that welfare policy changes and a favorable labor market have more than offset any decline in the labor market skills of leavers as more women have been moved off assistance. Another possibility is that because grant amounts are higher in Wisconsin than in much of the rest of the country, it takes a higher level of earnings to exit.

The analyses of NLSY and administrative data suggest that earnings play an important role in post-exit income. The potential role of macroeconomic conditions in accounting for the relative success of recent leavers is important. Erosion of employment opportunities could result in a substantially reduced level of earnings and income from that reported here. Families may be particularly vulnerable to fluctuations in earnings given the more limited access of families to cash assistance.

STUDIES OF THE POSTWELFARE EXPERIENCE IN OTHER STATES

The number of AFDC/TANF cases has declined sharply across the nation, from nearly 5.1 million cases in January 1994 to just over 3 million in June 1998. With this steep decline, many states in addition to Wisconsin have sought information on the condition (and sometimes the motivation) of those who have left their AFDC and TANF rolls. Cancian et al. (1998a) discussed recent studies of leavers in nine states: Iowa, Kentucky, Maryland, Michigan, New Mexico, South Carolina, Tennessee, Texas, and Washington. We summarize that discussion here.

These studies share common features but also differ on several dimensions. Most of the studies were performed either by university research centers within the respective state or by the state administrative agency responsible for public assistance; the exceptions were Texas (by the Texas Legislative Council) and Iowa (by Mathematica Policy Research). Most are based primarily on surveys (mail, telephone, in-home, or some combination), but the study in Maryland, like the Wisconsin study, relied on administrative data. In most of the studies, leavers include both families headed by a lone parent and two-parent families. Only the study of leavers in Washington, which focused on single-parent households, and the Wisconsin study, which considered just families headed by single adult women, were more restrictive. Moreover, in most of the states, the samples studied included leavers who exited for any reason.

The length of time off AFDC or TANF to reach "leaver" status differed among the studies. In most studies, nonreceipt of benefits for one month sufficed to create leaver status, although two consecutive months off AFDC was used in one study and six consecutive months in another. Some of the survey-based studies had fairly low response rates, by our calculations:[22] response rates ranged from a low of 12 percent (for a mail survey in New Mexico) to a high of 85 percent in the Iowa study. For the projects relying on administrative data in Maryland and Wisconsin, response rates were not, of course, an issue. The following paragraphs briefly describe key findings of the state studies of leavers.

Use of Means-Tested Programs

Only the studies in Maryland and Wisconsin considered the rate of return of leavers to AFDC or TANF, and those rates in the two states were quite close: about 20 percent returned in the first few months and much smaller percentages returned in subsequent months.

In all states which reported on use of food stamps and Medicaid, more leavers appeared to participate in Medicaid than in food stamps.[23] With the exceptions of Kentucky and Washington, at least two-thirds of leavers in each state reported participation in Medicaid, at least for the children in the case. With the exception of Washington, about one-half of leavers received food stamps.

Hours of Work, Wages, and Earnings following Exit

Percentage of Leavers Reported Working at Least Part-Time

In the three states that sampled only leavers whose cases had been closed for noncompliance, the percentage of leavers who were working at least part-time ranged from 42 percent to 53 percent. In states that surveyed all leavers, the percentage working at the time of the survey was generally higher, ranging from 49 percent to 70 percent. The two states that used unemployment insurance records to determine whether someone was working showed quite different findings: 55 percent had earnings in Maryland, compared with 72–75 percent in Wisconsin.

Hours of Work among Leavers Who Reported Working

The studies in Maryland and Wisconsin, which relied on administrative data from state unemployment insurance programs, could report only quarterly earnings, not the number of hours worked. The other states reported hours of work in different ways, which make comparisons among the states difficult. Overall, though, it appears that well over half the respondents who were working were doing so approximately full-time.

Reported Earnings and Wage Rates among Leavers Who Reported Working

States reported earnings in different formats, again making comparisons difficult. Among states reporting earnings, Iowa reported mean weekly earnings of $170, which would total $2,210 in quarterly earnings, about 7.5 percent less than the mean quarterly earnings reported in Maryland and some 15 percent less than the quarterly earnings reported in Wisconsin. The lower reported earnings for Iowa may not be surprising, since the sample in Iowa was of cases sanctioned for noncompliance, whereas Maryland and Wisconsin included voluntary leavers, some of whom probably left because they had found a job. The Iowa results are consistent with the Wisconsin results for sanctioned leavers, whose earnings were about 23 percent below the average of all leavers. Three of the states reporting hourly wages based on surveys seemed to cluster around $6.40 to $6.60 in mean hourly wages. The study in Washington showed significantly higher mean hourly wages among leavers, at $8.42.

Type of Employment among Leavers Who Reported Working

Most of the studies made an effort to assess the kinds of jobs leavers found. In classifying jobs, the investigators appeared generally to start with Standard Industrial Classification (SIC) codes, but the tendency of leavers to cluster in certain industries led all the investigators to use more detailed codes for some industries than others, and to do so in ways that probably made sense for that state but do not promote comparisons with other states.

Not surprisingly, most of the state studies reported heavy concentrations of leavers in food service and retail trade. The Washington study, which reported the highest mean wages, showed somewhat higher percentages of leavers who had found clerical/office and general labor/construction jobs (although, again, the different ways states combined SIC codes makes even this comparison conjectural).

CONCLUSION

We have presented a summary of what is known regarding the economic circumstances, employment, and patterns of benefit use among welfare recipients who have left the rolls in recent years. This analysis has drawn upon studies that used a wide variety of techniques for assessing these postwelfare economic circumstances: national longitudinal survey data, state administrative records, and state-based sample surveys. All of these efforts have limitations, and we have attempted to identify these. The various approaches chosen to assess the potential consequences of the 1996 welfare reform legislation are of necessity ad hoc, given the absence of a reliable national research effort for evaluating this policy change.

The primary dimensions on which these research approaches differ include 1) limitations in the variables measured, 2) limited response rates (and hence, potential selection biases), 3) attrition problems (and again, potential selection biases), 4) problems of limited sample sizes, and 5) the unreliability of some of the data collected. While national longitudinal survey data have extensive data on each family, there are difficulties in identifying "leavers," the responses regarding the receipt and value of benefits is often questionable, and the sample sizes are

often quite small. Administrative data from states have the most reliable information on benefits received, working, and earnings in
reported jobs; however, they lack information on family structure,
mobility, hours worked, and income sources apart from the earnings
and benefits of the leavers themselves. The administrative data are
accurate and available on a very timely basis, however. The state-level
sample surveys often have low response rates, and in some cases, the
samples selected are not representative of the general population of
those who have exited welfare.

In spite of the differences in approach and reliability, it is possible
to roughly summarize the findings regarding several important postwelfare economic effects across these studies.

To what extent do leavers continue to use means-tested benefits?

* About two-thirds of the leavers receive some type of welfare
  benefit (e.g., food stamps, Medicaid) after exiting AFDC in the
  first year after leaving. Medicaid is the most common type of
  noncash benefit received, but food stamp receipt is also common. Food stamp and Medicaid use decline as the time since
  exiting increases.

What proportion of the leavers work after exiting AFDC?

* About two-thirds of the women work after exiting AFDC, but
  most of them do not work full-time, full-year. In most of the
  studies, less than one-half of the leavers are full-time workers,
  although some of the state studies based on survey data suggest
  higher percentages of full-time workers. The "intensity" of
  work (hours worked per year) increases over time, as the share
  working full-time, full-year increases at the expense of part-
  time or part-year work.

How much do the leavers earn?

* Although the wage rates of leavers differ across states, they generally lie in the range of $6.50 to $7.50 per hour. The average
  wage rates increase with time, although not at rates substantially
  higher than the rates of increase for women's wage rates gener-

ally. Given these wage rates, the majority of leavers do not earn enough to support their families above the poverty line. Annual earnings average about $8,000 to $9,500, depending on the study; because of the growth in wage rates and especially in the intensity of work, the rate of growth of earnings is 6–10 percent per year.

How much family income do leavers have; are they able to escape poverty?

• Poverty rates were more than 50 percent for the leavers. However, because earnings rise over time and the number of leavers with partners increases over time, the poverty rate also falls over time. A few years after exiting, about 40 percent of the leavers remain poor. If one counts only the income (sum of earnings, cash benefits, and food stamps) of the leavers themselves, the poverty rate would be about 75 percent.

The research we have summarized gives a number of clues, but no definitive answers, about the effect of macroeconomic conditions on post-exit well-being. While higher unemployment is associated with less work and earnings, the coefficients are not always statistically significant and they are often small in magnitude. We speculate that these modest results are due to the inadequacy of county unemployment rates as a measure of the labor market conditions for women leaving welfare.

However, apart from the relationship between local unemployment rates and the economic performance of women who have exited welfare, the most important finding concerns the central role of own earnings in contributing to post-exit well-being. Because women's earnings are typically their most important post-exit income source, any downturn that limits earnings is likely to have a significant negative effect on their already-modest economic well-being.

Our findings underscore the challenges facing those who will leave cash assistance in the coming years. Many leavers remain poor, and many return to means-tested benefits after having attempted to leave. While average earnings grow over time, available evidence suggests this is largely due to increases in work hours rather than substantial growth in wages. If families are to move from welfare to self-sufficiency, their own earnings are likely to be insufficient.

The research findings that we have reviewed suggests substantial diversity among families leaving welfare in terms of economic performance and well-being. This suggests that high priority be given to expanding both data collection and evaluation; only with reliable cross-state and cross-time information will we be able to ultimately judge the success of current reform efforts and make informed decisions about future policy. Our review suggests that administrative data supplemented by survey findings is the best option for reliable research on post-exit outcomes. Over the next few years, a successful strategy for assessing the well-being of those who leave state TANF programs could combine analyses of state administrative data with improved state survey efforts designed to provide information not available from administrative systems. Some states have undertaken substantive survey efforts designed to enable the assessment of post-exit well-being and have been successful in raising their survey response rates to acceptable levels, at least for interviews of 15–20 minutes.[24] If this strategy can be successfully implemented more generally, it should be possible to generate a set of standard questions that have been validated in prior surveys to encourage assessment that is uniform across the states. Such questions could supplement what is generally available in administrative data and be sufficiently parsimonious as to enable the inclusion of other questions of special interest in a 20-minute interview.

Notes

The authors gratefully acknowledge the research assistance of Sandra Barone and Catherine O'Neill.

1. For example, in the Wisconsin results reported below, information on own quarterly earnings, but not on hourly wages, is reported. There is no information on whether the individual is married, and thus measures of family income are quite limited. Further, state databases do not include information on those who move out of state.
2. In this study, we define "exit" from welfare as not receiving AFDC for three consecutive months after a month of receipt.

3. Our definition of "family income" includes the income attributable to a woman, her husband/partner, and related children. For the definition of poverty, we have selected the official poverty threshold, despite its limitations (Citro and Michael 1995), because it is widely used in other research and hence facilitates a comparison of our results to those of others.

4. Another way to measure welfare use is to examine the percentage of family income derived from means-tested benefits: in the first year after exit, 28 percent of women received at least half their family income from means-tested benefits; in the fifth year, the percentage was identical.

5. Mean wages are, as expected, higher than median wages: they grow from $7.13 to $7.80 over the five years. This growth in real wages, it should be noted, contrasts with the stagnant wages faced by most men with low levels of education and experience during this period (Acs and Danziger 1993).

6. The figure uses average wages, the average of all wages earned in the year, weighted by hours worked in each job. The pattern is quite similar if we use wages in the most common job (the job in which the woman worked the greatest number of hours in the year). If we use the highest wage, the level is higher but the trend is remarkably similar.

7. Again, median values are lower than mean values. Mean family income grows from about $15,000 to $21,000–$22,000. We present a range of estimates because figures differ depending on the sample used. For example, median income among all those for whom we have income in the first year is $12,045; among those for whom we have income in all five years post-exit, it is about $11,742.

8. Recent studies of the impact of macroeconomic conditions on the probability of leaving welfare are reviewed in papers by Figlio and Ziliak and by Blank and Wallace in this volume.

9. In addition, the large sample can be used to analyze the impact of less common (but potentially important) types of recipients, such as women with children on SSI (Supplemental Security Income) and those with a foster child in the home.

10. Families who live in rural areas (66.8 percent) were the most likely to leave, while those in the largest urban area, Milwaukee, were least likely to leave AFDC (36.6 percent). Similarly, families that leave AFDC are likely to be those with the best work and marriage prospects. Throughout the state, women were more likely to leave AFDC if they 1) had higher levels of education; 2) were white, or to a lesser extent, Hispanic, and were U.S. citizens; 3) had fewer children, and there were other adults in the household; 4) did not receive SSI (neither the mother nor any child); and 5) had more work experience and higher total earnings in the two years (July 1993 to June 1995) prior to the July 1995 date when our sample was identified. Mothers who had been "sanctioned" for some failure to comply with the AFDC program were also more likely to leave, while those with a longer current spell of AFDC receipt were less likely to leave. (Sanction status is measured in July 1995 and refers to sanctions on the mother only.)

11. Seventy-three percent of our sample appeared in the data in each of the five quarters after they left AFDC, and about 8 percent never appeared in the database dur-

ing the entire 15 months after they left. These "disappearers" may have left Wisconsin. They also may still live in the state but may, for instance, have married and be relying on a husband's earnings or support from family and friends, or be in noncovered employment and not using public assistance. Nineteen percent of the sample are "partial disappearers," those who appear in the administrative data in some, but not all, of the quarters. The disappearers have been excluded from the findings we present here; the partial disappearers have been included only in the quarters for which we have data on them. Excluding cases that do not appear in any data set substantially increases the proportion employed (since disappearers, by definition, would otherwise enter as cases with no employment). Participation rates for AFDC, food stamps, and Medicare would also be higher were disappearers included. For a more detailed discussion of the sensitivity of results to these exclusions see Cancian et al. (1999).

12. "Work" is defined as having earnings that were reported to the Wisconsin Unemployment Insurance system.

13. Eighty-two percent of leavers who did not "disappear" worked in the first year post-exit.

14. Again, mean values are somewhat higher, in this case about $8,500.

15. Note that these growth rates are not the same as an average of individual rates of earnings growth, since the composition of leavers may be different in each quarter after exit. For some groups, moreover, rates start from a very low base. For example, women on SSI have a very high average quarterly growth rate of 12.4 percent, but start at $1,053, or about 44 percent of the median overall.

16. The categories are Nondurable Manufacturing; Wholesale Trade, Construction; Durable Manufacturing; Financial, Insurance, and Real Estate; Social Services, Public Administration, and Education; Health Services; Personal Services; Other Services; Agriculture, Forestry, and Mining; Retail Trade; Transportation, Communications, and Public Utilities; Restaurants; Hotels and Lodging; Business Services; and Temporary Agencies.

17. Note that this measure of income does not include income from spouses or cohabitants.

18. Family size matters considerably. Thirty-three percent of all leavers with one child (both those who returned to AFDC and those who did not) had cash incomes above the poverty level, compared with 15 percent of families with three children.

19. The period that we studied was one of substantial change in the Wisconsin AFDC program. From July 1995 to July 1996, single-parent AFDC caseloads in Wisconsin declined sharply, by 23 percent.

20. The best predictor of earnings after exit from AFDC was consistent employment in the two years before exit. Some groups of recipients—those on SSI, those sanctioned, and legal immigrants, for example—were less likely to work; however, the earnings of the immigrants who did work were significantly higher than those of native-born leavers. Those with more than three children were less likely to work than those with fewer children but, among those who worked, their earn-

ings were no lower. Earnings were lowest for the youngest mothers (18–24), and, to a lesser extent, for the oldest (over 40).

21. Even the one-third of all leavers who returned to AFDC worked a substantial amount after their return.

22. The response rates discussed here are based on our calculations from reports provided by the studies, and sometimes differ from response rates reported in the studies themselves. See Cancian et al. (1998a) for details.

23. A possible reason for this is that administrative records record eligibility for, rather than use of, Medicaid.

24. South Carolina, for example, achieved a 73 percent survey response rate for a sample that had been continuously off its TANF program for at least six months; regionally based employees of the state welfare department checked Medicaid and food stamp administrative records to obtain current phone numbers and addresses and went to the homes of sample members who had not responded after repeated telephone calls.

References

Acs, Gregory, and Sheldon Danziger. 1993. "Educational Attainment, Industrial Structure, and Male Earnings through the 1980s." *Journal of Human Resources* 28: 618–48.

Bane, Mary Jo, and David T. Ellwood. 1983. *The Dynamics of Dependence: The Routes to Self-Sufficiency.* Report prepared for the U.S. Department of Health and Human Services, Urban Systems Research and Engineering, Inc., Cambridge, Massachusetts.

Burtless, Gary. 1995. "Employment Prospects of Welfare Recipients." In *The Work Alternative: Welfare Reform and the Realities of the Job Market,* Demetra Smith Nightingale and Robert H. Haveman, eds. Washington, D.C.: Urban Institute Press.

Cancian, Maria, Robert Haveman, Thomas Kaplan, Daniel Meyer, and Barbara Wolfe. 1998a. "Work, Earnings, and Well-Being after Welfare: What Do We Know?" Paper presented at the "Welfare Reform and the Macroeconomy" conference, Washington, D.C., November 19–20, 1998.

Cancian, Maria, Robert Haveman, Thomas Kaplan, and Barbara Wolfe. 1998b. *Who Left Wisconsin's Welfare Rolls after 1995 and Who Stayed?* Report submitted to the Office of the Assistant Secretary for Planning and Evaluation, U.S. Department of Health and Human Services, from the Institute for Research on Poverty, University of Wisconsin-Madison, May.

Cancian, Maria, Robert Haveman, Thomas Kaplan, and Barbara Wolfe. 1999. *Post-Exit Earnings and Benefit Receipt among Those Who Left AFDC in*

Wisconsin. Special Report no. 75, Institute for Research on Poverty, University of Wisconsin-Madison, January.

Cancian, Maria, and Daniel R. Meyer. 1998. "Work after Welfare: Women's Work Effort, Occupation, and Economic Well-Being." Unpublished manuscript, July 1998.

Cheng, Tyrone Chi-Wai. 1995. "The Changes of Recipients Leaving AFDC: A Longitudinal Study." *Social Work Research* 19(2): 67–96.

Citro, Constance F., and Robert T. Michael, eds. 1995. *Measuring Poverty: A New Approach.* Washington, D.C.: National Academy Press.

Gritz, R. Mark, and Thomas MaCurdy. 1991. *Patterns of Welfare Utilization and Multiple Program Participation among Young Women.* Report to the U.S. Department of Health and Human Services, prepared at Stanford University.

Harris, Kathleen Mullan. 1996. "Life after Welfare: Women, Work, and Repeat Dependency." *American Sociological Review* 61: 407–426.

Hoynes, Hilary Williamson. 1996. *Local Labor Markets and Welfare Spells: Do Demand Conditions Matter?* IRP discussion paper 1104-96, Institute for Research on Poverty, Madison, Wisconsin.

Meyer, Daniel R., and Maria Cancian. 1996. *Life after Welfare: The Economic Well-Being of Women and Children following an Exit from AFDC.* IRP discussion paper 1101-96, Institute for Research on Poverty, Madison, Wisconsin.

Meyer, Daniel R., and Maria Cancian. 1998. "Economic Well-Being Following an Exit from AFDC." *Journal of Marriage and the Family* 60: 479–92.

Pavetti, LaDonna, and Gregory Acs. 1997. "Moving Up, Moving Out or Going Nowhere? A Study of the Employment Patterns of Young Women and the Implications for Welfare Mothers." Unpublished manuscript, October 1997.

Employer Demand for Welfare Recipients and the Business Cycle

Evidence from Recent Employer Surveys

Harry J. Holzer
Michigan State University

The extent to which the business cycle affects the labor market for welfare recipients has recently become an issue of major concern. A number of studies have tried to estimate the effect of the business cycle or local labor market conditions on welfare caseloads over the 1980s and 1990s (e.g., Hoynes 1996; Wallace and Blank 1999; Ziliak and Figlio 1999), but less evidence has been brought to bear directly on the question of how recipients' labor market outcomes are (or will be) affected. Ultimately, the labor market performance of welfare recipients should be our primary concern, since most welfare programs are now being viewed as *transitional* assistance for those who need help getting into the market rather than as permanent income support for those who are disengaged.

It is, of course, well-known that minorities and less-educated workers face relatively improved employment prospects in tighter labor markets (e.g., Freeman 1991; Bound and Holzer 1996), but we cannot necessarily infer from these studies the magnitudes of the wage or employment declines that welfare recipients will experience over the next cycle. What has been observed over the cycle for other disadvantaged groups might differ considerably from what welfare recipients will experience. Even among the recipients themselves, the declines in demand should vary according to their own personal characteristics and work histories.

Direct evidence on the labor market experiences of welfare recipients to date is quite limited (e.g., Burtless 1995; Pavetti 1997), and offers little insight into changes over the business cycle. Furthermore, earlier evidence on welfare recipients reflects those who "self-selected" into the labor market under a very different set of rules and incentives than the ones which current and future recipients will face, rendering the earlier evidence much less useful.[1] Recent efforts to analyze labor market changes for low-income or single mothers, many of whom may have been on welfare, are too indirect or reflect too many simultaneous labor market changes to be able to sort out cyclical from other causes.[2] And very little of the work to date considers the extent to which policy instruments might influence the demand for welfare recipients, or their earnings and employment, over the cycle.

In this paper, I hope to address some of these issues by analyzing recent data from employer surveys on the labor market demand for welfare recipients under a variety of conditions. My earlier work on employers (Holzer 1996, 1998b; Holzer and Danziger 1998) focused on how employer skill needs, geographic locations, recruiting/screening behavior, and attitudes influence the employment opportunities of minorities and disadvantaged workers more generally. But these efforts did not deal explicitly with demand for welfare recipients or how recipients might be affected by the business cycle. Likewise, some other recent surveys of employers deal with issues of skill needs, training, work organization, etc., and how these affect worker compensation and establishment productivity (e.g., Department of Employment, City of New York 1994; Osterman 1994; Cappelli 1996; Black and Lynch 1997), but they provide little evidence on disadvantaged workers or effects of the cycle and aggregate demand.[3]

Therefore, in this paper I focus on data from a new survey of employers that I administered in Michigan during the fall of 1997. The data focus specifically on the hiring of welfare recipients and include several measures of establishment-level labor demand (such as the job vacancy rate) that reflect the business cycle. I provide estimates of how these measures of demand affect the willingness of employers to hire welfare recipients and I use them to infer how their employment is likely to change over the cycle. The effects of certain policy measures, such as the activities of labor market intermediaries or employment subsidies/tax credits for welfare recipients, and how these effects might also vary over the cycle can be inferred from these data as well.

While I draw some very limited inferences about changes in the demand for disadvantaged workers over the cycle from comparisons of different surveys over time, the estimates presented below (and the resulting predictions regarding business cycle effects) are from a single cross-section of establishments.[4] While this procedure seems to generate quite plausible estimates of business cycle effects, some potential biases from using cross-sectional estimates to infer these effects over time are acknowledged and discussed below. I also analyze the self-reported willingness of employers to hire welfare recipients currently or in the future, as well as their having done so in the recent past. Thus, both prospective and actual employer demands for welfare recipients are considered here.

In the following sections of this paper, I describe the new employer data, particularly those presented below, in somewhat greater detail; present the empirical results; and then present the conclusions and some discussion of policy implications.

THE NEW EMPLOYER DATA

In the fall of 1997, I administered a new telephone survey to 900 establishments located in three metropolitan areas of Michigan: Detroit, Flint, and Grand Rapids. The survey was administered to the individual at each establishment who was responsible for entry-level hiring and to all establishments that had hired someone within the past two years. The response rate to the survey was over 70 percent.

The questions on the survey gauged a wide range of establishment characteristics, especially regarding their workforces. For instance, questions were included on the numbers of jobs in the establishment that require very few cognitive skills or credentials, overall hiring and employment growth rates, numbers of current job vacancies, and any difficulties they have recently had finding qualified workers (all discussed in greater detail below). A series of questions was also asked about the last worker hired into a job that didn't require a college degree.

Regarding welfare recipients, respondents were asked whether or not they had hired anyone in the previous two years who had been a welfare recipient; if so, they were asked a series of questions about the job filled and the workers' characteristics and performance. The respondent was asked whether or not they have had any contact with an agency trying to place welfare recipients, particularly a "Michigan Works!" agency; if so, they were asked whether or not they had hired any referrals from these agencies.[5] Finally, a series of questions was asked about their prospective willingness to hire welfare recipients, even if they had no high school diploma or recent work experience, either currently or over the next year.[6] If respondents indicated that they were willing to hire some, they were asked how many. These were converted into percentages of the total number of current jobs in each establishment (either filled or vacant) that were potentially available to unskilled welfare recipients. A series of questions was then asked about the chracteristics of the jobs most likely to be filled that way, about whether or not the employer would provide supports (such as training, child care, or transportation), and whether or not government policies (such as subsidies/tax credits or technical assistance) would make them any more likely to do so.

Below we provide summary data on these measures of potential job availability to welfare recipients, based on actual past hiring as well as prospective willingness to do so in the future. Summary measures are also provided on some measures of labor market tightness at the establishment level and of their employment of very unskilled workers. The extent to which these latter characteristics of establishments help to account for the observed availability of employment are then explored through a series of regressions that are described below.

EMPIRICAL RESULTS

Summary Findings

Table 1 contains data on the demand for welfare recipients at the establishment level. We present three measures of both actual and prospective demand for recipients: whether or not a welfare recipient has been hired at some point during the previous two years; whether the establishment would do so either now or over the next year; and, if so, how many they would hire in each case. Results are presented for all establishments; for three large industry groups (manufacturing, retail trade and service industries); for four establishment size catego-

Table 1 Demand for Welfare Recipients in 1997: Summary Results (%)

Demand measure	All	By industry			By establishment size				By location	
		Mfg[a]	RT[b]	Service	1–20	21–50	51–100	101+	CC[c]	Sub[d]
Percent of jobs in which welfare recipients could be hired										
Currently	3.2	1.4	5.0	2.7	5.4	2.6	2.8	1.4	3.0	3.3
Over next year	9.4	5.5	17.5	7.6	13.6	8.1	9.5	6.0	8.8	9.8
Percent of establishments that have hired recipients in the past 2 years	41.9	27.4	60.0	43.3	37.0	37.1	48.1	47.7	40.3	44.3

[a] Mfg = manufacturing
[b] RT = retail trade
[c] CC = central city
[d] Sub = suburb

ries (1–20, 21–50, 51–100, and over 100); and by location within the metropolitan area, i.e., central city versus suburbs.[7]

Employers report that they would be willing to fill over 3 percent of the jobs in their establishments with welfare recipients currently, and over 9 percent of the course of the next year. Also, over 40 percent of employers indicate that they have hired someone over the past two years whom they believe to be a welfare recipient.[8] By all three measures, demand seems highest in retail trade and lowest in manufacturing.[9]

The results in Table 1 also indicate some variation among establishments in their demand for welfare recipients by industry and establishment size. Establishments that are very small (20 or fewer employees) have much higher demand for recipients in percentage terms than do larger establishments.[10] Finally, demand for recipients seems a bit higher among establishments located in the suburbs than the central city, though this is not consistently true among metropolitan areas.[11]

Relative to the total number of welfare recipients who are projected to enter the labor force over the next few years (e.g., McMurrer, Sawhill, and Lerman 1997), these data suggest a fairly high degree of job availability. This is consistent with other evidence that the employment of welfare recipients to date (and single mothers more generally) has improved markedly since welfare reform legislation was implemented at the state and federal levels during the 1990s (e.g., Bishop 1998).

On the other hand, there are some reasons to be cautious about our interpretation of these numbers. The first two measures presented clearly represent prospective rather than actual demand and are based on subjective responses to hypothetical questions; these variables might therefore be measured with considerable error. Some employers might consider it more socially acceptable to answer such questions affirmatively, implying an upward bias in average estimates of such demand. And even our measure of the actual hiring of recipients in the recent past might be quite imperfect if employers are uncertain about who really has or has not been on welfare. On the other hand, the fact that the actual and prospective measures are correlated fairly highly with each other and with the establishment characteristics listed in

Table 1 gives us somewhat greater confidence that they are meaningful measures, with reasonably high ratios of signal to noise.[12]

Even if employer responses are accurate, competition for available job slots from other groups of unskilled workers would limit the actual availability of jobs for welfare recipients (Holzer and Danziger 1998). Given that most establishments and jobs are currently located in the suburbs, while long-term welfare recipients are disproportionately found in the poorest neighborhoods of central cities, the data suggest some potential mismatch between the locations of welfare recipients and the employers who would hire them; gaps between expected and actual skill levels and work performance are likely to materialize as well.[13] Thus, the extent to which these potential employment opportunities for welfare recipients will become realized remains uncertain.

Summary statistics on some likely determinants of employer demand for welfare recipients appear in Table 2, including measures of the extent to which establishments experience tight labor markets and unmet demand for labor. These measures include the current job vacancy rate for the etablishment (defined as the number of current vacancies divided by the total number of jobs, both filled and vacant); the percentage of establishments that have hired workers in the past two years with lower-than-usual qualifications and the percentage of all jobs filled by such workers; and the ease with which qualified applicants can currently be found to fill vacant jobs—in other words, whether it is very easy, somewhat difficult, or very difficult to do so. Also presented are measures of establishment-wide relative demand for unskilled labor.

By our measure, roughly 6 percent of jobs in these establishments are currently vacant, while unemployment rates in Michigan during this period have averaged just 3–4 percent. Even allowing for the fact that our measure of job vacancies differs slightly from those generally used in the past, this is an extremely high vacancy rate on jobs.[14] This portrait of a very tight labor market is confirmed by the other measures of market tightness, which show that over 40 percent of establishments have hired workers with lower-than-usual qualifications in the past two years; these workers account for about 7 percent of all filled jobs in these establishments. Also, we find that roughly 80 percent of establishments report some current difficulty finding qualified applicants, with almost 40 percent reporting great difficulty.

Table 2 Labor Market Tightness and Employment of Unskilled Workers in 1997: Summary Results (%)

Demand measure	All	By industry			By establishment size				By location	
		Mfg[a]	RT[b]	Service	1–20	21–50	51–100	101+	CC[c]	Sub[d]
Job vacancy rate	6.0	4.3	7.9	5.3	8.6	5.5	5.6	4.2	6.0	6.1
Have hired workers with lower qualifications than usual in past 2 yr.	41.9	49.2	55.0	33.9	39.7	44.3	44.9	40.9	39.7	43.3
Percent of jobs filled by workers with lower qualifications in the past 2 yr.	6.8	3.4	10.5	6.1	12.1	7.1	7.3	2.2	6.3	7.2
Ease of finding qualified workers currently:										
Very easy	18.9	14.6	14.4	23.6	16.5	19.0	19.1	20.8	20.5	17.9
Somewhat difficult	42.2	39.2	51.0	38.2	40.6	44.4	44.3	41.3	46.4	39.5
Very difficult	38.1	45.3	34.1	37.6	42.2	35.6	35.7	37.3	32.1	42.0
Percent of currently filled jobs that:										
Do not require education or experience	37.0	42.2	53.2	27.7	33.4	37.6	39.2	39.0	34.2	38.8

Also no reading, writing, or arithmetic	12.5	14.3	15.9	10.3	12.8	11.6	11.8	13.3	12.7	12.5
Also filled by women	6.2	5.9	8.7	6.2	5.7	5.5	6.1	7.0	6.6	5.9

[a] Mfg = manufacturing
[b] RT = retail trade
[c] CC = central city
[d] Sub = suburb

The data in Table 2 also indicate that 37 percent of currently filled jobs do not require workers with any particular levels of education or experience. Roughly a third of these also require no reading, writing, or arithmetic on a daily basis, and roughly half of the latter (or about 6 percent of jobs overall) are filled by women. Since these data refer to all current employment in these establishments (rather than the most recently filled jobs there) and since demand for skills among employers appear to be rising over time, these data appear to considerably overstate the *current* demand for unskilled workers in these establishments.[15]

By industry, small and/or retail trade establishments have the highest vacancy rates, the greatest difficulty finding qualified workers, and the lowest skill requirements for current employees. The difficulties that small establishments have finding qualified applicants, despite their relatively low formal skill requirements, reflect the smaller pool of applicants that they appear to draw, and perhaps their relatively greater use of informal hiring procedures as well (Holzer, Katz, and Krueger 1991; Holzer 1998a). All of these findings are also consistent with the relatively greater demand for welfare recipients, both actual and prospective, that we observe for these establishments in Table 1.

On the other hand, Table 2 indicates more mixed results for the manufacturing sector: vacancy rates are below average, but employers in that sector are experiencing somewhat greater difficulty finding qualified applicants than are other sectors. Somewhat mixed results are also found regarding relative demand for unskilled workers in manufacturing compared with the other sectors: the percentages of all employees in jobs that require no credentials or cognitive skills are somewhat high, but relatively few of these workers are women. These data, along with their relatively low implied demand for welfare recipients, suggest a rapid growth in skill demand among recent hires in manufacturing (Berman, Bound, and Griliches 1994). The data also indicate comparable or slightly higher levels of unmet demand in the suburbs than the cities, with relatively comparable demands for unskilled workers there.

Overall, these data imply very tight labor markets in Michigan with significant current demand for unskilled labor, particularly in small establishments and in the retail trade sector.

Regression Results: Determinants of Demand for
Welfare Recipients

Comparisons among industries and establishment size categories in Table 2 suggest that the very tight labor markets that we have recently experienced in Michigan help to account for at least some of the employer demand for welfare recipients that we observe in Table 1. The estimates presented in this section test this idea more formally.

In Table 3, we present results of estimated regression equations in which the dependent variable is the percentage of jobs that are currently available to welfare recipients in each establishment. The subjective nature of this variable, and any resulting measurement error, generally implies inefficient but consistent estimates when it is used as a dependent variable.[16] Independent variables include the current job vacancy rate at the establishment; the percentage of jobs that do not require education or previous training; and dummies for establishment size, industry, and location.[17]

The vacancy rate alone is used to capture the effects of labor market tightness on the establishment in these equations. The current vacancy rate should capture both the *frequency* with which firms have new vacancies as well as their average *duration*. The former should be a function of gross hiring activity at the establishment, reflecting both turnover and net employment growth, as well as the percentage of hires at each establishment that are at least temporarily vacant before they are filled. The duration of any given vacancy should then depend on the relative supply of applicants and their quality, as well as the costs of recruiting and screening them.[18] While at least some of these determinants of vacancy rates are separately measured in our data, their effects on demand for welfare recipients appear to be captured primarily by the vacancy rate, which therefore appears exclusively in these equations.[19] Likewise, the relative demand for unskilled labor at an establishment appears to be fully captured by the percentage of jobs with no formal education or experience requirements.[20]

Separate results are presented for the entire sample, for small establishments (50 or fewer employees), and for retail trade establishments. Results are also presented for equations estimated by OLS and by tobit, where the latter functional form is used to deal with the large

Table 3 Determinants of Current Demand for Welfare Recipients[a]

Variable	All		Small establishments		Retail trade	
	OLS	Tobit	OLS	Tobit	OLS	Tobit
Vacancy rate	0.276	0.599	0.222	0.699	0.582	0.849
	(8.212)	(7.820)	(8.048)	(5.085)	(10.281)	(9.150)
Percent of jobs that require	0.019	0.093	0.019	0.134	0.017	0.056
no education or experience	(1.994)	(4.147)	(1.238)	(2.850)	(1.216)	(2.259)
Establishment size	-0.002	0.001	-0.101	-0.015	-0.008	-0.013
(hundreds)	(1.615)	(0.068)	(2.633)	(0.129)	(1.645)	(1.214)
Industry:						
Manufacturing	-0.022	-0.051	-0.033	-0.097	–	–
	(1.249)	(1.208)	(1.106)	(1.100)		
Retail trade	0.003	0.016	0.005	0.012	–	–
	(0.203)	(0.412)	(0.215)	(0.167)		
Service	-0.009	-0.025	-0.016	-0.084	–	–
	(0.556)	(0.639)	(0.664)	(1.189)		
R^2	0.137	–	0.148	–	0.436	–
−log L	–	105.90	–	108.28	–	30.688
N	724	724	404	404	190	190

[a] t-Statistics are in parentheses. Regression equations also include dummies for other one-digit industries (construction is omitted); MSA, central-city locations, and their interactions; and a constant term.

numbers of zero values that are found in the dependent variable and the potential "censoring" that these values might imply.[21]

Table 3 shows that the job vacancy rate and the percentage of unskilled employees currently working at an establishment have strong positive effect on the employers' stated willingness to hire unskilled welfare recipients. These estimates are significant in both the OLS and tobit cases, but the tobit estimates are about twice as large for the vacancy rate and almost five times as large for skill levels of current employees. Establishment size, in contrast, has a significant effect only in the OLS equations. Interestingly, manufacturing establishments have lower demands for welfare recipients that are marginally significant, but the positive effect of being in retail trade disappears once we control for vacancy rates and skill needs. When separate equations are estimated for samples of small establishments or those in retail trade, the estimated effects of vacancy rates are larger, especially in the retail trade establishments.

The magnitude of the estimated coefficients for job vacancy rates at the establishment level imply large effects of labor market tightness on employer demand for welfare recipients. For instance, a 1-percentage-point increase in the job vacancy rate at any establishment implies that demand for welfare recipients will rise by 0.3–0.6 percentage points, and by 0.6–0.8 percentage points in the retail trade sector.

The results also imply possibly large effects of the business cycle on aggregate labor demand for welfare recipients. Most frequently, job vacancy rates during recessions average 1.2–1.3 percent (Abraham 1983; Holzer 1989), which might be anywhere from 2.8 to 4.8 percentage points lower than comparably measured current rates.[22] Using our cross-sectional OLS estimates, the results imply declines in demand for welfare recipients during the next recession of 0.8–1.3 percentage points (i.e., $0.276 \times 2.8 \cong 0.8$), or *25–40 percent of all current demand for recipients*. The tobit estimates imply effects roughly twice as large, though these are mostly relevant for the subset of establishments that have higher demand for welfare recipients at the outset.[23] The OLS estimates for the retail trade sector also imply business-cycle effects that are more than twice as large as those for the overall economy, relative to a starting level of demand (5.0) that is higher by 56 percent than the economy-wide mean (3.2; values found in Table 1).

Of course, there is some question as to whether the estimates generated from a cross-section of data are appropriate for inferring aggregate effects over time. For instance, job vacancy rates among establishments are likely to reflect relatively fixed firm-specific components (perhaps related most strongly to their job turnover rates) as well as more cyclical components. While only the latter is really relevant for the business cycle, our estimated effects of vacancies on employer demand for welfare recipients will confound the effects of both components, and it is possible that this could generate either an upward or downward bias in these estimates.[24] However, the estimates generated here are generally unaffected by the inclusion of additional controls for gross hiring or turnover (for the limited number of establishments where these responses are provided), and the estimates are fairly consistent with others that appear in the recent literature on how business cycle effects on employment vary by demographic group.[25] Thus, the estimates provided here are certainly plausible and possibly quite accurate.

Table 4 presents results from similar regression equations, in which the dependent variables are employers' prospective willingness to hire recipients over the next year and whether or not the employer has hired any welfare recipients during the past two years. The former equations are again estimated by both OLS and tobit, while the latter are estimated by OLS (and therefore represent linear probability models). Both equations represent demand for welfare recipients that is measured over a somewhat longer time period, and at least the latter measures actual hiring (as opposed to that which could prospectively occur).

The specifications of these equations are identical to those of Table 3 except for one change: I also include the dummy variable for whether or not the establishment has hired any workers who are less qualified than usual in the past two years as an additional independent variable in some equations. Given that both of these dependent variables are measured over somewhat longer time frames than current demand for welfare recipients, a stronger case can be made for including a measure of labor market tightness that captures the establishment's experience over a comparably longer period of time.[26] But, given that the current vacancy rate is correlated with this measure and may at least partly capture its effects, I present results from three spec-

Table 4 Determinants of Demand for Welfare Recipients: Next Year or Over the Past Two Years[a]

| | Next year | | | | | | Past two years (OLS) | | |
| | OLS | | | Tobit | | | | | |
	1	2	3	1	2	3	1	2	3
Vacancy rate	0.326	—	0.329	0.475	—	0.451	0.514	—	0.398
	(4.207)		(4.177)	(3.859)		(3.640)	(2.991)		(2.285)
Have hired workers with lower qualifications	—	0.016	0.005	—	0.054	0.040	—	0.126	0.119
		(1.018)	(0.320)		(2.161)	(1.599)		(3.762)	(3.489)
Percent of jobs that require no ed. or exp.	0.099	0.095	0.098	0.217	0.207	0.210	0.160	0.133	0.139
	(4.431)	(4.167)	(4.381)	(6.010)	(5.635)	(5.828)	(3.394)	(2.819)	(2.937)
Establishment size (hundreds)	-0.004	-0.005	-0.004	-0.003	-0.004	-0.003	0.004	0.001	0.003
	(1.732)	(2.104)	(1.751)	(0.764)	(1.113)	(0.815)	(0.696)	(0.175)	(0.519)
Industry									
Manufacturing	-0.040	-0.034	-0.019	-0.066	-0.062	-0.040	0.082	0.062	0.059
	(0.971)	(0.797)	(0.463)	(0.997)	(0.898)	(0.584)	(0.875)	(0.666)	(0.616)
Retail trade	0.048	0.064	0.069	0.059	0.081	0.091	0.367	0.370	0.357
	(1.211)	(1.544)	(1.709)	(0.926)	(1.220)	(1.388)	(4.097)	(4.168)	(3.900)
Service	-0.009	-0.000	0.014	-0.031	-0.015	0.007	0.223	0.218	0.217
	(0.229)	(0.012)	(0.346)	(0.495)	(0.238)	(0.114)	(2.533)	(2.496)	(2.409)
R^2	0.161	0.135	0.164	—	—	—	0.122	0.131	0.137
$-\log L$	—	—	—	145.53	146.704	140.241	—	—	—

[a] t-Statistics are in parentheses. Sample sizes are 850 and 533 for the regressions on hiring in the past two years and over the next year, respectively. Regression equations also include dummies for other one-digit industries (construction is omitted); MSA, central-city locations, and their interactions; and a constant term.

ifications of each equation: one including only the vacancy rate, one including only the dummy for having hired less qualified workers, and one including both. I also must note the greater potential for measurement error in the more subjective variable for less qualified hires and therefore for downward biases in the estimated effects of this variable on demand for welfare recipients.

The results in columns 1–3 of Table 4 do not differ dramatically from those presented in Table 3: the estimated coefficients on the current job vacancy rate are roughly similar to those in Table 3, the OLS estimate being a bit larger and the Tobit estimate somewhat smaller. The variable for having hired less qualified workers has positive and significant effects on the past hiring of welfare recipients and on prospective hiring in the Tobit equations.[27] The effects of skill requirements of jobs and establishment size are larger here than in the earlier table, as are some of the industry effects.

If we assume that, in addition to the declines in vacancy rates specified above, the tendency to hire less qualified workers will also decline by 50–100 percent during a recession (an admittedly arbitrary assumption), then the estimates in the right-most column 3 of Table 4 suggest that the tendency to have hired a welfare recipient over a two-year period will have declined by roughly 7–14 percentage points during a downturn. The prospective demand for welfare recipients over the next year will decline by 1.3–2.1 percentage points using the OLS column-3 estimates, and 3.3–6.1 percentage points using the tobit column-3 estimates.[28] These predicted changes over the business cycle are larger in absolute magnitude than those reported earlier, but somewhat smaller relative to the means of these variables that appear in Table 1.[29]

The smaller relative effects of the cycle, along with larger effects of skill needs and other establishment characteristics, suggest that estimates of establishment demand for recipients over a longer time period might approach some "equilibrium" level that is less sensitive to short-term cyclical conditions and more tied to underlying characteristics of the establishment and its workforce. Of course, our estimated effects of labor market tightness on the future demand for welfare recipients depends on the extent to which employers project current market conditions into the future, while estimated effects on past hiring also depend on the duration over which any current market tightness has been experienced. These issues add to our uncertainty over how to interpret these results.

Still, the values in Table 4 lend further support the notion that a business cycle downturn will have quite significant effects on the labor market demand for welfare recipients. Given that the measure of whether or not the establishment has hired someone with lower qualifications is relatively subjective and therefore likely measured with some error, the predicted effects of the cycle here are likely to be downward-biased. Furthermore, the estimates in Tables 3 and 4 only capture the effects of the cycle on new <u>hiring</u> activity and do not reflect its likely effects on the <u>retention</u> of those previously hired as layoffs rise; these estimates therefore will not fully reflect the cycle's effects on the overall employment of welfare recipients.[30]

The idea that aggregate labor market conditions affect employer willingness to hire less-skilled workers receives some additional support from comparisons between employer data collected in the Detroit metropolitan area in 1992-93 and those collected in 1997. The earlier data were collected just as the economy in Detroit was beginning to recover from the recession of the early 1990s; metropolitan-wide unemployment rates averaged about 7 percent over the course of that survey. Assuming that little else has changed in the labor market over this relatively short time period and that establishment and job characteristics in the two samples are fairly similar, comparisons between the two surveys should indicate the extent to which the business cycle affects hiring determinants and outcomes for unskilled workers.

Though still preliminary, the data suggest that employers in Detroit are more willing to hire workers into noncollege jobs that lack certain non-essential credentials, such as high school diplomas or previous experience, and that they are more willing to hire black (especially male) applicants.[31] These results confirm that, in the context of the much tighter labor market that characterizes Detroit in 1997, employers are more willing to hire less-credentialed or minority workers now than earlier in the decade, when the labor market contained a good deal more slack.

Regression Results: Determinants of Workplace Supports and Policy Responses

If employers are more willing to hire unskilled welfare recipients when labor markets are very tight, it might also be true that they are more willing to provide higher compensation or other workplace supports for these workers when markets are tight. They also might be more amenable to government programs or interventions that are designed to create employment for welfare recipients under these circumstances.

While the data do not support the notion that compensation of hired welfare recipients improves with labor market tightness, the other hypotheses listed above receive somewhat greater support.[32] Table 5 presents results from regressions in which the dependent variables are a series of dummies for whether or not the employer might be willing to help provide any welfare recipients whom they might hire with particular workplace supports, such as transportation, child care, or training (either basic skills or job-related). We also include regressions for whether employers might be more willing to provide such training to welfare recipients if they could receive either tax credits or technical assistance for doing so; whether they would be more willing to hire recipients if they could receive a 50 percent wage subsidy for one year; and whether they hired welfare recipients after having contact with a Michigan Works! agency (for those who, in fact, had such contact). These equations are estimated by OLS and have the same three specifications in each case as those presented in Table 4.[33]

The means in Table 5 indicate that relatively few employers would help provide transportation or child care to welfare recipients, though much larger percentages might provide training (especially if it is job-related). Many employers claim that their willingness to provide the latter would rise if they could receive tax credits or especially technical assistance.[34] Roughly one-third of employers report that they would increase employment of welfare recipients in response to wage subsidies; and a majority of the firms that had contact with a Michigan Works! agency did subsequently hire at least one welfare recipient.[35] The data therefore suggest that employers might be relatively responsive to a variety of policy interventions designed to raise the private sector employment and earnings prospects of the welfare population.

The results of Table 5 also indicate that the degree of labor market tightness facing establishments influences their willingness to provide workplace supports and their responsiveness to several potential government policy interventions. For instance, those that have hired workers in the past two years with lower-than-usual qualifications are more willing to provide each type of benefit or support and are more responsive to each of these government interventions.[36] Despite the crudeness of the dependent variables and the likelihood of measurement error (and therefore downward bias) in the independent variable measuring market tightness, these effects are increases of from 3 to 16 percentage points in the probabilities of providing supports or responding to government programs; relative to the means presented in the first column of Table 5, these are not necessarily small effects.

In addition, job vacancy rates at the firm also have positive and at least marginally significant effects on a firm's willingness to provide transportation or child care and on its responsiveness to subsidies or agency intermediation. Together with the results for hiring less qualified workers, these results imply that changes in these market tightness variables over the business cycle, of the magnitudes assumed earlier in this paper, would generate some significant differences in the provision of workplace supports and effectiveness of policy interventions on behalf of welfare recipients. For instance, the estimates imply that a recession would reduce the willingness of those who had contact with a Michigan Works! agency to hire recipients by roughly 7–9 percentage points (relative to the current level 0.59), and would reduce willingness to hire more recipients in response to subsidies by 4–6 percentage points (relative to its current level of 0.32). If anything, these estimates probably understate the effects of the cycle to a considerable degree.[37]

CONCLUSION

This paper presents data on employer demand for welfare recipients from a recent survey of employers in Michigan. We investigate the determinants of employers' willingness to hire welfare recipients either currently or in the future, as well as the tendency to have done so

Table 5 Determinants of Workplace Supports for Welfare Recipients and Responses to Policies

	Mean of dependent variable	Vacancy rate		Have hired less qualified workers		N	R^2
		β	t	β	t		
Would help provide transportation							
1[a]	0.170	0.402	2.959	–	–	784	0.044
2	0.170	–	–	0.058	2.129	784	0.034
3	0.170	0.356	2.595	0.047	1.705	784	0.046
Would help provide child care							
1	0.129	0.194	1.594	–	–	797	0.042
2	0.129	–	–	0.045	1.832	797	0.046
3	0.129	0.137	1.099	0.048	1.921	797	0.050
Would provide basic skills training							
1	0.468	0.119	0.616	–	–	817	0.038
2	0.468	–	–	0.082	2.240	817	0.043
3	0.468	0.055	0.281	0.092	2.463	817	0.046
Would provide job-related skills training							
1	0.887	-0.028	0.243	–	–	807	0.011
2	0.887	–	–	0.027	1.188	807	0.017
3	0.887	-0.026	0.222	0.025	1.06	807	0.012

Would be more willing to train if tax credit available							
1	0.550	0.078	0.365	–	–	528	0.028
2	0.550	–	–	0.101	2.262	528	0.030
3	0.550	0.023	0.104	0.095	2.081	528	0.038
Would be more willing to train if technical assistance was available							
1	0.657	-0.039	0.200	–	–	545	0.064
2	0.657	–	–	0.106	2.577	545	0.075
3	0.657	-0.101	0.528	0.107	2.572	545	0.077
Would hire more welfare recipients in response to 50% wage subsidy for 1 year							
1	0.322	0.454	2.641	–	–	829	0.027
2	0.322	–	–	0.120	3.552	829	0.033
3	0.322	0.389	2.226	0.105	3.072	829	0.039
Did hire welfare recipients after contact with Michigan Works! agency							
1	0.592	1.638	2.206	–	–	133	0.139
2	0.592	–	–	0.164	1.794	133	0.136
3	0.592	0.915	1.909	0.131	1.401	133	0.155

[a] Specifications 1–3 correspond to those in Table 4.

over the past two years. We focus specifically on how such demand is affected by establishment-level measures of labor market tightness, such as job vacancy rates and their recent need to have hired workers with lower-than-usual qualifications. We also explore the effects of these variables on employer willingness to provide a variety of workplace supports to any welfare recipients whom they might hire and on the extent to which their hiring or training of recipients might be affected by subsidies and credits, technical assistance, or labor market intermediation by local agencies.

The results of this study can be summarized as follows:

- Self-reported employer demand for welfare recipients is currently quite high in Michigan.

- Labor markets in Michigan are currently very tight.

- The tightness of the labor market accounts for significant portions of the current demand for recipients, which will likely disappear during the next recession.

- Labor market tightness makes employers more willing to provide workplace supports (such as training) to recipients whom they hire, and the employers are also more open to potential policy interventions on their behalf.

More specifically, employers in Michigan currently experience a considerable degree of labor market tightness. Job vacancy rates appear to be higher than current unemployment rates. About 80 percent of employers report at least some difficulty finding qualified applicants, and about 40 percent claim that they have hired workers recently with lower-than-usual qualifications. Regarding employer willingness to hire welfare recipients, they claim that they would be willing to fill about 3 percent of all of their jobs (or roughly half of their job vacancies) right away with recipients, even if the latter had no high school diploma or recent work experience, and that they would be willing to hire many more over the next year. Furthermore, roughly 40 percent of employers claim that they have already hired one or more welfare recipients during the past two years. On the other hand, long-term welfare recipients and especially inner-city minorities might have limited access to many of these jobs, for a variety of reasons.

To what extent do the hiring difficulties of employers that are attributable to labor market tightness affect their willingness to hire welfare recipients? Our measures of market tightness and of willingness to hire recipients are both particularly high in certain sectors of the labor market, such as small establishments and the retail trade sector. Yet, even controlling for these and other observable characteristics of establishments, we find that those with high vacancy rates (and, to some extent, those that have recently hired less-qualified workers) are more likely to hire welfare recipients, both currently and over the next year.

Using these cross-sectional estimates to predict the effects of the aggregate business cycle on hiring lead us to predict that a recession would reduce the current demand for welfare recipients by 25–40 percent, and longer-term hiring by somewhat greater absolute magnitudes (but smaller percentage ones). Estimated effects of demand conditions on small establishments, and especially those in retail trade, are even higher than those observed overall. Of course, there are potential problems with inferring aggregate time-series economic changes from a cross-section of data, though the biases caused here could go in either direction. Measurement error in our more-subjective dependent and independent variables likely generate inefficiency and/or downward biases in these estimates, which also fail to include the effects of the cycle on the employment of recipients through its effects on retention as well as hiring. Overall, the results should be interpreted as suggestive rather than definitive with regards to specific magnitudes of effects.

The data also imply that many firms might now be responsive to a wide range of potential government efforts to improve the employment prospects of welfare recipients. These include placement efforts by intermediaries, wage subsidies or tax credits for the hiring of disadvantaged recipients (provided they are "employer-friendly"), and tax credits or technical assistance for providing them with training. Furthermore, under tight labor markets, employers appear to be more willing than they otherwise would be to provide certain workplace supports (such as transportation, child care assistance, or training) to welfare recipients, and to respond to the kinds of government efforts mentioned above.

Overall, these results imply that the labor market difficulties of welfare recipients will almost certainly grow more severe during the next recession. There will likely be some need to provide countercyclical increases in labor demand (perhaps through some version of public service employment), or at least to improve the safety nets that welfare recipients will face during that time. The fact that some of the least-skilled welfare recipients have not yet entered the labor market, and may be reaching their time limits for assistance during the next economic downturn, renders these problems even more urgent.

Given the apparent openness of employers to policies aimed at improving the employment options of recipients in tight markets, and given that many long-term welfare recipients in inner-city will have limited access to available jobs (because of their poor skills, transportation or information problems, etc.), a strong case can also be made for funding some of these efforts right now, especially if they are accompanied by serious evaluation efforts. A fair amount of funding is potentially available during the current period of tightness, as many states and localities have surpluses to spend in their welfare budgets and are receiving "welfare-to-work" grants from the federal government. Of course, even if these programs are successful in improving the current labor market prospects of recipients, the extent to which those who achieve some success now will be retained by employers during the next downturn remains unclear, though at least some persistence of positive outcomes over the cycle should be expected.

This study also suggests the need for continued research on these issues. Data on prospective employer demand for welfare recipients during the next downturn is not a perfect substitute for data on actual demand when that downturn occurs. This is particularly true since the estimated effects of labor market tightness in a cross-section of firms might differ substantially from the effects of an aggregate downturn that affects all firms. Evidence on layoffs/retention (as well as on new hire rates) could be provided from such data, and we could also obtain data on the experiences of employers with the later entrants to the market, who are likely to be more disadvantaged than those whom we have observed to date. While many such experiences will be apparent from supply-side data on recipients and their labor market experiences, the data on employers can continue to provide insights on the demand-side factors that contribute to the outcomes we observe among these workers.

Notes

1. This self-selection generally implies that the average employment outcomes that we've observed for welfare recipients to date are biased upwards, though the estimated effects of labor market conditions or policy initiatives on these employment outcomes might not be.

2. See Eissa and Liebman (1996), Eissa and Hoynes (1998), and Bishop (1998) for evidence on the recent improvements in employment rates of single women. But, in these analyses of aggregate data over time, it is often difficult to disentangle the effects of the Earned Income Tax Credit, changes in Medicare coverage, welfare reform, and the business cycle.

3. One possible exception to this was a survey of establishments in Milwaukee, administered by the Employment and Training Institute of the University of Wisconsin at Milwaukee (Employment and Training Institute 1995). They gauged the number of job vacancies, both overall and in specific occupations, and compared them with the number of unskilled, unemployed workers in the metropolitan area. As of the mid 1990s, the number of unemployed workers continued to exceed the number of vacant jobs, despite the very low unemployment rates there.

4. Another wave of the survey will be administered to the same establishments in Michigan during the fall of 1999. The survey is currently being administered in several other metropolitan areas such as Chicago, Cleveland, Milwaukee, and Los Angeles.

5. Michigan Works! agencies are private contractors with the various Workforce Development Boards established at the county level by the Michigan Jobs Commission. For more detailed descriptions of their activities see Seefeldt et al. (1998).

6. The exact wording of these questions was as follows: "Suppose you were contacted by an employment agency that was trying to place welfare recipients who did not have a high school diploma or any recent work experience. Do you currently have any open positions that you might consider filling with these welfare recipients?" If yes: "How many of them would you consider employing right away?" For the following year: "Do you think you will have open positions during the next year that you might consider filling with these welfare recipients?" If yes: "How many of them would you possibly employ at any time during the next year?"

7. These three industries account for almost 80% of the establishments in the survey. Also, "central city" refers to the city of Detroit, as well as Flint and Grand Rapids, but does not include other municipalities that are officially designated as "central cities" by the Census Bureau in these areas, such as Dearborn or Pontiac.

8. We have set missing values equal to zero for the question of whether or not employers had hired welfare recipients over the previous two years; these account for roughly 20% of the sample in this case. The wages on jobs actually filled by recipients, as well as those prospectively available to them, averaged between $6.00 and 6.50, and about two-thirds offered some type of health care coverage.

9. Reported job availability for welfare recipients was particularly high in restaurants and in health care facilities and personal service establishments in the service sector.
10. Larger establishments are more likely to have hired at least one recipient, given that they engage in more hiring overall, but were not as high in terms of percentages of their respective workforces.
11. In Detroit, job availability for welfare recipients was actually higher in the central city than the suburbs, while the opposite was true in Flint and Grand Rapids.
12. The correlation between job availability currently and over the next year for welfare recipients is roughly 0.6, while the correlation between availability over the next year and the past two years is roughly 0.3.
13. In fact, the vast majority of available jobs for welfare recipients are in relatively small establishments (i.e., those with 50 or fewer employees), in suburban locations that are frequently not accessible to public transit, in establishments that recruit unskilled workers informally, or in establishments that frequently receive no applications from blacks (Holzer 1998b). Thus, many potentially available jobs will be relatively inaccessible to poor minority residents of inner-city areas, who constitute large fractions of long-term welfare recipients. The basic skills required on many of these jobs may also put some out of the reach of long-term recipients with poor cognitive abilities (Pavetti 1997).
14. See, for instance, Abraham (1983) and Holzer (1989) for evidence that unemployment rates usually exceed job vacancy rates by considerable amounts at all points in the business cycle. The question used in this survey to gauge job vacancies asks about all vacant jobs that the employer is currently trying to fill, while the question used in other surveys has generally also stipulated that these vacancies be available for immediate occupancy. It seems quite unlikely that a large percentage of vacancies that employers are currently trying to fill would only be available for future occupancy, though such a restriction might reduce the current vacancy rate to the 4–5% range.
15. For instance, when we analyze the most recently filled job in each establishment, we find that employers do not require (or even strongly prefer) high school diplomas, previous experience, or training in roughly 17% of these jobs, and they also do not require reading/writing or arithmetic in just 11%.
16. This assumes that the errors are not correlated with the independent variables of interest.
17. Dummies for all one-digit industries are included, with construction as the omitted category. Locational variables include dummies for metropolitan area, central city, and interactions between them.
18. See Davis, Holtiwanger, and Schuh (1996), Barron, Bishop, and Dunkelberg (1985), and Holzer (1994, 1996).
19. Measures of overall hiring activity or recent difficulty in finding qualified applicants did not generate significant estimates in these equations after controlling for the job vacancy rate.

20. The three measures of skill demand that appear in Table 1 all generated qualitatively similar estimates when used as independent variables in these equations.

21. The dependent variable might be censored if, for example, very weak demand generates "negative hiring" or layoffs of welfare recipients while measured willingness to hire is zero.

22. Given the discrepancy that we noted above between traditional measures of vacancy rates and those presented here (note 14), we assume that current rates could be in the range of 4–6% if measured comparably to more traditional measures.

23. Calculations of predicted values using tobit estimates must also allow for the probability that individual observations were censored at the outset. The sample-wide predictions here do not appear to differ substantially from those generated using the OLS estimates.

24. The estimates will be upward-biased if the firm-specific components of job vacancy rates have larger effects on demand for recipients than do the more cyclical components. This will be true if, for example, high-turnover firms regard welfare recipients as potentially more stable sources of labor than the ones on which they currently draw. But it is also possible that such firms have limited costs associated with such turnover, in which case temporarily high demand might be more costly and generate greater effects on their hiring behavior.

25. For instance, the figures presented in Freeman and Rodgers (1998) show that the employment rates of less-educated young black males (i.e., those aged 16–24 with 12 or fewer years of education) have varied by roughly one-fourth to one-third over the last few business cycles. Hoynes (1998) also shows that demand for less-skilled females is more cyclically sensitive than that of less-skilled males. Neither paper focuses exclusively on high school dropouts or other unskilled workers whose employment experiences might be more comparable to those of welfare recipients.

26. Indeed, these variables had little significant effect in any of the estimated equations for current willingness to hire welfare recipients but had more effect in equations for past or future hiring.

27. The percentage of jobs currently filled by workers with low qualifications also generated significant effects in the OLS version of the equation for future hiring, though it performed considerably less well than the dummy variable for any such hiring in some other equations presented below. While the continuous version of this variable might generally be preferred to the categorical one, it is likely that the former are measured with more error as well.

28. In other words, the lower end of the range of predictions was generated by using the lower bound changes in both independent variables, while the upper end of the predictions was generated using the upper bound changes in both cases.

29. For instance, the predictions from the OLS equations suggest that the probability of hiring any welfare recipient over a two-year period should decline by 17–33% in a recession, while the percentage of jobs available to recipients over the next year should decline by 14–22%.

30. The percentage decline in the overall demand for labor among welfare recipients will thus reflect the relative magnitudes of declines in retention as well as in new hiring. Davis, Holtiwanger, and Schuh (1996) suggest that the former are generally more important in explaining the variation in unemployment rates over the business cycle, as changes in movements "into" unemployment appear to dominate changes in movements "out."

31. For instance, specific experience was absolutely necessary or strongly preferred in 56% of non-college jobs filled in 1992–93 but only in 49% in 1997, even though the fraction of newly filled jobs that were white collar was higher in the earlier period. The ratio of the percentage of new hires that are black to the percentage of applicants that are black rose from 0.78 to 0.85 as well.

32. The effects of vacancy rates and the hiring of less-qualified workers on wage levels and provision of health benefits on jobs actually filled by welfare recipients and those prospectively available were generally negative but not significant, even after controlling for establishment characteristics such as industry, size, and location.

33. For the first six of these dependent variables, we assign the value of 1 to both "yes" and "maybe" responses and the value of 0 to "no."

34. The relatively small numbers of employers who answered "maybe" to these questions are counted among the positive answers here. Missing values are excluded from the sample.

35. More evidence on the likely effects of wage subsidies and intermediary efforts appears in Holzer (1998b). The magnitudes of the reported hiring increases in response to hypothetical wage subsidies are generally consistent with estimates of labor demand elasticities for unskilled workers. But, firms often showed little knowledge of existing federal tax credits for hiring welfare recipients and often seemed unwilling to claim these credits even when they were aware of them and eligible to receive them. These results suggest that tax credits might be much more effective when provided in an "employer-friendly" fashion and when accompanied by significant outreach efforts, perhaps by intermediaries who handle the paperwork (see also Katz 1998). While a majority of the firms that had contact with an agency hired recipients, only about 17% of the total reported any such contact.

36. Of all of these estimates, significant levels are marginal only in the case of job-related training.

37. For instance, the likelihood that establishments have contact with the agency at all probably declines in a recession as well, especially for those cases where the contact was initiated by the establishment rather than the agency.

References

Abraham, Katherine. 1983. "Structural-Frictional vs. Demand-Deficient Unemployment: Some New Evidence." *American Economic Review* 73(4): 708–724.

Barron, John, John Bishop, and William Dunkelberg. 1985. "Employer Search: the Interviewing and Hiring of New Employees." *Review of Economics and Statistics* 67(1): 43–52.

Berman Eli, John Bound, and Zvi Griliches. 1994. "Changes in the Demand for Skilled Labor within U.S. Manufacturing: Evidence from the Annual Survey of Manufactures." *Quarterly Journal of Economics* 109(2): 367–397.

Bishop, John. 1998. "Is Welfare Reform Succeeding?" Photocopy, Cornell University.

Black, Sandra, and Lisa Lynch. 1997. *How to Compete: The Impact of Workplace Practices and Information Technology on Productivity.* NBER working paper no. W6120, National Bureau of Economic Research, Cambridge, Massachusetts.

Bound, John, and Harry J. Holzer. 1996. "Demand Shifts, Population Adjustments and Labor Market Outcomes during the 1980's." NBER working paper no. 5685, National Bureau of Economic Research, Cambridge, Massachusetts.

Burtless, Gary. 1995. "The Employment Prospects of Welfare Recipients." In *The Work Alternative*, D. Nightingale and R. Haveman, eds. Washington, D.C.: The Urban Institute Press, pp. 71–106.

Cappelli, Peter. 1996. "Technology and Skill Requirements: Implications for Establishment Wage Structures." *New England Economic Review* (May/June): 139–154.

Davis, Steve, John Haltiwanger, and Scott Schuh. 1996. *Job Creation and Destruction.* Cambridge, Massachusetts: MIT Press.

Department of Employment, The City of New York. 1994. *New York City Employer Survey: Summary Report.* August.

Eissa, Nada, and Hilary Hoynes. 1998. *The Earned Income Tax Credit and the Labor Supply of Married Couples.* Working paper no. 4, Center for Labor Economics, University of California at Berkeley.

Eissa, Nada, and Jeffrey Liebman. 1996. "Labor Supply Response to the Earned Income Tax Credit." *Quarterly Journal of Economics* 111(2): 605–637.

Employment and Training Institute. 1994. "Survey of Job Openings in the Milwaukee Metropolitan Area: Week of October 24, 1994." University of Wisconsin at Milwaukee.

Figlio, David N., and James P. Ziliak. 1999. *Welfare Reform, the Business Cycle, and the Decline in AFDC Caseloads.* In this volume, pp. 17–48.

Freeman, Richard. 1991. "Employment and Earnings of Disadvantaged Young Men in a Labor Shortage Economy." In *The Urban Underclass,* C. Jencks and P. Peterson, eds. Washington, D.C.: The Brookings Institution.

Freeman, Richard, and William Rodgers. 1998. "Area Economic Conditions and the Labor Market Outcomes of Young Men in the 1990's Expansion." Unpublished document, Harvard University.

Holzer, Harry. 1994. "Job Vacancy Rates in the Firm: An Empirical Analysis." *Economica* 61(241): 17–36.

Holzer, Harry. 1989. *Unemployment, Vacancies and Local Labor Markets.* Kalamazoo Michigan: W.E. Upjohn Institute for Employment Research.

Holzer, Harry. 1996. *What Employers Want: Job Prospects for Less-Educated Workers.* New York: Russell Sage Foundation.

Holzer, Harry. 1998a. "Why Do Small Establishments Hire Fewer Blacks than Larger Ones?" *Journal of Human Resources* 33(4): 896–914.

Holzer, Harry. 1998b. *Will Employers Hire Welfare Recipients? Recent Survey Evidence from Michigan.* Discussion paper no. 1177–98, Institute for Research on Poverty, University of Wisconsin-Madison.

Holzer, Harry, and Sheldon Danziger. 1998. *Are Jobs Available for Disadvantaged Workers in Urban Areas?* Discussion paper no. 1157–98, Institute for Research on Poverty, University of Wisconsin-Madison.

Holzer, Harry, Lawrence Katz, and Alan Krueger. 1991. "Job Queues and Wages." *Quarterly Journal of Economics* 106(3): 739–768.

Hoynes, Hilary. 1998. "The Employment and Earnings of Less Skilled Workers Over the Business Cycle." Prepared for the Conference on "Labor Markets and Less Skilled Workers," Washington, D.C., November. Photocopy, University of California, Berkeley.

Hoynes, Hilary. 1996. *Local Labor Markets and Welfare Spells: Do Demand Conditions Matter?* NBER working paper no. 5643, National Bureau of Economic Research, Cambridge, Massachusetts.

Katz, Lawrence. 1998. "Wage Subsidies for the Disadvantaged." In *Generating Jobs: How to Increase Demand for Less-Skilled Workers,* R. Freeman and P. Gottschalk, eds. New York: Russell Sage Foundation, pp. 21–53.

McMurrer, Daniel, Isabel Sawhill, and Robert Lerman. 1997. *Welfare Reform and Opportunity in the Low-Wage Labor Market.* Research Center paper no. 7028, The Urban Institute, Washington D.C.

Osterman, Paul. 1994. "How Common Is Workplace Transformation and Who Adopts It?" *Industrial and Labor Relations Review* 47(2): 173–188.

Pavetti, LaDonna. 1997. *How Much More Can They Work? Setting Realistic Expectations for Welfare Mothers.* Research Center paper no. 6998, The Urban Institute, Washington D.C..

Seefeldt, Kristin, Sandra Danziger, and Jodi Sandfort. 1998. *Moving Towards a Vision of Independence: Local Managers' Views of Michigan's Welfare Reform.* Report of the Poverty Research and Training Center, University of Michigan.

Wallace, Geoffrey, and Rebecca M. Blank. 1999. *What Goes Up Must Come Down? Explaining Recent Changes in Public Assistance Caseloads.* In this volume, pp. 49–89.

Part III
How Are the States Responding?

What Will the States Do When Jobs Are Not Plentiful?

Policy and Implementation Challenges

LaDonna A. Pavetti
Mathematica Policy Research, Inc.

The Personal Responsibility and Work Opportunity Reconciliation Act (PRWORA) of 1996 ended the individual entitlement to welfare benefits under the 61-year-old Aid to Families with Dependent Children (AFDC) program and eliminated the companion welfare-to-work program, the Job Opportunities and Basic Skills (JOBS) training program created by the Family Support Act of 1988. PRWORA provides each state with a block grant to establish a Temporary Assistance for Needy Families (TANF) program.

In contrast to the AFDC program (which provided cash assistance for as long as needed) and to the JOBS program (which encouraged recipients to participate in long-term education and training programs), TANF provides short-term, work-oriented assistance to poor families with children. TANF recipients are required to work once they are job-ready or after receiving assistance for not more than 24 months (and less at state option), and persons are eligible to receive TANF assistance for only 60 months out of their lifetime. To ensure that state TANF programs emphasize work, PRWORA requires states to meet steadily increasing work participation rates to receive their full block grant.

WELFARE REFORM IN A ROBUST ECONOMY

Given that PRWORA mandates a work-oriented assistance system, the economic conditions under which states began their programs could not have been better. In most areas of the country, welfare offices shifted to a work-based system during a time when jobs were plentiful. When PRWORA was signed into law in August 1996, the unemployment rate was just 5.2 percent, down from almost 7 percent four years earlier. By October 1998, the unemployment rate had declined even further, to 4.6 percent; for women over the age of 20, the unemployment rate was just 4.0 percent. Although unemployment rates remain higher for population groups who traditionally have had a harder time finding employment, unemployment rates have declined for these groups as well. For example, persons over the age of 25 years of age without a high school diploma currently face an unemployment rate of 6.8 percent, down from 8.5 percent in August 1996, and African Americans face an unemployment rate of 8.6 percent, down from 10.7 percent (Bureau of Labor Statistics 1998). There are, however, areas of the country that have not shared in the good fortunes of the current economic boom; for example, former coal mining regions in Kentucky and Virginia are currently experiencing unemployment rates of nearly 20 percent.

A strong, robust economy with low inflation rates and unprecedented policy and programmatic changes in the welfare system have resulted in significant declines in the number of families receiving cash assistance; between January 1993 and June 1998, that number declined by 39 percent, from 4.96 million to 3.03 million families. Sixteen states experienced at least a 50 percent reduction in the number of families receiving assistance. However, with caseload declines of 18 and 24 percent, respectively, California and New York (the states with the two largest caseloads) experienced significantly smaller caseload declines than most other states and the nation as a whole. Hawaii, the only state with an increased caseload, provided cash assistance to 38 percent more families in June 1998 than in January 1993 (Administration for Children and Families 1998).

As a result of the steep decline in AFDC/TANF caseloads, most states have been able to implement major work-based reforms in a resource-rich environment. A recent General Accounting Office study (U.S. General Accounting Office 1998) found that the amount of TANF funds available to states for 1997 was $4.7 billion more than states would have had under the old AFDC formula. The median increase for states was 22 percent, with 46 states having more money than they would have had under AFDC formula. Since the enactment of PRWORA, states also have achieved budgetary savings by reducing state expenditures on welfare programs to the 75 or 80 percent "maintenance of effort" (MOE) required by federal law. Even with the state budgetary savings, 21 states are spending more per recipient than they were prior to the implementation of TANF (U.S. General Accounting Office 1998).

On top of their TANF funding, over the next several years states and localities will have access to close to $3 billion in additional funds from the Welfare-to-Work grants program (legislated in 1997) to implement work-based strategies for hard-to-employ welfare recipients. Some communities are using these funds to expand existing programs; others are using them to develop more intensive short-term training and/or supported work programs, or to provide existing and/or new services to underserved groups such as noncustodial fathers. Through the Child Care Development block grant, states also received additional funding to expand their child care programs for welfare recipients and/or for the working poor. Several states have used these additional funds to fully fund their child care program for welfare recipients and to eliminate or significantly reduce the waiting list for child care for working poor families.

Implementing work-oriented reforms in a resource-rich and job-rich environment has meant that states have been able to require the majority of TANF applicants or recipients to participate in work or work-related activities without developing long waiting lists, as was often the case under the JOBS program. Given the low unemployment rate, they have tended to rely on low-cost job search strategies while providing support services, especially child care and transportation assistance, to families who cannot afford to pay for these services on their own.

Now that caseloads have declined, many states have started to expand their welfare-to-work programs to help recipients retain jobs and advance to better jobs, instead of just focusing on getting recipients into jobs as they have in the past. For example, Rhode Island has implemented a statewide job retention unit to provide assistance to recipients who have been placed in employment and to employers who have hired recipients. Utah is providing training and paying for additional supervision for some welfare recipients who are placed in unsubsidized employment. Because many families remaining on the TANF rolls are harder-to-employ, some states have started to experiment with ways to help families facing a broad array of personal and family challenges make the transition from welfare to work. Oregon, North Carolina, Maryland, and New Jersey have implemented programs to identify and refer recipients to substance abuse treatment programs. Washington, Kansas, and Minnesota are implementing programs to identify and provide services to recipients with learning disabilities. Because they have multiple barriers to employment, many of the families left on the welfare rolls are likely to require more resources to make the transition to employment than those who have already left the rolls. For now, the extra resources that states and localities have at their disposal have created an environment that is welcoming of new ideas and supports investment in promising (but not yet proven) strategies to help welfare recipients with limited attachment to the labor force become self-sufficient.

IMPLEMENTING WORK-BASED REFORMS WHEN JOBS ARE MORE SCARCE

When the economy changes and firms are laying off more workers than they are hiring, federal, state, and local decision makers and program operators will face a different set of policy and programmatic choices than they face in the current environment. Given PRWORA mandates and that widespread support exists for a work-based assistance system, it is unlikely that a downturn in the economy will result in a shift away from the current emphasis on employment. Thus, the major challenge decision makers will face is identifying options for maintaining a focus on work in an environment where unsubsidized employment is more difficult to find, where welfare entrances will increase and exits will decrease, and where financial resources no longer expand to meet the increased demand for assistance.

PRWORA gave states unprecedented authority to decide how they would use their fixed TANF funds to meet the income, employment, and support service needs of poor families with children. PRWORA does, however, provide broad programmatic guidelines that have shaped the design of many state TANF programs and will affect states' ability to respond to an economic downturn. For example, PRWORA defines the activities that can count towards a state's work participation rate and specifies the number of hours a recipient must participate in allowable activities. PRWORA also set a lifetime limit on assistance and the fraction of a state's caseload that can be exempt from the time limit. As a result of the requirements PRWORA places on states, Congress and the federal government will have a major role to play in developing an appropriate response to an economic downturn, or states will face programmatic and financial difficulties.

Within PRWORA's framework, states and localities have implemented a variety of strategies to transform their cash assistance systems into systems that mandate and support work. Table 1 provides examples of the types of policies states have implemented. At the core of nearly all of these reform efforts are job search assistance and job placement programs, generally referred to as "Work First" programs. These programs range from independent job search programs (such as those implemented in Virginia, where recipients mostly are required to look for employment on their own and report regularly on their progress) to more structured group job search programs such as those implemented in Oregon and Nebraska (where recipients participate in structured job search activities such as how to complete an application, write a resume, and conduct themselves in a job interview). Even if different in their day-to-day operation, these programs share a common philosophy regarding world: any job is viewed as a good job, and program efforts are geared towards helping recipients enter the labor market as quickly as possible (Brown 1997; Holcomb et al. 1998).

In many states, the work expectations set forth through these programs have been reinforced with more stringent financial penalties for noncompliance (sanctions), more generous earned-income disregards that allow more recipients to continue to receive cash assistance while they are working, and time limits to create a new social contract that presents assistance recipients with a very different set of expectations and choices than they have faced in the past. While some states like California and Washington have relied primarily on incentives to encourage parents to enter the paid labor market, other states such as Wisconsin have relied more on penalties for not complying with work mandates. A number of states, like Massachusetts and Florida, have

Table 1 Examples of Key State Policy Choices under PRWORA[1]

State	Work requirement	Penalty for noncompliance (sanction)	Most stringent time limit	Earnings disregard policy
Alabama	Immediate job search	Initial benefit reduction, followed by loss of all cash assistance	60 months, followed by termination of benefits	100% of earnings in first 3 months, then 20%
California	Immediate job search; unsubsidized employment required at 18 months	Benefit reduction	60 months, followed by reduction in benefits	$225 and 50 percent of remainder
Colorado	Determined by individual counties	Initial benefit reduction followed by loss of all cash assistance	60 months, followed by termination of benefits	Varies by county
Florida	Immediate job search	Immediate loss of all cash assistance	48 months, followed by termination of benefits[2]	$200 and 50 percent of remainder
Massachusetts	Work or community service required within 60 days for families with a child over the age of 6; no job search or work require-ment for other families	Initial benefit reduction followed by loss of all cash assistance	24 months out of 60, followed by termination of benefits	$120 and 50% of remainder
Michigan	Immediate job search	Initial benefit reduction, followed by loss of all cash assistance	None	$200 and 20% of remainder

Minnesota	Job search for 8 weeks, followed by assessment and a range of potential program activities, including short-term education or training	Initial benefit reduction, followed by loss of all cash assistance	60 months, followed by termination of benefits	36%
Mississippi	Immediate job search	Immediate loss of all cash assistance	60 months, followed by termination of benefits	100% for first 6 months if full-time employment is obtained within 30 days after job search is required; otherwise $90
New Jersey	Immediate job search, followed by various work readiness activities	Initial benefit reduction, followed by loss of all cash assistance	60 months, followed by termination of benefits	100% for first month, then 50 percent
New York	Determined by counties; immediate job search and community work experience are common	Benefit reduction	60 months, followed by reduction in benefits[3]	$90 and 42% of remainder
Texas	Job search immediately	Benefit reduction	60 months, followed by termination of benefits	$120 and 1/3 of remainder for four months; $120 for eight months; then $90
Washington	Job search or other work activities after assessment and development of an Individual Responsibility Plan	Benefit reduction	60 months followed by termination of benefits	50%

(continued)

Table 1 (continued)

State	Work requirement	Penalty for noncompliance (sanction)	Most stringent time limit	Earnings disregard policy
Wisconsin	Work or community service required immediately	Benefit reduction or loss of all cash assistance[4]	60 months followed by termination of benefits.	No disregards

Source: Gallagher et al. 1998.

[1] Information is presented for the 13 states that are a part of the Urban Institute's "Assessing the New Federalism" project, a multi-year project designed to examine state choices and outcomes associated with the implementation of PRWORA.

[2] In addition to the 48-month lifetime limit, Florida also has a 24-out-of-48-month time limit for job-ready recipients and a time limit of 36 out of 72 months for long-term recipients with poor job skills and little work experience.

[3] In addition to benefits being reduced, payments are provided in the form of vendor payments to cover the family's major expenses such as rent or utilities.

[4] Wisconsin uses a "pay for performance" system of determining benefits. If a recipient works some, but not all of the required hours, their grant is reduced by the minimum wage for every hour not worked. If a recipient does not work any of the required hours, they do not receive any of their cash assistance.

combined incentives and penalties. With a few exceptions, most states have imposed lifetime limits on the number of months families can receive TANF assistance. These limits have created a sense of urgency not found in previous welfare-to-work programs.

When the economy weakens, decision makers and program operators are likely to face five key challenges: 1) reallocating program expenditures to account for larger assistance caseloads; 2) reassessing what constitutes work participation and for whom participation is required; 3) identifying strategies for continuing to provide work incentives and work supports when resources are limited; 4) reassessing time limits to take into account the more limited availability of jobs; and 5) maintaining a focus on strategies to help the hardest-to-employ find jobs and to help recipients keep their jobs longer and move into better jobs. Politics, fiscal realities, programmatic goals, and administrative capacity all are likely to influence the way in which states and localities resolve these challenges.

Reallocating Program Expenditures to Account for Larger Assistance Caseloads

States have had additional resources to spend on welfare-to-work activities and supportive services for welfare recipients because they are spending less money providing cash assistance to families. When jobs are not as readily available as they are now, caseloads are likely to begin to increase. It is possible that cash assistance caseloads will not increase to their previously high levels. Nonetheless, because welfare-to-work program activities and support services are now essential components of state TANF programs, for the first time states will be forced to weigh the tradeoffs between allocating resources to cash grants and other services that help parents to find and maintain work.

Although states and localities now have the authority to deny cash assistance to families seeking assistance if expenditures for cash benefits begin to exceed budget allocations, there are no indications that states will pursue this course of action. Even though PRWORA ended the entitlement to cash assistance, states have continued to treat the receipt of TANF benefits as an entitlement; that is, all families who apply for assistance and meet the eligibility criteria (including any work requirements) receive cash assistance.

Some states, however, have tightened the eligibility requirements, resulting in a smaller pool of eligible families. For example, Idaho's caseload declined by 77 percent between January 1997 and June 1998, primarily because the state began to count income from the Supplemental Security Income (SSI) program when determining eligibility for TANF cash assistance. Most states that have tightened eligibility requirements have done so by imposing work-related requirements on families when they apply for assistance. For example, 16 states require parents to look for work before their application for assistance is approved (Maloy et al. 1998). If caseloads begin to increase rapidly during a recession, other states may begin to include additional sources of income when determining eligibility. However, states may be less inclined to impose work requirements as a condition of eligibility since fewer applicants are likely to find jobs and more families are likely to turn to the welfare system because they have just lost a job.

Because TANF funding is fixed, if states continue to maintain the entitlement to cash assistance and caseloads begin to increase, states are likely to begin to look for "non-essential" services that can be reduced or eliminated in order to meet the cost of providing cash assistance to a larger number of families. In addition, states that have shifted primary responsibility for the design and implementation of TANF programs to county governments or other local entities are likely to face difficult decisions about how to allocate limited resources to local entities with very different needs and priorities. To further complicate the situation, states are likely to be making these decisions at the same time they are required to place large numbers of their TANF caseloads in acceptable work activities. This complex set of circumstances is likely to result in a search for new and cheaper alternatives for maintaining a focus on work.

Reassessing What Constitutes Work Participation and for Whom It is Required

Several key features that have distinguished current welfare-to-work programs from their predecessors are likely to form the basis of discussions about how to maintain an emphasis on work when fewer jobs are available and resources are more limited than they are now. Chief among those features are the emphasis on job search and other work activities, the expansion of work participation requirements to the majority of welfare recipients, and the emphasis on personal responsibility. All of these issues are likely to be revisited if the economy weakens. However, given that states have approached welfare reform differently, the extent to which each of these issues is revisited is likely to vary from state to state.

PRWORA is explicit in its definition of what constitutes participation in work activities. In contrast to the former JOBS program that emphasized placement in long-term education and training activities, the allowable activities under TANF are much more directly oriented toward work. Activities that can count toward a state's work participation rate include: 1) unsubsidized or subsidized private or public sector employment; 2) on-the-job training; 3) work experience; 4) job search and job readiness assistance for up to six weeks; 5) community service programs; 6) provision of child care services to an individual participating in a community services program; and 7) vocational educational training (limited to 12 months for any individual and to 30 percent of those required to participate).

Under the JOBS program, only a small fraction of the AFDC caseload (less than 10 percent) was mandated to participate in program activities, primarily because all families with children aged three and younger were exempt from participation. In addition, due to limited resources, many parents who were required to participate spent long periods of time on waiting lists and never actually participated in program activities.

Under TANF, mandatory program participation has been extended to a substantially larger share of the TANF caseload. PRWORA gives states the option to exempt parents from participating in work activities if their youngest child is under the age of one. Only five states have chosen to exempt families caring for a child over the age of one year from their work participation requirements;[1] 22 states require parents with children under a year to participate in program activities. In 1997, among the 39 states for which data is currently available, 61.5 percent of TANF adults were subject to the TANF participation rates (Administration for Children and Families 1998).

Over time, as Table 2 shows, the share of the caseload required to participate in program activities and the intensity of participation increases. In FY 1997, states were required to have 25 percent of all

Table 2 Annual Work Participation Requirements

	All families		Two-parent families	
Fiscal year	Participation rate (%)	Hours of work required per week to count toward rate	Participation rate (%)	Hours of work required per week to count toward rate
1997	25	20	75	35
1998	30	20	75	35
1999	35	25	90	35
2000	40	30	90	35
2001	45	30	90	35
2002	50	30	90	35

families participating in work activities for a minimum of 20 hours per week; by FY 2002 the participation requirements increase to 50 percent of the caseload participating in work activities for a minimum of 30 hours per week. States also are required to meet significantly higher two-parent participation rates.

Underlying the shift to a mandatory work-based assistance is the belief that it is reasonable to require families to meet a set of expectations in exchange for government assistance. Given the time and energy local offices have invested in changing recipient and worker expectations, states and localities are likely to be quite reluctant to shift away from an emphasis on work and personal responsibility, even in an economic downturn when fewer jobs are available. Instead, states and localities will be faced with a difficult set of choices around how and whether to redefine what constitutes program participation, how to expand community work experience and subsidized work opportunities, and whether to reduce the pool of recipients required to participate in program activities. The experiences of states to date provide some indication of the magnitude of this challenge.

The strength of the economy has made it possible for many states to meet their work participation requirements for all families primarily through a "pro rata reduction" in the participation rate to account for the decline in a state's caseload, unsubsidized employment, and participation in job search. Participation in other work activities such as subsidized employment or community work experience has been less common.

The data presented in Table 3 illustrate the importance of the pro rata reduction and the extent to which states have been able to rely on the strength of the economy to meet the TANF work participation rates. Because of its significant caseload decline, Wisconsin was only required to have 8 percent of its TANF caseload that is subject to the TANF work participation requirement participating in work activities; with 53 percent of families participating in work activities, Wisconsin far exceeded the participation rate for FY 1997. The majority of families in Wisconsin worked in unsubsidized jobs or participated in job search, although a sizable number also participated in work experience. Although California met its work participation requirement, it did so only by a small margin. Unlike Wisconsin, California primarily met its work participation targets through unsubsidized unemployment; only a small fraction of parents met the participation requirement by participating in job search, and an even smaller fraction met the requirement by participating in subsidized employment, on-the-job training, work experience, or community service.

Even during an economic downturn, job search programs are likely to remain at the core of state efforts to help welfare recipients find jobs. Although it is likely to take many recipients longer than the six weeks currently allowed under PRWORA to find employment, a substantially higher unemployment rate will not mean that such programs will need to come to a halt. Although few new jobs may be created during an economic downturn, normal job turnover, especially in low-wage jobs, will continue to produce job openings for welfare recipients to fill. In fact, it is easy to imagine a scenario in which welfare recipients, with better access to job search assistance and job developers who have cultivated relationships with employers, may have an easier time finding employment than other low-skilled, unemployed persons who are left completely on their own to find employment in a slack labor market.

Even if job search remains the core of state and local welfare-to-work efforts, when fewer jobs are available, there is likely to be a greater need for alternative work-related activities such as community work experience or subsidized employment programs. A comparison of two localities in Virginia with dramatically different labor markets illustrates this point. In Virginia, TANF recipients with a child 18 months or older

Table 3 TANF Work Participation for All Families, Fiscal Year 1997

	Adjusted work participation standard[a] (%)	State participation rate 1997 (%)	Adults participating in selected program activities[b] (%)			
			Unsubsidized employment	Job search	Subsidized employment, work experience, on-the-job training, or community service	
Alabama	17.1	42.3	67.7	22.9	9.3	
California	19.5	20.6	94.7	1.9	0.9	
Colorado			Data not available			
Florida	16.4	28.4	75.7	12.7	7.3	
Massachusetts	12.6	31.5	38.6	8.8	25.5	
Michigan	13.3	41.1	86.2	13.0	3.0	
Minnesota			Data not available			
Mississippi	16.3	17.2	62.6	13.1	25.8	
New Jersey	16.9	20.7	34.3	11.7	54.3	
New York	19.6	27.9	39.2	13.6	43.3	
Texas	14.6	19.4	42.7	36.1	20.6	
Washington	22.0	24.0	63.3	22.4	14.3	
Wisconsin	8.0	52.8	59.4	52.3	30.1	

SOURCE: Administration for Children and Families 1998.

[a] The adjusted work participation rate takes into account the "pro rata reduction" that the state received due to the decline in its TANF caseload.

[b] Recipients may be participating in more than one activity; thus, the data presented here reflects a duplicated count of participants.

are required to look for work for 90 days and then work for pay or participate in a Community Work Experience Program (CWEP) where they "work off" their grant. Recipients who work for pay can continue to receive their full cash assistance grant as long as their income remains below the poverty line, creating an unambiguous incentive for anyone who can work for pay to do so. A year after Lynchburg—a community of 66,000 people with an unemployment rate of 3.3 percent in 1995—implemented welfare reform, 54 percent of the parents enrolled in the locality's welfare-to-work program had found full-time work and 14 percent part-time work; only 7 percent had participated in CWEP. In stark contrast, a year after Wise County—a rural community of 40,000 people with an unemployment rate of 17 percent in 1995—implemented welfare reform, 27 percent of parents had found full-time work, 24 percent had found part-time work, and 26 percent had participated in CWEP.

Because states have been successful at placing recipients in unsubsidized jobs, only a few states have developed alternative work activities for recipients who have not found employment.   Oregon, Massachusetts, Mississippi, Vermont, and Washington have developed subsidized employment programs where TANF grants are used to reimburse employers for recipients' wages; however, all of these programs are quite small. New York City is the only locality that operates a large CWEP program. Most recipients who participate in the program work alongside city workers, cleaning parks or helping with clerical tasks such as filing; some also work for nonprofit organizations. Because these programs have been used so little, few states or localities will have an infrastructure in place that will facilitate the placement of large numbers of recipients in alternative work activities when it becomes more difficult to place recipients in unsubsidized jobs.

The experience of states with subsidized employment and community work experience programs is one of implementation difficulties, even on a small scale (Holcomb et al. 1998). It is often difficult to recruit employers to participate in subsidized employment programs, especially if substantial paperwork is required. Community work experience programs are somewhat easier to implement because recipients continue to receive their TANF grant. However, CWEP placements often pose a significant management challenge, especially if placements are limited in duration and the recipients placed in the program face substantial barriers.

The data in Table 4 suggest that if caseloads stayed at their current level, many states would have to substantially increase the number of parents participating in work activities to meet the 50 percent work participation standard that will be expected in FY 2002. California, for example, would need to more than double its current participation rate. There are, however, states such as Alabama, Michigan, and Wisconsin that could meet the FY 2002 work participation standard with their current level of participation in work activities. Because the high participation rates in these states reflect large numbers of parents who are working in unsubsidized employment, when fewer jobs are available these states may find themselves facing very similar issues as states that currently have lower participation rates.

Table 4 Hypothetical TANF Work Participation in Fiscal Year 2002

	Adjusted work participation standard FY 2002[a] (%)	Participation rate achieved FY 1997 (%)	Additional participation needed to meet 2002 standard[b] (percentage points)
Alabama	42.1	42.3	0
California	44.5	20.6	23.9
Colorado	Data not available		
Florida	41.4	28.4	13.0
Massachusetts	37.6	31.5	6.1
Michigan	38.3	41.1	0
Minnesota	Data not available		
Mississippi	41.3	17.2	24.1
New Jersey	41.9	20.7	16.9
New York	44.6	27.9	16.7
Texas	39.6	19.4	20.2
Washington	47.0	24.0	23.0
Wisconsin	33.0	52.8	0

[a] The FY 2002 adjusted work participation standard assumes the TANF caseload remains at its current level. To reflect the increase in the work participation rate, this adjusted rate is 25 percentage points higher than the FY 1997 adjusted standard.

[b] The increase in participation is obtained by substracting the FY 2002 adjusted work participation standard from the 1997 state participation rate.

Implementing large-scale employment programs when financial resources are tight and work participation rates are increasing is likely to pose significant challenges—and may, in fact, be impossible. Job search programs are low cost because services can be provided in a large group setting with limited individualized assistance. Because subsidized employment or community work experience programs require more attention to individual circumstances and needs, they will cost substantially more than the job search programs most localities are currently operating. A lower-cost alternative would be to require recipients to participate in less-structured community activities that they arrange on their own. Michigan operated such a program as the first stage of reforming its welfare system. Recipients were required to sign a "social contract" in which they agreed to participate in activities that made a positive contribution to the communities in which they lived. Participating on a resident council of a public housing development, volunteering at Head Start or a child's school, or volunteering at one's church are examples of the kinds of activities that could count toward a recipient's social contract obligation. Recipients were required to submit a form indicating they had completed their social contract activities, but only minimal enforcement and monitoring occurred (Pavetti, Holcomb, and Duke 1995).

Without some type of backup program requirement such as Michigan's social contract in place, states may have a difficult time emphasizing work, at least to the degree that it is currently emphasized. Localities that are currently operating alternative work programs, even if on a small scale, are likely to face far fewer challenges when jobs are much less available than those states and localities that have no knowledge of what it takes to operate such programs. Nonetheless, they too will face significant issues operating programs that are substantially larger than those currently in place.

Currently, states can place 30 percent of those required to participate in work activities (i.e., 30 percent of 25 percent in FY 1997, or 7.5 percent) in education or vocational education programs. Relaxing this constraint to allow more parents to participate in these activities would provide states with additional program alternatives for recipients who are unsuccessful at finding employment. Expanding the definition of activities to include more traditional education programs (such as adult basic education or GED preparation programs) would increase these options even further. The advantage of allowing education and training programs to count as allowable program activities is that these programs exist in most local communities and can often expand in a relatively short time to meet excess demand.

At the federal level, and in many states, the current emphasis on work was hard-won, and there is likely to be substantial resistance to broadening the definition of work activities to include additional educational activities or increasing the fraction of recipients who can participate in vocational training programs. States already approach education and training quite differently. Those that currently view education or training as an acceptable program activity are more likely to support making education and training available to more of the caseload during a recession. Illinois has recently proposed extending the time limit for recipients who want to further their education. In Nebraska, education or training is an acceptable program activity as long as it can be completed within the state's 24-month time limit. However, in Virginia, participation in an education or training program is only permitted if it is combined with work. In the end, the decision on whether such expansions are appropriate even when jobs are not available is likely to be influenced by fiscal realities. To the extent that welfare offices can rely on educational programs that already exist in local communities, these programs may be substantially cheaper than developing new alternatives.

Instead of redefining what constitutes work participation or expanding expensive subsidized employment or community service programs, it is possible that Congress and the states would opt to reduce the pool of recipients required to participate in work activities. The 22 states that require parents with children under the age of one to participate in program activities could decrease the pool of recipients required to participate in work activities without changes in federal law. However, changes in federal law would be required to exempt families with children over the age of one. Especially in states where the emphasis on work over education and training is especially strong, reducing the pool of persons required to work may be more feasible politically than changing the definition of what constitutes work.

Continuing to Provide Work Incentives and Work Supports

Work incentives in the form of earned income disregards and work supports such as child care and transportation have been an important component of state efforts to reform the welfare system. They have provided recipients with an incentive to go to work and TANF workers with a tool to reward recipients in their efforts to find work. Although recent research shows that, when combined with other program components such as sanctions or time limits, work incentives result in higher levels of employment and higher income (Miller et al. 1997; Bloom et al. 1998), it may be difficult to maintain these investments when there is more competition for a fixed set of financial resources. Although the fraction of the caseload that combines work and welfare is larger than it was prior to the expansion of earned income disregard policies, working recipients still account for a minority of TANF recipients. Between July and September 1997, 18 percent of the total TANF caseload was working. The variation from state to state was substantial: only 3 percent of recipients were working in Texas compared with 47 percent in Connecticut. As suggested by Wise County's experience, in a slack labor market it is possible that more families will only be able to find part-time work, resulting in an increase in the number of families who combine welfare and work. If this occurs, there may be pressure to control the costs of offering this additional assistance to working families. On the other hand, working recipients could help a state meet their work participation rates; the cost of providing partial grants to more recipients might be cheaper than implementing and managing large-scale subsidized work or CWEP programs.

The reduction in TANF caseloads has allowed many states to shift financial resources from providing cash grants to families to programs that help families pay for child care and transportation. Under the JOBS program, limited funds for these supportive services often resulted in long waiting lists. Even when families could identify education or training programs in the community in which they could participate at little or no cost, limited funds for child care often made it impossible for them to do. We are likely to see similar situations occurring if caseloads begin to increase, although it will occur in a more complex environment. Some states have used a portion of their TANF funds and their additional child care dollars to eliminate waiting lists for child care for working poor families. If more families begin to receive cash assistance and are required to participate in program activities almost full-time, child care resources will undoubtedly be stretched. Because child care is no longer an entitlement for cash assistance participants, families receiving cash assistance and working poor families will are likely to find themselves in direct competition for the same child care dollars.

Reassessing Time Limits

Although it is impossible to predict when we might begin to see a downturn in the economy, it is likely to occur around the same time that time limits begin to kick in and high work participation rates are in effect. Although there is reason to be concerned about what will happen when time limits hit, many states have implemented extension policies that will provide them with procedures to address the situations of recipients who have looked for work but have been unable to find it. Virginia, for example, provides unlimited extensions to families who hit the time limit in areas with high unemployment rates. Some states with extension policies in place have already made widespread use of those extensions for families who have played by the rules (Bloom et al. 1998), which may set the tone for other states to do so as well.

If the economy weakens and remains weak for an extended period of time, there may be a need to examine the possibility of allowing for extensions to the federal time limit and/or increasing the fraction of the caseload who can be exempted from the time limit. Currently, PRWORA allows states to exempt 20 percent of their caseload from the 60-month lifetime time limit, meaning that 20 percent of a state's caseload can receive benefits for more than 60 months. It is up to states to decide who will be exempted from the time limit. Although PRWORA does not make a distinction between extensions and exemptions, states do make this distinction. Parents exempted from the time limit are parents who are not expected to meet the state's work requirements. Common exemptions include advanced age and a parent who is disabled or caring for a disabled child. Extensions to the time limit are generally granted to parents who are expected to work but have been unable to find work. Even if the 20 percent exemption ends up being sufficient to cover the number of families who are not expected to work, it is unlikely to be sufficient to cover the additional needs of families who can work but can't find jobs.

Due to the extremely strong emphasis on work and personal responsibility, it is possible that gaining political consensus to extend time limits may be less difficult than gaining consensus to expand the definition of what constitutes participation in work activities. In most states, time limits have been implemented in conjunction with full family sanctions. This means that if policies are implemented as they are intended, the only families that will be affected by time limits are families that have played by the rules and have been unable to make it on their own. Families that do not play by the rules will have lost their benefits due to sanctions long before time limits hit. While there may be some opposition to extending time limits when jobs are not available (and especially when resources are limited), time limits may be less of an issue during an economic downturn than we might initially anticipate, especially if states are able to continue to mandate participation in work activities for families who have exhausted their time limit.

It is too early to have learned very much about how time limits have affected the behavior of recipients. However, early implementation analyses suggest that time limits have created a sense of urgency in local welfare offices and local communities that did not exist prior to welfare reform (Bloom and Butler 1995; Holcomb et al. 1998). One dilemma decision makers will face when jobs are not available is how to extend time limits for families who are unable to find employment while maintaining the sense of urgency that time limits have created. That sense of urgency has brought many communities together to identify opportunities for collaboration and to create common program goals, building on each organization's strengths to provide welfare recipients with the resources they need to succeed on their own. If time limits are relaxed and the sense of urgency is reduced, it is unclear whether community-based reform efforts will have garnered sufficient momentum to continue. It is interesting to note that in Wise County, Virginia, where recipients who exhaust their time limit will be eligible for benefits for an extended period of time because of the high unemployment rate, the community has banded together to bring jobs to the area and to create opportunities for recipients to work in CWEP positions that might lead to future employment. The sense of urgency that exists in the county mirrors that found in other counties with significantly lower unemployment rates.

Maintaining a Focus on Job Retention, Job Advancement, and Strategies for the Hard-to-Employ

Concerns about long-term welfare dependency provided the catalyst to dramatically alter the purpose and structure of providing cash assistance as an entitlement. In spite of this focus on reducing long-term welfare dependency, most state and local efforts have emphasized reductions in caseload, not distinguishing which types of welfare recipients were leaving the welfare rolls. To increase work among welfare recipients, most states have focused on strategies that have worked for recipients with moderate, but not more severe, barriers to employment. Many of these recipients probably would have had relatively short stays on welfare without any assistance or prodding. Those in the midst of long stays on welfare are most likely to still be on the welfare rolls today.

Now that caseloads have declined and states have more financial resources per recipient available, many states have turned their attention to strategies to help the hardest-to-employ, many of whom are long-term welfare recipients. Some states are working on integrating substance abuse treatment into their welfare-to-work programs by co-locating substance abuse professionals on site; others are trying to identify recipients with learning disabilities and provide accommodations such as specialized testing or job coaches for them; others are developing supported work programs, building on programs developed for persons with developmental disabilities or chronic mental health problems. Except in a few isolated programs, these strategies were not part of earlier welfare-to-work efforts.

Prior to the current round of reform, many hard-to-employ recipients were exempt from participating in welfare-to-work activities; others who were not exempt languished in a holding status because TANF workers had neither the time nor the resources to work with them. The current resource-rich environment provides states and localities with an unprecedented opportunity to identify promising strategies for working with this group of families. A downturn in the economy has the potential to stall or significantly reduce these efforts. We know little about what strategies might work best for this group of families; in times of competition for scarce resources, states will be far less likely to invest in strategies that do not have a proven track record than they are in the current environment.

Similarly, the decline in caseloads has allowed states to begin to think about longer-term strategies for helping welfare recipients stay employed longer and move into better paying jobs. If resources become strained, these efforts are likely to be perceived as luxuries rather than necessities. Thus, like efforts to find promising strategies for the hard-to-employ, these efforts are likely to be halted if the economy weakens.

FACTORS AFFECTING THE MAGNITUDE OF THE POLICY AND IMPLEMENTATION CHALLENGES

Many factors will undoubtedly affect how policymakers and program administrators respond to a change in the economy. Two factors stand out as especially important: the extent to which caseloads increase when the unemployment rate begins to climb and the extent to which states and localities have created a stable infrastructure to support their current reform efforts.

How Much and How Fast Caseloads Increase

The magnitude of the problems states will face in maintaining a focus on work will largely depend on how much and how fast caseloads rise. The more caseloads rise, the fewer resources states will have for providing alternative work or training activities for families unable to find employment in the paid labor market, for providing earned income disregards and work supports, and for maintaining their current efforts to promote job retention and identify strategies for the hardest-to-employ. Although research based on historical data suggests that caseloads will rise substantially when the unemployment rate rises, there are several reasons why these models may overestimate caseload increases in the current policy environment.

First, if a substantial fraction of recipients have left welfare for work and the economy continues to stay strong for awhile, we should expect some families who lose their jobs during an economic downturn to qualify for unemployment insurance. Only after an extended period of unemployment should these families need to turn to the welfare system for support. While it is too early to tell how many families may fall into this category, as more employment data becomes available for recipients who have left the welfare rolls, it should be possible to estimate the fraction of recipients who appear to meet the eligibility criteria for unemployment insurance and will not immediately need to turn to the welfare system for support. However, in a recession, many workers exhaust their unemployment insurance benefits. This will be more of a problem if the recession is deep and long.

Second, assuming states continue to mandate participation in employment-related activities and impose full family sanctions, families who are unwilling or unable to comply with these requirements will continue to be ineligible for benefits. Although there is no research that examines how much full family sanctions or noncompliance with applicant job search requirements have contributed to the decline in the AFDC/TANF caseload, the large number of families sanctioned would suggest they have played a nontrivial role. If work requirements become less stringent or are expanded to allow broader participation in education and training activities, it is possible that some families who previously failed to comply with work requirements may return to the welfare rolls. In addition, if sanctioned families are now relying on family and friends who fall on hard times, they are likely to return to the welfare system if no other alternatives are available to them.

Third, with a more stringent work mandate in place, more recipients may find work in an economic downturn than would have prior to the implementation of such mandates. That is not to say that recipients will not find it very difficult to find employment. However, if recipients are required to look for work even in times of high unemployment, the speed with which and rate at which families leave welfare for work should be higher than they would have been during earlier years with similarly high unemployment rates when such mandates were not in place. Again, Wise County is a case in point. Although Wise County's caseload has not declined as fast as the state as a whole (40.2 percent), between June 1995 and April 1998 the county's caseload declined by 18.5 percent.

The Stability of the New Welfare Infrastructure

States and localities are all at different stages of shifting to a work-based assistance system. While some states started to implement major reforms only recently, others implemented major reforms long before welfare reform passed at the federal level. States and localities that have a longer history of implementation will not be immune to the policy and implementation issues that all states and localities will face during an economic downturn. However, they are likely to be in a better position to develop alternative program strategies and to redeploy staff resources. Organizations that are still in flux and have not yet developed a new, stable infrastructure to accommodate a focus on work will face an especially difficult time in responding to a downturn in the economy. Change takes time and is difficult for most staff, even when they believe the changes are positive. Implementing new changes before the first changes take hold could prove to be a disaster for local offices that are still trying to create an environment that promotes and supports work.

If TANF caseloads increase, food stamp and Medicaid caseloads will undoubtedly increase as well. While states have dealt with increases in these programs in the past, the environment in which these programs are currently operating has changed to accommodate the implementation of a work-based assistance system for families with children. To provide TANF program workers with reduced caseloads that make it feasible for them to focus on work-related and eligibility activities, many offices have increased the caseloads of workers who work with food stamp and Medicaid recipients not receiving TANF benefits, making it far more difficult for the latter workers to increase their caseloads any further.

Although states with lower caseload declines are likely to have a more difficult time meeting work participation rates in the short term, their current experiences may put them in a better position to adjust to a downturn in the economy. The strategies they are implementing are less likely to rely on the availability of the "extra" resources that states with very large caseload declines have available. In addition, they are more likely to have (or be putting into place) strategies that will help them to meet the work participation rates, without the advantage of an extremely large caseload reduction credit. For example, Kentucky and New York primarily have met their work participation requirements through actual participation rather than caseload reduction credits. New York operates a large community work experience program; Kentucky makes extensive use of vocational education and work experience in addition to unsubsidized employment.

CONCLUSION

A downturn in the economy is inevitable; at some point, policymakers at the federal, state, and local levels will be faced with decisions about how to sustain a work-based assistance system when jobs are less readily available. While it seems unlikely that policymakers or program operators would shift away from a focus on work, it may be necessary to broaden the definition of what constitutes participation in a work activity. Such a definition might include more liberal use of vocational education or training programs and might also include active participation in community activities such as volunteering in a child's school. The other alternative will be to develop more alternative program activities such as community work experience or public service employment programs, but these programs often are costly to operate. With a fixed level of funding, states and localities will be faced with difficult choices about how to balance competing interests and program goals. Although it is impossible to fully prepare for an economic downturn, the choices states and localities make now will significantly affect the issues they will face when jobs are not as readily available as they are now. Given the range of choices available to them about how to spend their TANF and Welfare-to-Work dollars, it is probably in every state's interest to begin, even if on a small scale, the development of a community service, work experience, and/or subsidized employment program now while the economy is still strong. Developing the infrastructure for such a program in a resource-rich environment is likely to be far less daunting than it will be when resources are tight and employment opportunities are limited. States and localities have made significant progress in shifting to work-based assistance; nonetheless, welfare reform remains a work in progress. The ability to weather an economic downturn will be an important test of whether it is possible—and what it takes—to sustain an employment-focused assistance over the long term.

Note

1. Although states can choose to exempt families with a child over the age of one from participating in work activities, these families are included in the state's base of families who are subject to a work requirement for purposes of calculating a state's work participation rate.

References

Administration for Children and Families. 1998. *Characteristics and Financial Circumstances of TANF Recipients, July–September 1997.* Washington, D.C.: U.S. Department of Health and Human Services.

Bloom, Dan, and David Butler. 1995. *Implementing Time-Limited Welfare: Early Experiences in Three States.* New York: Manpower Demonstration Research Corporation.

Bloom, Dan, Mary Farrell, James J. Kemple, and Nandita Verma. 1998. *The Family Transition Program: Implementation and Interim Impacts of Florida's Initial Time-Limited Program.* New York: Manpower Demonstration Research Corporation.

Brown, Amy. 1997. *Work First: How to Implement an Employment-Focused Approach to Welfare Reform.* New York: Manpower Demonstration Research Corporation.

Bureau of Labor Statistics. 1998. "Labor Force Statistics from the Current Population Survey." Http://stats.bls.gov/. May.

Gallagher, Jerome, Megan Gallagher, Kevin Perese, Susan Schreiber, and Keith Watson. 1998. *One Year after Federal Welfare Reform: A Description of State Temporary Assistance for Needy Families (TANF) Decisions as of October 1997.* Occasional paper no. 6, The Urban Institute, Washington, D.C. June.

Holcomb, Pamela A., LaDonna Pavetti, Caroline Ratcliffe, and Susan Riedinger. 1998. *Building an Employment Focused-Welfare System: Work First and Other Work-Oriented Strategies in Five States.* Research Center paper no. 7477, The Urban Institute, Washington, D.C., 109 pp.

Maloy, Kathleen, LaDonna Pavetti, Julie Darnell, Peter Shin, and Lea Scar-pulla-Nelson. 1998. *Description and Assessment of State Approaches to Diversion Programs and Activities Under Welfare Reform.* Washington, D.C.: The George Washington University Medical Center, Center for Health Policy Research, August.

Miller, Cynthia, Virginia Knox, Patricia Auspos, Jo Anna Hunter-Manns, and Alan Orenstein. 1997. *Making Welfare Work and Work Pay: Implementation and 18-Month Impacts of the Minnesota Family Investment Program.* New York: Manpower Demonstration Research Corporation.

Pavetti, LaDonna A., Pamela Holcomb, and Amy-Ellen Duke. 1995. *Increasing Participation in Work and Work-Related Activities: Lessons from Five State Welfare Reform Demonstration Projects.* Vol. 1, Summary Report no. 6405, Washington, D.C.: Urban Institute, September.

U.S. General Accounting Office. 1998. *Early Fiscal Effects of the TANF Block Grant.* Report to the Chairman, Subcommittee on Human Resources, Committee on Ways and Means, House of Representatives. Washington, D.C.: U.S. General Accounting Office.

Cyclical Welfare Costs in the Post-Reform Era

Will There Be Enough Money?

Phillip B. Levine

Wellesley College

and

National Bureau of Economic Research

Although an economic downturn causes hardship for many individuals, those at the bottom of the income distribution are particularly hard hit. Poverty rates typically climb, and many of the newly destitute turn to the government for assistance, increasing the costs of safety net programs at precisely the time when the slowdown in economic activity leads to a reduction in tax revenues. Through 1996, the federal government covered at least half of these costs in the main cash assistance program, Aid to Families with Dependent Children (AFDC), and the states made up the difference. Sweeping welfare reform legislation enacted in that year replaced AFDC, however. The new cash assistance program, Temporary Assistance for Needy Families (TANF), provides each state with a federal block grant, the amount of which does not depend upon the business cycle.

This new system creates potential difficulties for a state's ability to finance benefit payments during a recession. AFDC represented a very small share of the federal budget, and cyclical fluctuations in its costs were a tiny contributor to the annual budget deficits that ballooned during the past two recessions. Because the federal government can easily obtain credit on financial markets, financing these additional costs was a trivial issue. States, on the other hand, face constraints that the federal government does not. In fact, many states have balanced budget requirements that do not allow them to spend more than the tax revenues they collect. The debate preceding welfare reform recognized this problem, and the 1996 legislation created a contingency fund to provide additional resources to states experiencing serious economic downturns.

This paper will address the burden imposed on states by cyclically induced increases in the demand for welfare. The first part will estimate how much states likely will be forced to spend on additional welfare payments in the event of an economic downturn. I use data from 1976–1996 on welfare expenditures and economic activity in all 50 states and the District of Columbia and estimate the sensitivity of overall (state and federal) welfare costs to a recession. Then I review the specific details of the TANF program and the federal contingency fund that will determine how these costs will be split between federal and state governments. My findings indicate that the financial burden imposed upon some states is likely to be quite high because payments from the contingency fund will be inadequate to cover the welfare-related costs of a recession. Moreover, payments from the fund will not commence until well into a recession.

The high burden imposed upon states raises the question of the manner in which they will fund these cyclical expenditures. Although welfare reform may have been too recent for states to establish mechanisms to address this problem, other state-administered programs, like the unemployment insurance (UI) system, have similar difficulties. This system has been in place long enough that the experiences with it may serve as a relevant example.

The second part of this paper, therefore, examines the financing of UI, with particular emphasis on the ability to cover the additional benefit payments that are required during a recession. After providing details of the institutional arrangements of the financing system, I explore the historical ability of the system to provide adequate resources to fund high cyclical expenditures. I then simulate the resources required to weather recessions of different magnitudes in the future and determine whether current funding patterns are sufficient to meet these needs. Unfortunately, the results of this analysis do not bode well for many states' abilities to save for a rainy day.

HOW MUCH DOES A RECESSION COST?

Research addressing the cyclical pattern of welfare activity has largely focused on changes in the size of the welfare caseload.[1] For instance, several recent studies indicate that a 1-percentage-point rise in the unemployment rate increases the number of people on welfare by roughly 4 to 6 percent (Blank 1997; Council of Economic Advisers 1997; Levine and Whitmore 1998; Blank and Wallace, this volume; and Bartik and Eberts, this volume). Although such an expansion of the welfare rolls probably will have similar effects on expenditures, the cyclical effects may differ somewhat if the composition of the caseload changes (towards, say, larger families) or if states impose cyclical adjustments in the generosity of their benefits. Therefore, this section of the paper replicates a common approach taken to examine caseload cyclicality, but focuses on actual welfare spending instead.

Specifically, the methodology employed is analogous to that used in Council of Economic Advisers (1997) and Levine and Whitmore (1998), which focused on explaining trends in the size of the welfare caseload. Using federal fiscal-year data from 1976–1996, I estimate OLS regression models of the following form:[2]

Eq. 1 $\quad \ln E_{s,t} = \alpha + U_{s,t}\beta_1 + U_{s,t-1}\beta_2 + U_{s,t-2}\beta_3 + \ln B_{s,t}\beta_4$
$$+ \gamma_s + \gamma_t + trend \times \gamma_s + \varepsilon_{s,t}$$

where

$\quad E_{s,t} \quad$ = AFDC expenditures in state s in fiscal year t,
$\quad \alpha \quad$ = the intercept,
$\quad U \quad$ = the fiscal year unemployment rate,
$\quad B \quad$ = real maximum AFDC benefits in 1996 dollars for a three-person family,
$\quad \gamma_s$ and γ_t = state and year fixed effects, respectively, and
$\quad \varepsilon \quad$ = a residual.

Lagged values of the unemployment rate are included along with the contemporaneous level because individuals may exhaust other sources of support before turning to the welfare system for help. Because Blank (1997) reported that welfare caseload effects hit their peak 18 months following an increase in unemployment, I include up to two-year lags with the annual data available here. The year fixed effects capture time-varying factors that affect all states in a given year. Such factors might include changes in welfare policy (like OBRA 1981 or the Family Support Act of 1988), other changes in policies targeted to low-income individuals (like the Earned Income Tax Credit or Child Care and Development Block Grant), or changes in national attitudes regarding welfare receipt that may have been linked to the welfare reform debate. The state fixed effects control for time-invariant differences among states, such as differences in industrial composition that may affect less-skilled workers or attitudes towards welfare recipients. A state-specific linear trend is included to capture typically slow-moving changes in the characteristics of the low-income population, like teen and nonmarital birth rates, that may differ among states.[3]

Consistent with Blank's findings, I indeed find a lag in the impact of a recession on welfare expenditures (Table 1). In the year the unemployment rate begins to rise, no statistically significant effect on expenditures occurs. These effects become significant in the following year and even bigger in the year after that (although differences between the two lagged coefficients are not statistically significant). To interpret these findings, consider a 1-percentage-point increase in the unemployment rate that lasts at least two years. Summing the three coefficients indicates that three years into a recession, annual welfare expenditures would have increased by almost 4.75 percent. As expected, benefit generosity is strongly positively correlated with expenditures; a 10 percent increase in the maximum welfare benefit yields an identical increase in welfare spending.

Table 1   Coefficients for the Effect of Economic Activity on Welfare Expenditures[a]

ln of maximum AFDC benefit	Unemployment rate in year t	Unemployment rate in year $t-1$	Unemployment rate in year $t-2$
104.8[b]	0.51	1.49**[c]	2.78**
(5.25)	(0.45)	(0.59)	(0.42)

[a] The dependent variable is the total expenditure on welfare by the federal and state governments, measured in natural logarithms. Estimates are obtained from a model including state and year fixed effects along with state-specific trends.

[b] Coefficients are multiplied by 100; standard errors are in parentheses.

[c] **= significant at the 5% level

In Table 2, I apply the estimates from this model to simulate the additional welfare costs of a recession based on 1997 spending levels.[4] I consider the additional spending that would be generated by recessions equal in magnitude to the three most recent cyclical downturns. Unemployment rates in these recessions peaked in 1975, 1982, and 1992 at 8.5, 9.7, and 7.5 percent, respectively, providing a range of levels of hardship. In each case, welfare expenditures are assumed to begin at the 1997 level of about $23 billion in total welfare spending before the recession begins. Additional expenditures are calculated as the unemployment rate rises from its low point in the first row of the table. These calculations are made for the following five years, because most of the additional costs resulting from a recession are accrued over this period. The costs vary from $6.8 billion to $13.7 billion in 1997 dollars.

These results must be interpreted with some caution because the underlying data cover the 1976–1996 period, in which the welfare system was significantly different than it is now in the aftermath of welfare reform. In particular, the emphasis on moving recipients to work may increase the sensitivity of welfare costs to the business cycle. To the extent that potential welfare recipients are successful in obtaining employment during an expansion, these individuals are at a greater risk

Table 2 Unemployment Rates in Past Recessions and Five-Year Welfare Spending Costs

Unemployment rate in	1973–79	1979–85	1989–95
Year 1	4.9%	5.8%	5.3%
Year 2	5.6%	7.1%	5.6%
Year 3	8.5%	7.6%	6.8%
Year 4	7.7%	9.7%	7.5%
Year 5	7.1%	9.6%	6.9%
Year 6	6.1%	7.5%	6.1%
Year 7	5.8%	7.2%	5.6%
Total five-year costs (billions of 1997 dollars)[a]	$11.5	$13.7	$6.8

[a] Costs are calculated from year 2 to year 7.

of experiencing unemployment during a recession and may find themselves requesting assistance from the welfare system (Gustafson and Levine 1998).[5] This suggests that the estimates in Table 2 of cyclical increases in welfare costs are likely to be understated.[6] Nevertheless, these estimates provide a basis upon which to evaluate the financing of welfare spending in future recessions.

WHO WILL PAY THESE COSTS?

In previous recessions, states were significantly shielded from the excess welfare costs during an economic downturn because the federal government reimbursed the state according to a formal schedule (called the Medicaid matching rate) that mandated higher rates of reimbursement for states with lower per capita income. The federal government paid half the costs of welfare payments in wealthier states, like California and Connecticut, and up to about three-quarters of the costs in poorer states, like Arkansas and Mississippi.

Welfare reform replaced this system with one based on annual block grants to states. Through the 2003 fiscal year, each state will receive a lump-sum payment equal to the amount of federal funds it received under the old formula in the 1994 fiscal year (with no adjustments for inflation). Note that these payments are unrelated to the actual welfare expenditures made by the state.

Although it appears that state governments will face all additional welfare costs brought about by a recession under this block grant, two important features of TANF may mitigate these costs.[7] First, the federal government established a $2 billion contingency fund designed to provide resources to states should the economy experience an economic downturn. A state may use the contingency fund if its own expenditures exceeded the 1994 level and one of the following two conditions are met: 1) the state's unemployment rate over a three-month period exceeds 6.5 percent and is at least 10 percent higher than that in the corresponding period in either of the two preceding calendar years, or 2) the state's food stamp caseload exceeds the 1994 or 1995 level by 10 percent.[8] Once triggered, contingency funds will be used to match additional state expenditures at the Medicaid match rate.[9]

Second, some states will enter the next recession with unexpended funds allocated in earlier years that can help finance higher cyclical welfare costs. The availability of these funds is the result of the decline in welfare rolls over the past few years. Nationwide, the number of people receiving welfare fell by over 40 percent between January 1994 and June 1998; the decline in some states was even greater. The number of welfare recipients in Wyoming and Idaho fell by more than three-quarters, and even some larger states such as Florida and Massachusetts experienced about a 50 percent decline. But the 1996 welfare reform legislation requires states to maintain spending of their own funds on TANF and other welfare-related programs (called "maintenance of effort" or MOE) at between 75 and 80 percent of their 1994 expenditures. For those states with large declines in caseloads, maintaining the required level of state spending while using all of the federal funds allocated to them would force them to spend considerably more on each case still on the rolls. Alternatively, states may choose to spend less of the federal funds than they are entitled to and save the remainder for future needs, such as a recession. Current law requires that any unspent funds remain in the federal treasury, but they are earmarked for future TANF spending by those states with claims on them.

Unfortunately, these sources of funds will not provide sufficient assistance for many states in meeting the higher demand for welfare during a recession. Two limitations of the contingency fund will reduce its value in helping states. First, the federally matched reimbursement system, in essence, replicates the approach used to fund all cyclical welfare costs prior to welfare reform, except that the federal obligation is capped at $2 billion. Therefore, only a small share of the cost of an economic downturn, which I conservatively estimate as $6.8 to $13.7 billion, will be covered. More importantly, funds from this source are only available to states that spend at least as much of its own funds as it did in 1994 (i.e., 100 percent MOE). With average state caseload declines to date of 40 percent, substantial increases in state spending will be required before reaching this level, indicating that states may not be able to access the federal contingency fund until well into a recession, if at all. As for previously unexpended funds, they currently exist only for those states that have experienced very steep declines in caseloads. Many states, including California and New York, currently have no such funds available.

These issues are highlighted in Table 3. The number of welfare recipients fell by 20 percent nationwide between January 1994 and January 1997, while the average decline was only 14 percent in the 10 states shown. The two largest states, California and New York, experienced relatively small declines of 5.5 and 13.5 percent, respectively. Column 2 shows each state's 1997 annual expenditure of its own funds for TANF.[10] Column 3 shows the amount that each state would have to spend to hit 1994 levels and satisfy the 100 percent MOE required by the federal contingency fund. The values in column 4 (calculated as the difference between columns 2 and 3) represent the shortfall in state TANF spending that would need to be eliminated before federal contingency funds could be activated. The last row of column 4 indicates that all states would need to increase spending by $3 billion, with additional spending of $729 million and $562 million required in California and New York alone. These levels are surely higher today based on the continuing decline in caseloads in 1998; therefore, $3 billion is a minimum figure.

Columns 5 through 7 of Table 3 report the extent to which states are spending the federal funds allocated to them. In the 1997 fiscal year, about $13.4 billion was awarded to all states and the District of Columbia, but $1.3 billion was never spent. This money will be available in future years to those states in an amount commensurate with their balance. However, not all states share in this surplus equally; in particular, states with higher welfare expenditures are less likely to benefit in the future from current savings. The 10 highest spending welfare states saved less than half of the total unspent, even though they account for over two-thirds of the federal allocation. Even within this group, savings are largely limited to Florida and Massachusetts, two of the states in this group with very large reductions in caseloads. Of the two highest spending states, California used all of its funds, while New York saved less than $100 million (about 2 percent) of its annual welfare spending.

The results of this analysis suggest that many states are still likely to be responsible for the vast majority of additional welfare expenditures. In states that have experienced very large caseload declines, or for those who will do so in the near future, the savings from previously unexpended federal awards that have accrued before a recession hits may provide a strong buffer from the higher anticipated costs at that

Table 3 FY 1997 Financial Data for the 10 States with the Highest TANF Awards

State	Col. 1 Reduction in number of welfare recipients, 1/94–1/97 (%)	2 1997 Full-year equivalent state TANF expenditures[a] ($)	3 1994 State spending ($)	4 Shortfall in state TANF spending (%)	5 Federal TANF block grant ($)	6 1997 Expend. of federal funds ($)	7 Balance ($)
California	5.5	2,915	3,643	729	3,148	3,148	0
New York	13.5	1,719	2,281	562	1,982	1,899	84
Michigan	31.3	486	625	138	775	698	78
Ohio	25.0	441	521	80	728	728	0
Florida	30.6	392	495	103	562	356	207
Massachusetts	31.4	330	479	148	459	459	0
Texas	21.3	280	314	35	432	432	0
Pennsylvania	21.3	434	543	109	418	343	76
Wisconsin	42.6	159	226	67	318	186	133
New Jersey	23.5	304	405	101	293	293	0
Sum for top 10	–[b]	7,459	9,531	2,072	9,116	8,539	577
All 50 states + D.C.	20.0	10,851	13,913	3,062	13,360	12,106	1,255

SOURCE: All of the data was obtained from the U.S. Department of Health and Human Services (1998).
[a] TANF expenditures reported in column 2 are computed as full-year equivalents because states had until the end of the 1997 fiscal year to implement their TANF program. Expenditures of federal funds include unliquidated obligations.
[b] Weighted average for top 10 states is 13.9%.

time. The need for resources from the contingency fund may not come until late in a recession, if at all, by the time these states use up their unexpended funds and increase their own spending back to 1994 levels. In states that have experienced only moderate declines in their welfare caseloads, including many of the largest states like California and New York, little will likely be available in the form of previously unexpended federal funds. Significant additional state spending will be required before money from the federal contingency fund can be released, and that money will cover just a small share of the additional welfare costs incurred during a recession. These are the states that are the most at risk in the event of a cyclical downturn.

FINANCING CYCLICAL COSTS IN THE UNEMPLOYMENT INSURANCE SYSTEM

The results presented so far indicate that some states, particularly many of the larger ones, will face the burden of paying for a large share of the costs of increased welfare benefits during a recession. In these states, a state-level rainy-day fund would be required to weather the storm without facing the difficult decision of cutting back on welfare at a time when it is needed most or finding other sources of funding at a time when tax revenues are falling. (Some critics of the 1996 reform have expressed concern that the new law may lead states to stop enrolling new cases or to cut benefits significantly when faced with increased demands for welfare during a recession.) Although some states have already established such funds, few of the large states have done so. In addition, the level of savings is small in these funds.[11]

Because welfare reform is so recent and states have had no experience with TANF in a cyclical downturn, it is understandable if states are not fully prepared for the next recession. To determine whether or not states are likely to learn to effectively manage these costs in the long-run, I compare states' experiences with financing another program that involves large cyclical cost increases, the unemployment insurance (UI) system.[12] Although UI and welfare are very different programs with different target populations and institutional arrangements, such a comparison may help gauge states' degree of foresight in planning for the increased costs of transfer payments during a recession. Therefore, I will begin by describing the institutional features of the UI system and the historical patterns of solvency, and then present an analysis of whether or not state UI programs are adequately prepared for a future recession.[13]

The UI system pays weekly benefits to individuals with a sufficient work history who lose their jobs through no fault of their own. Because rates of job loss and the length of time it takes to find a new job increase during recessions, the cost of providing UI benefits varies with the business cycle in much the same way as welfare costs. The financing to pay for these benefits is obtained through a tax on employers. The federal tax is equal to 6.2 percent of their federal taxable payroll.[14] However, a tax credit of 5.4 percent is available to firms in states that have met federal guidelines which require that, among other things, states utilize some form of experience rating (i.e., tax rates must be lower for firms that lay off fewer workers). Because all states meet these guidelines, the *de facto* federal component of the UI tax is 0.8 percent of federal taxable payroll. Part of the federal revenues collected in excess of federal administrative expenses goes into a trust fund used to finance loans to states whose trust funds have become insolvent.

The tax revenue that the states collect is deposited into a UI trust fund; fund balances are called net reserves. As the economy expands, net reserves typically grow, and they are drawn down during a recession. A commonly reported statistic that normalizes net reserves to the size of the state's workforce is the "reserve ratio," the ratio between net reserves and total payroll in the state.

HISTORICAL PATTERNS OF UI TRUST FUND ADEQUACY

Figure 1 displays the reserve ratio aggregated across all 50 states and the District of Columbia from 1961 through 1996.[15] As expected, a strong cyclical pattern is observed. The reserve ratio grew during the expansions of the 1960s, late 1970s, mid to late 1980s, and the mid 1990s and declined in the years surrounding cyclical troughs of 1971, 1975, 1982, and 1991. Although savings accumulate during expan-

Figure 1 Ratio of Net Reserves to Total Payroll

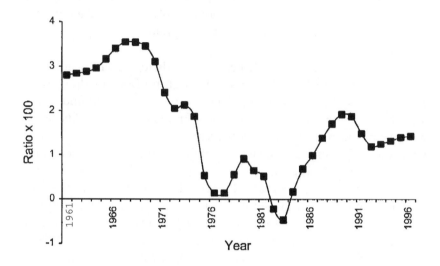

sions, they have not always been sufficient to pay the greater costs incurred during a recession. A large number of states experienced a deficit during the 1975 recession and were forced to borrow funds from the federal government. Federal funds were available interest free at that point, but the extent of borrowing led to 1981 legislation that instituted interest payments on loan balances. This policy change occurred too late to forestall the massive borrowing that took place during the recession in the early 1980s; net reserves aggregated over all states were in deficit at that time.

UI trust funds weathered the recession in the early 1990s rather well compared with the experience of the previous two recessions. Several factors may explain this positive outcome. First, the incentive to generate a larger trust fund (brought about by interest charges on federal borrowing) led states to change their tax and benefit structures so as to accumulate greater reserves. Second, the economy underwent a lengthy and robust expansion in the mid to late 1980s that generated extra revenue through larger taxable payrolls and fewer and shorter unemployment spells. Third, the subsequent recession was rather mild compared with the two preceding it.

A final factor that may have led to the maintenance of positive net reserves during this last recession is the declining share of unemployed workers who collect UI benefits. As shown in Figure 2, throughout the mid 1970s, upwards of 60 percent of unemployed workers received UI. Through the early 1980s, however, that share fell to about 40 percent and has remained roughly constant since then. A substantial literature trying to explain these trends over time has found that they may be attributable to declining unionization, the changing industrial structure of the economy, the taxation of UI benefits, and other factors (Corson and Nicholson 1988; Blank and Card 1991; Vroman 1991; Anderson and Meyer 1997). Regardless of the reason, the smaller the share of unemployed who collect UI, the lower the benefit payouts are. A recession of any particular magnitude as measured by total unemployment will now draw down net reserves in the UI trust fund at a slower pace.

Based upon the strong performance of the UI financing system from the mid 1980s through the recession of the early 1990s, a puzzling trend in the past few years is the rather anemic growth in trust funds in the presence of a strong economy. The absolute increase in

Figure 2 Insured Workers as a Percentage of Total Unemployment

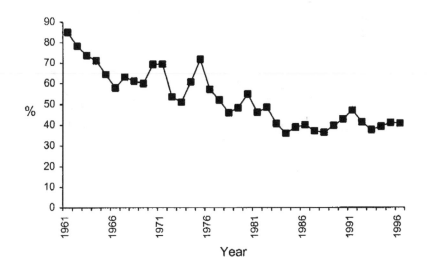

the reserve ratio between 1993 and 1996 was considerably smaller than that observed in past expansions of this length and size.

In fact, these statistics aggregated over the entire country mask even more startling patterns that are seen when looking at individual states. Figure 3 displays funding patterns for three larger states (New York, Maryland, and Texas). The main cyclical discrepancy between these states is the prolonged recession observed in Texas through the 1980s in response to low oil prices. Nevertheless, by the early 1990s, all states had UI trust funds that were at similar levels. Although trust funds in Maryland appear to have grown at a rate similar to those observed across the nation in past expansions, trust funds in New York and Texas have barely increased at all. Not only are their reserves growing very slowly, they are also very small in absolute terms, and New York and Texas are not alone. Other states like California, Connecticut, and Missouri all have reserve ratios below 1, an unusually low level for this stage of an economic expansion.

Figure 3 Ratio of Net Reserves to Total Payroll, Three States

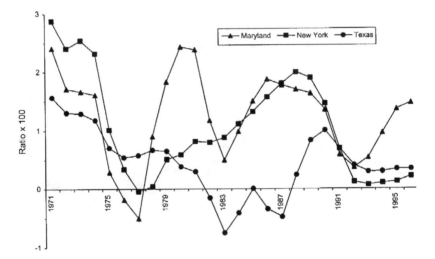

ARE STATE UI TRUST FUNDS BIG ENOUGH?

Low levels of reserves do not necessarily indicate that state funds are at risk of insolvency in future recessions. States could be responding to trends in the labor market—like the declining share of unemployed workers who collect UI—which imply that benefit payments in future recessions will be less costly than in the past. To examine this possibility in more detail, I simulate the drain on UI trust funds brought about by future recessions of various magnitudes.

The methodology employed here is similar to that used to estimate the costs of additional welfare spending during a recession. Specifically, I estimate a model of the form:

Eq. 2 $$RR_{s,t} = \alpha + IUR_{s,t}\beta_1 + IUR_{s,t-1}\beta_2 + IUR_{s,t-2}\beta_3$$
$$+ \gamma_s + \gamma_t + \text{trend} \times \gamma_s + \varepsilon_{s,t}$$

where IUR represents the insured unemployment rate, which equals the number of UI recipients divided by the number of employees covered by the UI system, multiplied by 100. This specification represents a reduced form model, as parameters of state UI systems (like tax rates and benefit levels) are not included.[16]

The results, reported in Table 4, show that unlike for welfare spending, the costs of a recession for the UI system begin mounting right away. The coefficient on unemployment in year t is negative and significant. Individuals who lose their jobs may be less reluctant to apply for UI benefits, perhaps because of less social stigma compared to collecting welfare, and may not wait to draw down their resources before filing a claim. Also, some welfare recipients apply for assistance only after they exhaust UI benefits. Therefore, as soon as job loss begins to rise, claims for UI begin to rise. The costs continue to mount over the next two years as job-finding rates for the unemployed may be slow to recover following a cyclical trough. These results indicate that a 1-percentage-point increase in insured unemployment rates that persists for at least two years will lower the UI reserve ratio by about 0.9 percentage points.

Table 4 Coefficients for the Effect of Economic Activity on the UI Reserve Ratio[a]

IUR in year t	IUR in year $t-1$	IUR in year $t-2$
−0.314	−0.285	−0.266
(0.033)	(0.043)	(0.032)

[a] Estimates are obtained from a model including state and year fixed effects along with state-specific trends.

The impact of recessions of different magnitudes, based on these estimates, is reported in Table 5. The top panel gives the insured unemployment rates before, during, and after the past three recessions. Comparing these values with those reported in the top panel of Table 2, which lists comparable values for the total unemployment rate, provides important insights. First, Table 2 indicates that the recession in the mid 1970s was less severe than that in the early 1980s. Unemployment peaked at an annual average of 8.5 percent in the former, compared with an average of almost 10 percent for two consecutive years in the latter. Yet structural changes in the labor market and the UI system that have led to a smaller share of unemployed workers receiving benefits occurred over this period. As a result, the insured unemployment rate in the mid 1970s recession far surpassed that in the early 1980s. In 1975, the total unemployment rate reached 8.5 percent and the insured unemployment rate climbed to 6.1 percent, indicating a ratio of insured to total unemployment of over 72 percent; that ratio had fallen dramatically, to 48 percent, in 1982 (4.7/9.7). This comparison highlights the importance of the declining share of insured to total unemployment. Even though the recession of the early 1980s was more severe, it was less costly to the UI system than the previous recession.

The bottom rows of Table 5 reports the estimated reduction in the UI reserve ratio that would result based on each of these three recessions. The high ratio of insured to total unemployment in the mid 1970s recession makes that the most costly: the reserve ratio is estimated to fall by 1.89 percentage points. The early 1990s recession, which was relatively mild and followed the decline in the ratio of insured to total unemployment, had a considerably smaller effect, lowering the reserve ratio by 0.75 percentage points.[17]

Table 5 Insured Unemployment Rates in Past Recessions and UI Reserve Ratio

Insured unemployment rate in	1973–79	1979–85	1989–95
Year 1	2.5%	2.8%	2.1%
Year 2	3.4%	3.9%	2.4%
Year 3	6.1%	3.5%	3.2%
Year 4	4.4%	4.7%	3.1%
Year 5	3.7%	3.9%	2.6%
Year 6	2.8%	2.7%	2.4%
Year 7	2.8%	2.8%	2.3%
Drop in the UI reserve ratio at trough	1.89	1.10	0.75
Lower bound of 95% confidence interval	1.61	0.94	0.69
Upper bound of 95% confidence interval	2.17	1.26	0.81

How would UI reserves weather a recession in the future? In 1996, the reserve ratio aggregated over all states stood at 1.43. Therefore, even a recession as severe as that experienced in the early 1980s would not deplete aggregate UI trust funds. These results suggest that the reserve ratio would fall by 1.10, leaving a positive balance of 0.33 across the country as a whole. Alternatively, based on patterns of UI receipt in the mid 1970s, a recession could exhaust the fund, as the estimated decline in the reserve ratio of 1.89 is greater than the present level. Such an outcome seems rather unlikely, however, under the present circumstances. Even if the ratio of insured to total unemployment reached 50 percent (which has not happened in almost 20 years; see Figure 2), the peak insured unemployment rate of 6.1 percent recorded in 1975 would amount to a total unemployment rate of 12.2 percent. Levels of unemployment that high have not been recorded since the Great Depression. These results suggest that UI trust funds aggregated over all states are likely to remain solvent through the next recession despite the relatively low rate of savings throughout the current recovery.

This conclusion is somewhat misleading, however, because it ignores the variation in current levels of trust fund reserves among states. Table 6 presents values of the reserve ratio for all 50 states and the District of Columbia in 1996, ranked from lowest to highest. Five states (New York, Texas, Missouri, Connecticut, and the District of Columbia) have reserves that are low enough that even a mild recession, coupled with a low ratio of insured to total unemployment (like the experience of the early 1990s), would exhaust their trust fund; compare their reserve ratios in Table 6 with the 0.75 value in Table 5 (rightmost column, first row below divider). An experience similar to that of the early 1980s would wipe out all savings in four additional states, including California. However unlikely it is that the experience of the mid 1970s would be repeated, in a nationwide recession of that size, more than half of the states' trust funds would become insolvent. Regardless of the size of the recession, some of the states that are in the most perilous position regarding UI financing, like California and New York, are the same ones that might expect future difficulties in financing cyclical welfare costs.

One additional exercise that may be of interest is to determine the states that are very unlikely (with less than a 5 percent probability) to experience a deficit in their UI trust fund during recessions of different magnitudes. To do this, I constructed 95 percent confidence intervals around the point estimates of the effect of the different recessions on reserve ratios. The high end of the interval is of most interest because it tells us the largest fall in the reserve ratio that we may reasonably expect based on past recessions (Table 5, last row). The results indicate that no additional states are at risk or falling into deficit in a mild recession, although California is close to the cut-off. In a moderate recession (at least in terms of UI receipt) like that of the early 1980s, five additional states, including Massachusetts and Illinois, fail to meet this stricter test of having sufficient fund reserves. In the most severe recession considered, 34 states are at risk of depleting their UI trust funds, including all the larger states with the exception of Virginia.

What do these results regarding the UI system tell us about states' ability to plan for higher cyclical transfer payments in general and, perhaps, welfare spending in particular? It appears that a number of states have sufficient foresight that they will be able to cover the higher UI costs associated with a recession. One may infer that over time these states will apply similar thinking in planning for higher cyclical welfare costs. On the other hand, some states exhibit far less fiscal fore-

Table 6 Reserve Ratios in 1996, by State

State	Reserve ratio	State	Reserve ratio
New York	0.22	Pennsylvania	1.79
Texas	0.34	North Carolina	1.85
Missouri	0.59	South Carolina	1.89
Connecticut	0.60	New Jersey	2.00
District of Columbia	0.75	Hawaii	2.02
California	0.87	Montana	2.03
Minnesota	0.95	Georgia	2.10
South Dakota	0.97	Indiana	2.13
Arkansas	1.08	New Hampshire	2.23
Massachusetts	1.13	Oklahoma	2.34
North Dakota	1.14	Kansas	2.49
Illinois	1.16	Washington	2.53
Colorado	1.18	Delaware	2.83
Maine	1.19	Iowa	2.91
West Virginia	1.33	Utah	2.95
Rhode Island	1.36	Idaho	2.99
Alabama	1.38	Wisconsin	3.00
Maryland	1.47	Oregon	3.03
Ohio	1.52	Mississippi	3.05
Florida	1.53	Louisiana	3.35
Nebraska	1.56	New Mexico	3.38
Arizona	1.57	Alaska	3.39
Tennessee	1.58	Wyoming	4.21
Kentucky	1.61	Vermont	4.49
Michigan	1.68	Virginia	7.07
Nevada	1.76		

Source: U.S. Department of Labor (various dates).

sight in UI and may not be expected to save sufficient funds to pay for higher welfare costs in the event of a recession. Unfortunately, two of these states include California and New York, that together account for about 40 percent of total welfare spending.

DISCUSSION AND CONCLUSIONS

Many states, particularly the larger ones, will be liable for a large portion of cyclically related increases in welfare spending. The existence of the federal welfare contingency fund, which provides resources to states during bad times, is designed in such a way that accessing these funds will be difficult. States will be required to spend a considerable amount of their own money before federal money can be obtained, and then it is only provided on a matching basis. Some states will be able to take advantage of federal funds that had previously been allocated but were unused because of very large declines in caseloads. Many of the largest states, including California and New York, have experienced more moderate caseload declines, however, and have not been able to save much (if any) of their federal allocation. In these states, the burden of facing the welfare cost increases associated with a cyclical downturn largely will be borne by them.

Because the absence of state-level rainy-day funds to cover these additional costs may be attributable to inexperience, I considered states' ability to establish sufficient fiscal discipline to cover cyclically related cost increases observed in the UI system. The record of the UI system should not leave one with tremendous optimism that states will be able to weather the financial storm that a recession will bring in terms of additional welfare spending. In the two recessions preceding the relatively mild downturn of the early 1990s, many states exhausted their UI trust funds. Although two prolonged recoveries have surrounded the last mild recession, state trust fund reserves are not substantial and have been growing very slowly over the past several years. The fact that a smaller share of unemployed workers collect UI today than 20 years ago has helped; funding requirements for future recessions are not quite as substantial as they once were. Nevertheless, anything other than a very mild recession will still cause financial difficulties for UI systems in many states. In fact, the larger states like California and New York, which are particularly at risk in terms of financing cyclically related welfare costs, are among the weakest in terms of the financial stability of their UI systems.

Moreover, UI enjoys considerably greater popular support compared to welfare. In light of states' reasonably poor record of financing the costs of additional UI spending during a recession, it seems unlikely that they will do a better job of accumulating funds to cover additional welfare spending. States will, therefore, be faced with the reality of raising taxes when such increases are likely to be quite unpopular, reallocating funds from other areas of its budget during a time of general revenue shortfalls, or cutting benefits precisely at the time that need will be the greatest.

Alternatively, states may be playing a sophisticated game of "chicken" with the federal government in much the same way that they do in the UI system. During periods of high unemployment, job seekers are much more likely to exhaust their UI benefits simply because jobs are not available. States could accumulate greater reserves in anticipation of this and extend the maximum benefit duration to help compensate those unable to find work, but they do not do this. Instead, they wait for the federal government to provide extended benefits at no cost to the states, which it has done in virtually every recession in the past 40 years.[18] The fact that states like California and New York seem destined to face a shortfall of welfare funding when a recession occurs may simply indicate that they are anticipating a bailout by the federal government. Even if states win at this game, the victory will not come without costs. Based on the track record of the UI system, when additional welfare funding is provided by the federal government in an economic downturn, this assistance is likely to be poorly timed, commencing months or years after a recession begins. In the interim, states will still be faced with difficult choices that may not benefit those in need.

Notes

I thank Patty Anderson, Sheldon Danziger, Wayne Vroman, and conference participants for comments.

1. Boyd and Davis (1998) estimated the effect of a recession on welfare expenditures, but they assumed that costs per case remain constant and applied previous estimates of the sensitivity of the welfare caseload to changes in unemployment.
2. These regressions are weighted by the state population in each year to yield parameter estimates that are representative of the entire country.
3. If differences among states over time are nonlinear, they will not be captured by these trends and, if these differences are correlated with the unemployment rate, the estimated effect of the business cycle on welfare expenditures will be biased.
4. The level of spending used here is based on 1997 full-year equivalent state TANF expenditures, as well as state expenditures of federal block grant funds as reported in columns 2 and 6 of Table 3. For additional details, see the discussion of that table and its notes.
5. This effect may occur even if employment gains do not generate caseload declines. If welfare recipients are successful in gaining part-time employment that reduces, but does not eliminate, their need for public assistance during an expansion, an economic downturn will likely increase their level of need.
6. In the somewhat more distant future, a countervailing effect may occur as more and more people reach their lifetime limit on benefit receipt and will not be able to return to welfare when the economy turns down.
7. A report by the U.S. General Accounting Office (1998) provides more detail on the institutional arrangements discussed here.
8. The exact requirements that must be met before contingency fund money may be released to a state are actually somewhat more stringent. Welfare reform legislation allows states to use their own funds to establish welfare-type programs outside the scope of the TANF program. States that spend at least 75 to 80 percent of their fiscal year 1994 expenditures on TANF and these other programs are in compliance with federal guidelines. To access the contingency fund, however, states must spend at least 100 percent of their 1994 expenditures on state TANF programs only, not including state spending on these other programs.
9. Payments from the fund are limited to 20 percent of the state's grant for that year.
10. Welfare reform legislation allowed states until the end of the 1997 fiscal year to institute their own TANF programs; therefore, reported TANF spending for 1997 only reflects the portion of the year following each state's implementation. For purposes of comparison, all 1997 state expenditures reported here have been converted into " full-year equivalent" spending.
11. The U.S. General Accounting Office (1998) reports that among 10 states surveyed (California, Colorado, Connecticut, Louisiana, Maryland, Michigan, New York, Oregon, Texas, and Wisconsin), only Colorado, Maryland, Texas, and Wisconsin have created state-financed rainy-day funds specifically targeted to cover cycli-

cally related welfare expenditures. In each case, the amount saved represents only a few percent of annual operating costs.

12. Vroman (1995) also used the UI system to draw lessons for funding welfare payments in an environment with federal block grants.

13. Vroman (1998) provided an alternative treatment of the topics addressed here and arrived at similar conclusions.

14. For additional discussions of UI financing issues, see Blaustein, Cohen, and Haber (1993), Levine (1997), Miller (1997), and Miller, Pavosevich, and Vroman (1997).

15. When the current UI system first began operating in the 1930s, pessimistic actuarial assumptions based on unemployment patterns from the Great Depression and the full employment economy generated by World War II led to a very large surplus in state trust funds. Through the 1950s, states increased benefit generosity without increasing tax liabilities to bring down these surpluses. Because of these events, trust fund reserves did not begin to show the expected cyclical sensitivity until the 1960s, so the analysis reported here uses data beginning in 1961. All UI data was obtained from the U.S. Department of Labor, Employment and Training Administration.

16. I have also estimated alternative specifications that include these program parameters and obtained similar results to those reported. Although any exercise that includes parameters such as these runs the risk of introducing a "policy endogeneity" (policy responding to market conditions), the problem is particularly severe in UI. For instance, many states have tax schedules that depend upon the level of reserves in the state's UI trust fund. As reserves fall, scheduled tax rates rise, making identification of the effect of taxes on reserves difficult. For this reason, I have chosen to report the more parsimonious specification.

17. These findings are based on point estimates and do not take into consideration the fact that a standard error is associated with the estimated effect of a recession on the UI reserve ratio. Because these parameters are estimated with some error, a state with, say, a reserve ratio of 0.9 may still run out of funds in a mild recession (like that of the early 1990s) that is estimated to reduce the reserve ratio only by 0.75.

18. A formal federal system of extended benefits has been in place since 1970, but changes in the labor market have made it virtually impossible to activate these additional payments (Woodbury and Rubin 1997).

References

Anderson, Patricia and Bruce D. Meyer. 1997. "Unemployment Insurance Takeup Rates and the After-Tax Value of Benefits." *Quarterly Journal of Economics* 112(3): 913–938.

Blank, Rebecca M. 1997. *What Causes Public Assistance Caseloads to Grow?* NBER working paper no. 6343, National Bureau of Economic Research, Cambridge, Massachusetts, December.

Blank, Rebecca M., and David E. Card. 1991. "Recent Trends in Insured and Uninsured Unemployment: Is There an Explanation?" *Quarterly Journal of Economics* 106: 1157–1189.

Blaustein, Saul J., Wilbur J. Cohen, and William Haber. 1993. *Unemployment Insurance in the United States: The First Half Century.* Kalamazoo, Michigan: W.E. Upjohn Institute for Employment Research.

Boyd, Donald J., and Elizabeth I. Davis. 1998. "Welfare Reform and Expenditure Pressures in the Next Recession." *National Tax Association Proceedings – 1997,* Washington, D.C.: National Tax Association, pp. 3–14.

Corson, Walter, and Walter Nicholson. 1988. *An Examination of Declining UI Claims during the 1980s.* Unemployment Insurance occasional paper no. 88-3, U.S. Department of Labor, Washington, D.C.

Council of Economic Advisers. 1997. *Technical Report: Explaining the Decline in Welfare Receipt, 1993–1996.* Washington, D.C.: Council of Economic Advisers, May.

Gustafson, Cindy, and Phillip B. Levine. 1998. *Less-skilled Workers, Welfare Reform, and the Unemployment Insurance System.* NBER working paper no. 6489, National Bureau of Economic Research, Cambridge, Massachusetts, March.

Levine, Phillip B. 1997. "Financing Benefit Payments." In *Unemployment Insurance in the United States: Analysis of Policy Issues*, Christopher J. O'Leary and Stephen A. Wandner, eds. Kalamazoo, Michigan: W.E. Upjohn Institute for Employment Research, pp. 321–364.

Levine, Phillip B., and Diane M. Whitmore. 1998. "The Impact of Welfare Reform on the AFDC Caseload." Proceedings of the National Tax Association Meetings, 1997. Washington, D.C.

Miller, Mike. 1997. "Appendix to Chapter 8: The Role of Federal Financing in the Unemployment Insurance System." In *Unemployment Insurance in the United States: Analysis of Policy Issues*, Christopher J. O'Leary and Stephen A. Wandner, eds. Kalamazoo, Michigan: W.E. Upjohn Institute for Employment Research, pp. 355–361.

Miller, Mike, Robert Pavosevich, and Wayne Vroman. 1997. "Trends in Unemployment Benefit Financing." In *Unemployment Insurance in the United States: Analysis of Policy Issues*, Christopher J. O'Leary and Stephen A. Wandner, eds. Kalamazoo, Michigan: W.E. Upjohn Institute for Employment Research, pp. 365–421.

U.S. Department of Health and Human Services. 1998. *Temporary Assistance for Needy Families (TANF) Program: First Annual Report to Congress.* Administration for Children and Families, Office of Planning, Research and Evaluation, Washington, D.C.: Government Printing Office, August.

U.S. Department of Labor. *Unemployment Insurance Financial Data (ET Handbook 394)*, 1983 and annual supplements, Washington, D.C.: Government Printing Office.

U.S. General Accounting Office. 1998. *Welfare Reform: Early Fiscal Effects of the TANF Block Grant.* Washington, D.C.: Government Printing Office, August.

Vroman, Wayne. 1991. *The Decline in Unemployment Insurance Claims Activity in the 1980s.* Unemployment Insurance occasional paper no. 91-2. U.S. Department of Labor, Washington, D.C.

Vroman, Wayne. 1995. "Rainy Day Funds: Contingency Funding for Welfare Block Grants." In *Welfare Reform: An Analysis of the Issues*, Isabel V. Sawhill, ed. Washington D.C.: Urban Institute.

Vroman, Wayne. 1998. *Topics in Unemployment Insurance Financing.* Kalamazoo, Michigan: W.E. Upjohn Institute for Employment Research.

Woodbury, Stephen A., and Murray A. Rubin. 1997. "The Duration of Benefits." In *Unemployment Insurance in the United States: Analysis of Policy Issues*, Christopher J. O'Leary and Stephen A. Wandner, eds. Kalamazoo, Michigan: W.E. Upjohn Institute for Employment Research, pp. 211–283.

The States, Welfare Reform, and the Business Cycle

Howard Chernick
City University of New York

Therese J. McGuire
University of Illinois at Chicago

The Personal Responsibility and Work Opportunity Reconciliation Act of 1996 (PRWORA) dramatically changed the financial arrangement between the federal government and the states concerning cash assistance for poor families. Previously, Aid to Families with Dependent Children (AFDC) was jointly financed by the two levels of government through a federal matching-rate grant at an average matching rate to the states of about 60 percent. Under this arrangement, when the economy contracted and AFDC spending rose, the federal government was responsible for 60 cents of each dollar in increased spending in the average state. Under the new arrangement, the federal government provides a fixed amount under a block grant set equal to the level of the federal AFDC grant amount in 1994. Because most states had relatively high case loads and correspondingly high spending in 1994, the block grant amounts are quite generous relative to Temporary Assistance for Needy Families (TANF) spending requirements in the prosperous years since passage of the 1996 act, but prosperous times will not last forever. Under this new arrangement, when the economy next contracts and the demand for income assistance increases, the states will be solely responsible for each dollar increase in spending on cash assistance.

Our purpose in this paper is to speculate on the cyclicality of state fiscal responses under this new regime. In particular, how will they respond during the next recession? We draw lessons from several strands of the literature, including estimates of the spending responses of governments to matching and block grants, and we consider some new evidence. We also summarize studies that examine the incentives states have to mimic their neighbors' spending levels, as well as studies of the substitutability of spending across programs. We conclude that the "price effect" of the shift from matching grants to block grants is likely to be small, at least in the short run; that the strength of the "neighbor effect," and thus the likelihood of a race to the bottom, is also small if not uncertain; and that the evidence that different welfare programs are close substitutes for one another in a state's budget is suggestive, but tentative.

We also review the literature on how state revenues and expenditures vary over the business cycle and during contractionary periods. This research, although recent and sparse, generally finds that states that rely on progressive income taxes and narrowly based sales taxes have revenue systems that exhibit high cyclical variability. Thus, during economic contractions, such states are less able to maintain spending programs without adjusting tax rates upward. Definitive evidence on spending is more difficult to come by because of the difficulty of generating policy-free measures of expenditures. Still, part of the interest is in examining the decisions made by policymakers in the face of recession; preliminary evidence indicates that most states maintain or increase spending (and revenues) virtually across the board in contractions. While this finding of countercyclical spending is not surprising for the matching-rate program (AFDC), it is interesting that other state spending not stimulated by matching rates also tends to be countercyclical. Cautious speculation based on these findings, coupled with the emerging consensus that the price effect may be small in the short run, leads us to hazard a guess that state spending on welfare may not decline as greatly as some have predicted when the next recession occurs.

Trends in state and local welfare spending from 1980 to 1995 are displayed in Table 1. As shown in the first column, cash assistance as a share of total expenditures fell from 3.3 percent in 1980 to 2.2 percent in 1994. It is particularly notable that cash assistance declined as a share of the budget between 1990 and 1995, despite a sharp increase in the number of recipients. The decline reflects cuts in the maximum benefit over this period and the decision by a number of states to drop their General Assistance programs during the recession.[1]

In contrast to cash assistance, total welfare expenditures grew as a share of state and local expenditures, from 10.5 percent in 1980 to 14.3 percent in 1995. The increase was particularly pronounced in the

Table 1 State and Local Outlays on Public Welfare[a]

Year	Total state and local expenditures on public welfare			State and local own-source expenditures on public welfare[b]		
	Share of total state and local expenditures (%)		Public welfare share of personal income (%)	Share of own-source revenues[c] (%)		Public welfare share of personal income (%)
	Cash assistance	Public welfare		Cash assistance	Public welfare	
1980	3.3	10.5	2.0	2.0	5.6	0.9
1985	2.9	10.6	2.0	1.6	5.0	0.9
1990	2.5	11.3	2.3	1.4	5.6	1.1
1995	2.2	14.3	3.1	1.3	6.5	1.3

Source: Personal income: Economic Report of the President, 1998, Table B–2. Total state and local expenditures: *Statistical Abstract of the United States, 1998*, Table #499 and 1989, Table #446. Public welfare expenditures, own-source revenues, and public welfare from federal government: *Statistical Abstract of the United States, 1998*, Table #506 and 1989, Table #453. Cash assistance: *Statistical Abstract of the United States* 1998, Table #508, and U.S. House of Representatives 1996, Table 8–1.

[a] Public welfare includes both cash assistance to needy persons and vendor payments for medical care and other services to needy persons; it excludes completely federal welfare programs, such as food stamps.

[b] State and local expenditures on public welfare minus federal intergovernmental revenues for public welfare.

[c] Own-source revenues include taxes and other non-intergovernmental grant revenue sources, such as charges and fines.

1990s, increasing from 11.3 percent to 14.3 percent. Welfare expenditures also grew as a share of personal income, increasing by almost a percentage point between 1990 and 1995. The increase in total welfare spending is due primarily to the rapid growth in Medicaid, reflecting an increase in mandated coverage, increases in utilization and reimbursement, and rapid medical price inflation (Coughlin, Ku, and Holahan 1994). State and local own contributions to cash assistance also fell from 1980 to 1995, while own contributions to total welfare spending increased slightly, from 5.6 percent of own-source revenues in 1980 to 6.5 percent in 1995.

LESSONS FROM THE LITERATURE ON GRANTS-IN-AID AND COMPETITION AMONG NEIGHBORING STATES

In this section, we describe federal and state cash assistance programs and we review the literature on the effects of matching and block grants on spending, neighborhood effects, and program substitution.

Federal Financial Incentives for Cash Assistance Programs

Under the TANF program, states receive a block grant that is approximately fixed in nominal terms. TANF replaced the AFDC program, which provided open-ended matching assistance to states. To receive its full block grant allocation, a state is required to contribute overall state funding equal to at least 80 percent of the sum of FY 1994 expenditures on AFDC, JOBS, emergency assistance, and welfare-related child care programs; this is known as the Maintenance of Effort (MOE) requirement.[2] Not only do states lose a dollar of TANF funds for every dollar they fall below the MOE requirement, but they are then obliged to raise spending beyond the MOE level to offset the federal penalty.

In the AFDC program, the mean federal matching rate was 60 percent, with states paying 40 cents for an additional dollar of cash assistance. With TANF, the marginal price has risen to 1. If the stimulative price effect of open-ended matching aid exceeds the lump-sum grant effect for nonmatching categorical assistance, then over time one would expect TANF to induce a substantial reduction in state spending on cash assistance.

Given the price increase, the crucial parameters in predicting and explaining the expenditure response of states to the TANF block grants are the elasticity of benefits and of total expenditures with respect to the matching rate. These elasticities must be compared with the expenditure response per dollar of nonmatching categorical aid for welfare. The price elasticity can, in principle, be estimated using variations in state matching rates. However, we have no direct experience with cash assistance as a block grant, so to predict the effect of the block grant, we must also examine the state spending response to nonmatching aid for other categories of welfare spending.

State spending on AFDC or TANF is also influenced by the availability and benefit levels of other federal welfare programs. The existence of multiple programs with overlapping coverage and differential federal financial sharing rules provides a fiscal incentive for states to substitute among programs, with the goal of maximizing the federal contribution per dollar of own resources. The strongest incentive for substitution is between the federally funded Food Stamp and Supplemental Security Income programs and cash assistance. Almost all recipients of cash assistance are eligible for and receive food stamp benefits. Because food stamps are close to cash in their effect on recipient budgets, state policymakers are likely to view the two forms of assistance as fairly close substitutes. Food stamps are indexed to inflation and impose an implicit tax on recipients in terms of reducing food stamps by 30 cents for each additional dollar of cash benefits provided by the states. This tax implies that, so long as the level of cash assistance under AFDC or TANF exceeds the food stamp disregard of $134 per month, the cost to the states of raising total cash benefits by a dollar is approximately $1.43.[3]

At any point in time, few AFDC/TANF recipients also receive benefits under the federal Earned Income Tax Credit (EITC) (Liebman 1996). Hence, for any given recipient, states cannot directly substitute the EITC for cash benefits, as they can in the case of food stamps. However, the expansion in EITC benefits in the 1990s has substantially increased the value to TANF recipients of moving from not working to part-time work (Coe et al. 1998). The lower a state's cash benefit level, the greater the increase in family income from part-time work. By contrast, a low-benefit reduction rate as earned income increases tends to reinforce the EITC work incentive. Thus, the decisions of a number of states to both decrease their maximum benefit levels and increase their income disregards may be partly a response to the EITC.[4]

Previous Estimates of Matching-Rate Price Effects

Benefit Levels

Many studies attempt to explain variation among states and over time in AFDC benefit levels, caseloads, total spending, and spending on welfare more broadly defined. AFDC benefits (total expenditures) are assumed to depend on state income, the federal matching rate, demographic controls, and, in some models, other welfare programs and benefit levels in neighboring states.

The major studies have been summarized in several review papers (Chernick 1998; Ribar and Wilhelm 1999). Results from some frequently cited studies are shown in Table 2, which reports estimates of the income and price elasticities and of the food stamp substitution effect. There is considerable variation in the estimated elasticities. The price elasticity is relatively large in Baicker's (1998) analysis of the period 1948–1963, in the Gramlich and Laren study (1984), and in a Craig and Inman (1986) analysis of total welfare expenditures. By contrast, price elasticities are small, and sometimes positive, in Moffitt (1990) and the Ribar and Wilhelm papers (1994, 1999).

Ribar and Wilhelm (1994, 1999) provided a careful econometric review and replication of most of the studies of AFDC benefit level determination. They concluded not only that matching rate effects are small, but also that, controlling for unobserved characteristics of states through state fixed effects and common national trends through year dummies, income elasticities are substantially less than 1. For example, in an OLS specification, they found that the income coefficient is reduced from 0.593 to 0.357 with the addition of state fixed effects. The general implication of the Ribar-Wilhelm analysis is that state AFDC benefit levels are much less sensitive to economic variables than earlier studies indicated.

The Gramlich and Laren (1984) estimates, which received considerable attention, found large effects of federal matching rates and sub-

Table 2 Estimates of the Price and Income Elasticity of Welfare Benefits

Study	Dependent variable	Sample	Price elasticity with respect to state share	Income elasticity	Food stamp substitution
Baicker (1998)	AFDC spending	48 states, 1948–63	[−0.48, −0.92]	[−0.9, −0.2]	Not applicable
	AFDC recipients,		−0.55	−0.98	
	AFDC benefit per recipient		−0.37	−0.08 (insignif.)	
Gramlich and Laren (1984)	AFDC guarantee, adjusted for state implicit tax rates	33 states on Medicaid formula, 1974–81.	−0.67 Migration parameter: elasticity of benefits w.r.t. neighboring state benefits: 0.61	0.15	Not considered
Craig and Inman (1986)	Total state welfare spending (AFDC, GA, Medicaid, Other)	States using Medicaid formula, 1965–80	−0.17 Long run impact: spending per grant dollar = $1.35	0.45	Additive to total welfare spending, i.e, low substitution
Moffitt (1990)	AFDC guarantee, family of four	48 states, 1960, 1984	−0.17* (not significant)	0.98	Full substitution of food stamps and Medicaid

(continued)

Study	Dependent variable	Sample	Price elasticity with respect to state share	Income elasticity	Food stamp substitution
Craig (1993)	Total state welfare spending, AFDC spending, AFDC average benefit level	48 states, 1965–89	No effect on total public welfare spending	0.31	Partial offset of AFDC expenditures for a dollar increase in food stamps
			No effect on total AFDC spending	0.33	Released funds remain in the total welfare budget
			Benefits increase by $2.10 per dollar of matching aid	0.34	
Ribar and Wilhelm (1994)	AFDC benefit per recipient	50 states and District of Columbia	*		Little or no substitution of Food Stamps or Medicaid
		1969–75	[−0.043, −0.162]	[0.09, 1.35]	Food stamp offset only tested for period 1969–75
		1976–81	[−0.09, −0.19]	[0.33, 1.47]	
		1982–89	[−0.08, +0.239]	[0.23, 1.34]	
Ribar and Wilhelm (1999)	Same as above	1982–92	[−0.08, +0.02]	[0.35, 0.52]	Not directly tested

Moffitt, Ribar, and Wilhelm (1998)	AFDC benefits per recipient	50 states, 1969–92	[–0.05, –0.08*]	[–0.016, +1.867]	Not considered
	Public welfare share of state general expenditures	Same	–0.07 0.06*	–0.6	
	AFDC expenditures per capita	Same	–0.10 0.20	[–0.77, –1.05]	

* Price defined as state matching share × recipient ratio.

stantial neighbor effects. Their model is based on the concept that while more recipients increases the cost of raising benefit levels, higher benefits in turn increase the number of recipients, both from within a state and by encouraging migration from other states. The conventional way to estimate such a model is to find variables that affect benefits but not the number of recipients and other variables that affect recipients but not benefits. Such variables serve as instruments to identify the two equations. Given the difficulty in finding acceptable instruments, Gramlich and Laren estimated a reduced form model using the same variables (income, price, unemployment, and neighbor benefits) for each equation. They then used the model's structure to infer the extent to which the pure price and income effects on benefit levels are dampened by the fact that any increase in benefit levels brings with it an increase in the number of recipients.

Gramlich and Laren's model was estimated for the period 1974–1981 and used a restricted sample of 33 states that were on the open-ended Medicaid matching formula at that time. Chernick (1999) reestimates the Gramlich-Laren model for the period 1984 to 1995, using the full sample of states. This reestimation yields substantially lower price elasticities than in the earlier period, and higher income elasticities. Price effects are significant at conventional levels only when the dependent variable includes food stamps. In general, reestimation supports the conclusion of Ribar and Wilhelm that price effects are small in the 1980s and 1990s.

Total Welfare Spending

The evidence suggests that higher benefit levels lead to higher numbers of recipients (Blank 1997). Therefore, if higher federal matching rates do have a positive effect on benefit levels, we would expect matching rates to have a bigger effect on total spending than on benefit levels alone. While studies using data from earlier periods (Gramlich and Laren 1984; Craig and Inman 1986; Baicker 1998) support this expectation, more recent evidence does not. For example, Moffitt, Ribar, and Wilhelm (1998) found that the elasticity of AFDC expenditures with respect to the state share is –0.1, while Craig (1993) found no effect of matching grants on AFDC expenditures. The small effects in the Moffitt, Ribar, and Wilhelm study reflect the very low estimated price elasticities for benefits; in the Craig study, they reflect the offsetting effect of higher matching rates raising benefit levels but lowering caseloads. This evidence reinforces the conclusion that, on average, the short-run effects of eliminating matching rates will be small.

Estimation Issues

The AFDC matching rate (the Federal Medicaid Assistance Percentage) is inversely correlated with state personal income per capita. Collinearity is not perfect because the formula sets an upper bound for the state share at 50 percent. This collinearity makes it difficult to disentangle the true price and income effects. We can write the benefit equation as

Eq. 1 $\ln B = a_1 \ln S + a_2 \ln Y(S)$

where B is the benefit level, S is state share, and Y is state income per capita. $Y(S)$ is the inverse of the formula determining the relationship between state share and income. The estimated price effect will be equal to

Eq. 2 $\varepsilon_{B,s} = a_1 + a_2 \varepsilon_{Y,s}.$

Because $\varepsilon_{Y,S}$ is negative, the stronger the income elasticity a_2, the smaller will be the estimated price effect. In typical specifications of the benefit model, both state share and income have significant positive effects on benefit levels. Once state fixed effects and time variables are controlled for, the coefficient on state share remains positive but has a much smaller size and is no longer significant.

One way to identify the price effect is to define price as the (per capita) cost of raising benefits by a dollar for all recipients:

Eq. 3 $p = (1 - m)\left(\dfrac{R}{N}\right)$

where m is the federal matching rate, R is the number of recipients, and N is the population. This approach imposes the restriction that the marginal effect of a change in the matching rate be the same as the effect of a change in the number of recipients. However, if the response to a matching rate change is not the same as a response to variation in the recipient ratio, then it is incorrect to infer the effect of matching rate changes from this multiplicative term. A second problem is that the recipient ratio is endogenous to benefit level decisions, imparting an upward bias to the estimated price effect. Ribar and Wilhelm (1999) presented an extensive set of tests of for price exogeneity. They concluded that their findings of modest income effects and weak price effects are not very sensitive to the choice of instruments.

An alternative approach to identifying the matching rate effect is to exploit the fact that the matching rate has a lower bound of 50 percent. For the 11 states at this lower bound (in 1996) it is possible to estimate a pure income effect. This method, proposed by Craig (1993), yields a significant matching rate effect on AFDC benefit levels for the period 1965–1989. However, in a replication of the Craig study for the period 1981–1995, Chernick (1999) finds that the matching rate has no effect on either benefits or total expenditures.

A Consensus of Sorts

A prior review paper (Chernick 1998) concluded that the appropriate range for the price elasticity estimates was from 0.2 to 0.3. These estimates imply a predicted decline in average benefit levels as a result of shifting from matching to block grants of somewhere between 15 and 30 percent, and a slightly higher decline in total expenditures. The high-end estimates from the literature, which would imply reductions in spending of as much as 75 percent, are rejected by Chernick because they used selected sub-samples of states and failed to identify the key parameters. Very low estimates are rejected on the grounds that the price term (state share times the recipient ratio) was misspecified.

The econometric evidence on matching rate effects is buttressed by considering state fiscal responses to the federal SSI program, established in 1974. SSI is similar in fiscal structure to a block grant. The analysis found that when public assistance to the aged, blind, and disabled (AABD) was converted from a matching grant to states to an indexed grant going directly to individuals, states responded by gradually reducing their share of total funding and their absolute dollar commitment. By 1996, the value of state supplementation had fallen by 21 percent.

The most recent statistical analyses find lower matching rate elasticities, ranging from zero to about 0.15. Chernick (1999) attempts to replicate the major prior studies with data from 1983 to 1995 and finds that estimated elasticities were smaller than before. The reduced effects of matching could reflect a real behavioral change in how states respond to federal matching rate subsidies, or they could reflect an increase in the offsetting role of state income in determining benefits and expenditures. The implicit food stamp tax on AFDC, by raising the price of benefits in all states, may further obscure the role of matching rate variation in state spending decisions. Taken at face value, the matching rate estimates imply that the equilibrium reduction in average benefit levels from ending the matching subsidy would be no more than approximately 10 percent. This reduction would in turn imply a reduction in the state contribution to cash assistance of at most 25 percent.

However, this conclusion is subject to a number of caveats. First, the increase in the price of cash assistance under the block grant is far larger than the prior variation in price under the AFDC program. Our only recent experience with such a substantial change comes from the SSI program, and (as discussed above) this program has been accompanied by a substantial decline in state contributions. This decline is particularly telling in that SSI recipients are mostly viewed as the "deserving poor," and are likely to be treated more favorably by states than mothers on welfare. Historical analyses (Wallis and Oates 1998; Baicker 1998) suggest that matching grants played a crucial role in expanding state commitments to assist the needy. These analyses suggest that the relatively small predictions from the recent literature, while they may be a good guide to the short run behavior of states, probably underestimate the long-run expenditure adjustments that will take place under the TANF block grant.

A second caveat is that the TANF legislation gives states much greater flexibility in determining public assistance spending. Under AFDC, the main margin along which spending could be adjusted was changes in benefit levels, while under TANF there are more margins of response. For example, states can set shorter time limits and adjust income disregards. Some states have saved money by setting shorter time limits but spent money by allowing recipients to keep more of each dollar earned. These changes make it more difficult to use fiscal response parameters estimated under the prior regime as predictors of behavior under the block grants.

The initial fiscal response to TANF has been dominated by a sharp drop in caseloads. Between 1994 and mid 1998, AFDC/TANF case-loads fell by 40 percent, and by June of 1998 were at their lowest level since 1972. This sharp drop, due partly to the strong economy and partly to state policy choices (Levine and Whitmore 1998; Blank 1997; Figlio and Ziliak 1998) means that public assistance costs have declined dramatically in most states. Because the state MOE requirement must be satisfied in each year, while federal TANF funds can be banked for use in future years, states have tended to use their own funds first to satisfy the MOE and then draw down TANF funds.[5] Thus, the drop in state spending under TANF is primarily a reflection of declining caseloads rather than the long-run response to the price effect of the block grants.

Neighbor Effects

If there is significant mobility of potential recipients in response to benefit level differentials, then welfare spending in each state may be influenced by spending in neighbor or competitor states. Even if actual migration effects are small, state politicians may feel particularly vulnerable to the charge that the state is attracting indigents from other states by virtue of its generous benefits. This interdependence could be exacerbated by the fact that under TANF the federal government will no longer share in any increase in state expenditures, while states will realize 100% of the savings from reduced spending.

A simple test of whether competitive pressures have increased in recent years is to examine variation in benefit levels across states. Between 1984 and 1995, the mean of state maximum benefits adjusted for inflation declined by about 10 percent, but the coefficient of variation remained at 36 percent. However, the variation in AFDC benefits plus food stamps was not only lower than for AFDC alone but showed some decline, from 19 percent to 16 percent. This suggests that in the 1980s and 1990s there has been a small amount of convergence in the total benefit package across states.

The most powerful test for the race to the bottom would come from evidence that the number of recipients in a given state is positively affected by benefit differentials between that state and its "neighbors," however defined. A weaker test would be provided by evidence that benefit levels move in tandem with those of their neighbors. The latter evidence is more difficult to interpret. Such behavior could represent one state responding to the decisions of other states; alternatively, it could imply that both are subject to common economic or political influences.

Evidence on the migration effect is mixed. Aggregate studies covering the 1980s and early 1990s show no evidence that a state's ratio of AFDC recipients to population was sensitive to benefit level differentials, whereas there is some evidence of sensitivity in prior periods. (Gramlich and Laren 1984; Ribar and Wilhelm 1994; Shroder 1995). Among the aggregate studies, both Gramlich and Laren (1984) and Ribar and Wilhelm (1994) found that AFDC recipiency ratios are sensitive to neighbors' AFDC benefit levels in the period 1976 to 1981. However, data from the 1980s (Ribar and Wilhelm 1994; Schroder 1995; Craig 1993) exhibit no such evidence. The lack of effect could reflect the narrowing of the combined AFDC-food stamp differentials referred to above.

Using micro data to study the interstate migration effect, Gramlich and Laren (1984) and Blank (1988) found that in the 1970s, though only a very small proportion of welfare recipients move between states in any given year, those moves are much more likely to be from low-benefit to high-benefit states. Levine and Zimmerman (1995), covering the period 1979–1992, and Walker (1994), using 1980 data, found little or no support for the welfare magnet theory. Borjas (1997) found that recent immigrants are disproportionately attracted by California's high benefit levels. Reviewing these papers, Brueckner (1998) noted the contradictory nature of the evidence on welfare migration. Except for the Borjas study of immigrants in a single state, the evidence does not indicate an increase in such migration in the 1980s.

The evidence on strategic interaction between states in benefit levels is stronger than the direct evidence on migration. For the 1980s, Ribar and Wilhelm (1994) found that a dollar increase in geographic neighbor benefits leads to an increase in own benefits that ranges from 23 to 55 cents. In a recent review paper, Brueckner (1998) cited papers by Figlio, Wolpin, and Reid (1998) and Saavedra (1998) as providing "strong evidence that a given state's benefit choice is affected by benefit levels in nearby states." A consensus estimate from this literature would be that a dollar change in neighbor benefits leads to about a 30-cent change in own benefits.

In Chernick's (1999) investigations of the neighbor effect, the neighbor results are found to be quite sensitive to specification. For example, when both own and neighbor benefits are measured by combined AFDC plus food stamp benefits and the model is estimated in first-difference form, neighbor effects have a negative rather than a positive effect on own benefits. When maximum AFDC benefits are adjusted for implicit tax rates, the neighbor effect is insignificant. Instrumental variables estimation yields similar results. It is only when published maximum benefits is the benefit measure that the strong strategic interaction effect is apparent. These preliminary results suggest that in the most visible aspect of welfare policy, the maximum benefit, changes are indeed copied by neighbor states. However, using a broader measure of state "generosity," the links are much weaker.

Even if neighbor effects are important, it is not an automatic implication that the block grants will lead to a race to the bottom. A necessary condition for that race to occur is for the price elasticity to be of some reasonable magnitude. If the price response is small, then even if the interstate competition effects are potentially large, the leapfrogging effect of a race to the bottom will not be triggered. Because the consensus price elasticity estimates are rather low, this suggests that the block grant alone will not be sufficient to kick off a strong race to the bottom.

Program Substitution

As discussed above, the fact that most AFDC recipients are automatically eligible for food stamps and Medicaid provides an opportunity and an incentive for states to substitute both of these programs for cash benefits. Several studies suggest that this substitution is important.

Moffitt (1990) argued that observed declines in AFDC benefits could reflect a substitution of food stamps and Medicaid for AFDC, rather than a decrease in generosity towards the poor. To test this hypothesis, he compared combined benefits for AFDC, food stamps, and Medicaid in 1984 to the benefit level that would be predicted based on an earlier year (1960), prior to the introduction of food stamps and Medicaid. He found that actual benefit levels for the sum of AFDC, food stamps, and Medicaid were within $10 of predicted benefit levels. In a replication of the Moffitt approach for the years 1983 and 1993, Chernick (1999) finds that the 1983 structure overpredicts the 1993 combined AFDC, food stamp, and Medicaid benefits by between 7.5 and 9 percent. Thus, in the period 1983 to 1993, program substitution can explain most (but not all) of the decline in AFDC benefits.

The Moffitt and Chernick findings are relevant to PRWORA because they show substantial program substitution even when cash assistance was matched by federal dollars. With the conversion of federal aid for cash assistance from matching to lump-sum grants and the fact that states can now use a portion of the block grant money for in-kind expenses such as child care and training, we expect even stronger substitution in favor of Medicaid and food stamps under PRWORA.

Recent research by Katherine Baicker investigated federal mandates aimed at changing state spending on specific categories of welfare and their effect on state budget allocations across other categories of spending. This research is relevant to understanding the implications of PRWORA, because the act requires states to move recipients into employment, a requirement that is likely to involve increased spending by states on training, placement, and child care. In an examination of the effect of federal Medicaid expansions on state budgets over the period 1983 to 1995, Baicker (1998) found that states tended to accommodate required increases in spending for health care for the indigent by decreasing spending on other components of the broader state welfare budget. State tax revenues and spending on nonwelfare categories of the state budget were largely unaffected. These results should be treated with caution because of difficulties in interpreting the data on Medicaid spending. Nonetheless, the findings indicate some amount of "stickiness" in state budgets; i.e., federally mandated increases on one program for the needy are likely to result in state decisions to decrease spending on related programs, in some cases without much of an effect on overall welfare spending.

THE VOLATILITY OF STATE REVENUES AND EXPENDITURES OVER THE BUSINESS CYCLE

The federal welfare reform debate and the resulting legislation, as well as state-instigated welfare changes enabled by federal waivers, have occurred against the backdrop of one of the longest continuous economic expansions in modern U.S. history. The inevitability of a recession at some point compels the question of how state welfare spending under the new policies is likely to respond to the accompanying fiscal stress. Indeed, because of the strong economy, the switch from a matching grant under AFDC to a block grant under TANF will not have significant consequences for the states until the next recession occurs. A nascent literature examines the revenue-readiness of states to weather a turn in the business cycle, the fiscal experience of the states during previous recessions, and state spending on welfare over the business cycle.

Sobel and Holcombe (1996) used national measures of income and retail sales to proxy state revenue bases and estimated short-run elasticities to capture the cycle-related variation in the major state tax sources. They found that corporate income is the most volatile component of the tax base, followed by nonfood retail sales. Personal income and retail sales including food exhibit similar short-run elasticities of approximately 1, while motor fuel usage and liquor sales are the least volatile. The elasticity estimates are relatively stable over time and thus can be used to inform the design of tax policy to address future economic contingencies.

Dye and McGuire (1998) argued that the structure of state taxes is important to determining their volatility. They proxied the structures of the personal income and general sales taxes—the two largest revenue raisers for state governments—of each of the 48 states having these taxes and estimated state-specific cyclical elasticities, assuming that each state's income distribution and personal consumption patterns (the bases for the two taxes) are the same as those for the nation. Their analysis recognized that when the next recession occurs, the states will be responsible for any increase in spending beyond the level of the TANF block grant. Their aim was to assess which states are likely to be the most resilient to economic downturns (i.e., to have the least volatile revenues over the cycle).

The most salient feature of state personal income taxes for determining short-run elasticity is the progression in their rates; thus the building blocks of an estimate of the volatility of a state's income tax consist of different income categories. Dye and McGuire found that the short-run elasticity rises monotonically from near zero for the lowest income group to over 4 percent for the highest income group. When they applied the different state tax structures to these income components, they found that the cyclical elasticity estimates for the individual income tax range from 0.95 to 1.68. Because of the monotonicity with respect to income brackets of the elasticity estimates, states with a greater degree of progression in their income tax systems (e.g., Connecticut and Nebraska) have more volatile income taxes.

A similar analysis for the general sales tax, where differential treatment of various categories of spending distinguishes the different state tax structures, results in cyclical elasticity estimates for the general sales tax in the range of 0.85 to 1.37. The states with the most volatile sales taxes have narrow bases that exclude food for home consumption (e.g., Maryland and Vermont). California has both a progressive income tax and a narrow sales tax base, resulting in the distinction of having the highest cyclical elasticity for the combined income and sales taxes. By this measure, California is the state most vulnerable to the next recession and thus least able to pick up where federal block grant dollars will leave off.

Mattoon and Testa (1992) examined the fiscal experience of state and local governments during each contractionary period over the last 50 years. They found that fiscal behavior is countercyclical (i.e., expenditures rise relative to revenues during downturns), indicating perhaps that elected officials are keen to maintain services in recessions. Blackley and Deboer (1993) attempted to explain the decisions by states to increase revenues during the most recent 1990–1991 recession. They found that both political and economic forces were behind the discretionary state revenue increases of the early 1990s and that the depressing effect of the recession explained a fair portion of the revenue increases.

Three recent papers examine welfare spending over the business cycle and during periods of contraction; they take quite different approaches but present findings and conclusions that are mutually supportive. Powers (1998) simulated spending on AFDC/TANF over a recent 20-year period under different financing scenarios and calculated a measure of variability that relates each state's expenditures on welfare to its unemployment rates. Boyd and Davis (1998) also simulated spending on AFDC/TANF but restricted attention to the two recent recessionary periods. The third paper, by Dye and McGuire (forthcoming), examines actual state revenue and expenditure streams during state-specific business cycles and periods of recession.

Powers (1998) compared actual spending on AFDC over the period 1976–1995 to simulated spending on TANF programs under two different assumptions about state responses to the shift in federal financing from a matching grant to a block grant. The "lower bound" simulations assume that states are quite sensitive to the price increase associated with the financing change and that states will choose to spend only the bare minimum required by the federal government. The optimistic "upper bound" simulations assume that each state will choose to maintain total spending on TANF programs to the level under the AFDC program regardless of the declining support of the fixed federal block grant over time (declining because of inflation). Powers was most interested in comparing the overall level of spending on welfare of these two TANF regimes to the actual level of spending under AFDC over the period, but she also calculated a measure of variability for each state under each scenario from a regression of the log change in expenditures on the log change in the unemployment rate over the period 1976–1995. She found that the estimated relationship under each of the three scenarios is zero for most states, suggesting that AFDC/TANF spending is not related in a systematic way to the cycle. The reliability of this result is weakened by the fact that the effects of unemployment are estimated contemporaneously, while other studies show that the biggest effect of unemployment on caseloads occurs some 18 months after an increase in unemployment.

Boyd and Davis (1998) focused on the national recessions of 1980–1982 and 1990–1991 and calculated the amount by which state spending on welfare would have increased due to rising unemployment if TANF had been in place (i.e., if states had been solely responsible for increased spending at the margin) and states had provided benefits to the resulting new cases consistent with existing state-specific benefit levels. In other words, they calculated the expenditure increase needed to maintain welfare spending during the past two recessions under a TANF-like regime. They allow the severity of recessions to vary from state to state according to actual experience, but the assumed responses under a TANF regime are not allowed to vary. Thus, their findings reflect how states with varying economic conditions, benefit levels, and caseloads might have reacted had TANF been in place during the past two recessions.

It is useful to compare these assumed responses under Boyd and Davis to actual state behavior during the most recent recession. California and Michigan both cut their nominal benefit levels substantially, though California had a big increase in caseloads (37 percent from 1990 to 1994) while Michigan's caseloads were approximately constant. New York and Texas kept nominal benefits unchanged despite substantial caseload growth. Thus, there was substantial variation in state responses to recessionary conditions.

Boyd and Davis found a wide range of expenditure increases across the states, reflecting the differences in the severity of recession and the generosity of welfare programs across the states. On average, the deeper recession of the early 1980s would have resulted in an increase in welfare expenditures (as a percentage of state general fund budgets) of 1 percent. This figure seems small, but when compared with an average of 3 percent for state expenditures on AFDC as a percentage of state general fund budgets, it can be viewed as important. Some states are hit much harder than others. California, in particular, was estimated to experience expenditure increases of over 2 percent in each of the recessions, due to its higher-than-average benefit levels, higher-than-average case loads, and higher-than-average increase in unemployment during the recession of the early 1990s. In contrast, states in the southeast (with the exception of West Virginia) were estimated to experience below-average increases in expenditures as a share of their budgets under recession, in large part because of their low benefits.

Extrapolating from these findings to the next recession, Boyd and Davis seem to assume that states will succumb to fiscal pressures and reduce spending on welfare, but it is still an open question whether states will, in fact, choose to cut back welfare spending when the next recession occurs in the brave new world defined by TANF.

Dye and McGuire's (forthcoming) analysis attempts to shed some light on this open question. They examine actual revenues and expenditures, with an explicit focus on years of recession for each of the 49 states that experienced contractions during the period 1977–1995 (Florida did not experience a decline in gross state product [GSP], the measure of recession employed in the study, for any year during this period). The use of actual revenues and expenditures (as opposed to measures free of policy changes) is dictated by the lack of policy-fixed data for expenditures. An advantage to using actual revenues and expenditures is that they reflect not only automatic changes due to changes in economic conditions, but also the discretionary decisions of state decision makers, which is of interest in a study of the responses of states to economic distress.

For each state, Dye and McGuire calculate an elasticity of actual revenues (or expenditures) with respect to (declines in) GSP as the ratio of the percentage change in revenues (or expenditures) with respect to the percentage change (decline) in GSP.[6] They find that the calculated elasticity is negative for the individual income tax, the general sales tax, and total tax revenues for many states and on average, indicating that discretionary decisions are taken to counter the effects on revenues of the economic downturn. Similar calculations result in negative elasticities on average for total nonwelfare spending (–1.68), public welfare spending (–7.58), AFDC spending (–1.27), expenditures on K–12 education (–1.02), and expenditures on higher education (–3.01), indicating that states on average increase spending on these categories during contractionary periods.[7] The fact that AFDC spending is countercyclical on average is not surprising given the nature of the program, but the fact that education and other nonwelfare spending is also countercyclical for most states is surprising. Dye and McGuire interpret this preliminary evidence as supportive of the idea that states tend to maintain spending across the board during recessionary times. Since spending on nonwelfare programs is not financed by federal matching grants, it may not be unreasonable to expect states to increase taxes in order to maintain spending (including spending on welfare) even under TANF.

Dye and McGuire caution that their results are preliminary and require greater exploration. In particular, state-specific behavior often differs from average behavior and is oftentimes not easily explained.

For example, in contrast with the countercyclical findings for education spending for the U.S. average, the elasticity during recessions for K-12 education spending in Massachusetts is calculated to be cyclical, while the elasticity for higher education is weakly countercyclical.

Taken together, the studies of actual state fiscal behavior during recessionary periods and the studies simulating state welfare spending under the new TANF block-grant arrangement point to a cautious conclusion that the next recession need not result in large cuts in welfare spending, and may well result in an effort by most states to maintain their welfare policies and programs even as new cases are generated by the economic contraction. This conclusion is cautious for several reasons: 1) simulations outside of actual experience are always subject to wide margins of error; 2) the federal funding change for AFDC/TANF programs is dramatic and not just a change at the margin; and 3) several states (for example, Mississippi, Idaho, and Pennsylvania in Dye and McGuire's analysis) do exhibit cyclical (as opposed to noncyclical) spending on welfare, even under the AFDC matching-rate funding arrangement.

In assessing the impact of the change from federal matching grants to block grants on state spending and revenues, bear in mind the small share of total state expenditures attributable to AFDC/TANF spending. The largest state public welfare program by far is Medicaid, and it is still financed by a matching grant from the federal government. Thus, overall spending on public welfare programs is likely to continue to be highly countercyclical.

Finally, we comment on the likely efficacy of the contingency fund implemented as part of the 1996 welfare reform act and designed to provide additional federal funding for states experiencing dire economic conditions. Both Powers and Boyd and Davis note that states must spend at 100 percent of their 1994 levels in order to qualify for the contingency fund, a restriction that is likely to keep many states from qualifying. On the other hand, the argument that the fund at $2 billion is insufficient to cover the increased spending of states in a recession is not wholly convincing, given Boyd and Davis's estimate of an expenditure increase for the aggregate of all states of $2.5 billion due to the recession of the early 1990s.

Boyd and Davis' estimate of $2.5 billion is significantly smaller than Levine's (1998) estimate of $7.3 billion over five years. The major reason for this difference is that Levine estimated a much larger expenditure response for a given increase in unemployment than the consensus estimates employed by Boyd and Davis. Second, Levine's estimates assumed sustained increases in spending over a longer period than Boyd and Davis. Levine's aggregate expenditure response appears implausibly high in light of the smaller state-specific responses simulated by Boyd and Davis. This conclusion is reinforced by the fact that Boyd and Davis assume that states would have maintained benefit levels and covered all eligible recipients with their own revenues, if TANF had been in place during the previous two recessions. This is a generous assumption about state spending behavior. If states choose instead to cut benefit levels, as some did during the most recent recession, then the aggregate spending increase would be even smaller.

CONCLUSIONS AND FUTURE RESEARCH

A consensus seems to have emerged concerning the likely impact on welfare spending of a switch from matching to block grants. Recent econometric estimates suggest that the elasticity of spending with respect to matching rates is small, ranging from zero to 0.15. If correct—and there remains considerable uncertainty about the exact magnitude of the price effects—these elasticities imply cuts in benefit levels of no more than 10 percent and declines in the state share of 25 percent at most. Even this relatively modest response will not occur immediately, because the sharp drop in welfare caseloads has yielded a block grant windfall and reduced the budgetary pressure on states from welfare spending.

With regard to competition with other states, states do seem to follow their neighbors in making adjustments to benefit levels. However, the results on this type of interdependency are weak enough—and the importance of unmeasured state characteristics strong enough—that we do not predict the dramatic convergence in benefit levels implied by the phrase "race to the bottom."

Regarding program substitution, over a 20-year time period, evidence suggests that there has been considerable substitution between federal programs such as food stamps and SSI and shared state-federal programs. This substitution should accelerate under the incentives of a fixed block grant. Thus, looking ahead, say, 10 years or more, we speculate that state-financed cash assistance will be lower as a share of total welfare expenditures, including food stamp and Medicaid outlays.

We stress that considerable caution is warranted in predicting government behavior under any radical change in institutional setting. We have had several decades of experience with federal financing of AFDC under a generous matching grant; we have had less than two years of experience of federal financing of TANF under a generous block grant. Patience and diligence in monitoring state responses are called for.

At the same time, analyses of actual state fiscal behavior during recent periods of economic contraction are somewhat sanguine about the ability of the state sector to weather the next recession under the new TANF regime. This literature is very new and many unanswered questions remain. In addition, much of the analysis has not adequately accounted for behavioral changes in response to the new financing arrangements. The most encouraging evidence that state spending on welfare may not be dramatically reduced during the next (and first post-TANF) recession is provided by Dye and McGuire (forthcoming), who find that, with notable exceptions, most states did not reduce spending on nonwelfare programs, including K–12 and higher education—programs not financed by matching grants from the federal government—during recent recessions. These results are provocative rather than definitive (there are some puzzling results state by state), but they suggest that state spending behavior during periods of declining gross state product (periods of economic and fiscal distress) may differ greatly from secular trends in spending and from state spending behavior in good times. Additional research is needed to understand the causes and consequences of decisions made by individual states concerning welfare spending in difficult economic times.

Notes

We thank Sheldon Danziger, Greg Duncan, Julie Cullen, and Bob Schoeni for helpful comments.

1. Between 1991 and 1994, 11 states actually cut the nominal value of their maximum benefit level, while only 6 states increased benefits enough to maintain their real value.
2. The MOE requirement falls to 75 percent for states that meet federal work participation rate requirements.
3. Under the AFDC matching rate regime, if a state cut benefits by a dollar or moved a recipient from AFDC to SSI, it saved only 40 cents for every dollar of reduced spending. Under TANF, it saves a full dollar. If the recipient also gets food stamps, when the states cuts cash benefits by a dollar, food stamp benefits go up by about 30 cents.
4. Disregards still vary substantially across states. For example, in California a family gets to keep the first $225 in earnings per month and loses 50 cents per dollar thereafter. In Washington state, TANF benefits are reduced by 50 cents from the first dollar of earnings.
5. In FY97, 28 states reduced their own expenditures to the MOE minimum, 18 states were below their 1994 level but above the minimum, and 5 states increased their expenditures relative to their 1994 levels of spending (Lazere 1998).
6. The authors experiment with different lag structures for spending and GSP and find the results to be fairly robust on average.
7. The findings of countercyclical spending on average are consistent with the results in Mattoon and Testa (1992).

References

Baicker, Katherine. 1998. "Fiscal Federalism and Social Insurance." Unpublished dissertation, Department of Economics, Harvard University, Cambridge, Massachusetts.

Blackley, Paul R., and Larry Deboer. 1993. "Explaining State Government Discretionary Revenue Increases in Fiscal Years 1991 and 1992." *National Tax Journal* 46(1): 1–12.

Blank, Rebecca. 1988. "The Effect of Welfare and Wage Levels on the Location Decisions of Female Headed Households." *Journal of Urban Economics* 24: 186–211.

Blank, Rebecca. 1997. *What Causes Public Assistance Caseloads to Grow?* NBER working paper no. 6343, National Bureau of Economic Research, Cambridge, Massachusetts, December.

Borjas, G. J. 1997. "Immigration and Welfare Magnets." Unpublished paper, Harvard University.

Boyd, Donald J., and Elizabeth I. Davis. 1998. "Welfare Reform and Expenditure Pressures in the Next Recession." *Proceedings of the National Tax*

Association's Ninetieth (1997) Annual Conference, Washington, D.C.: National Tax Association, pp. 3–14.

Brueckner, Jan. 1998. "Welfare Reform and the Race to the Bottom: Theory and Evidence." Photocopy, The Urban Institute, Washington, D.C.

Chernick, Howard. 1998. "Fiscal Effects of Block Grants for the Needy: An Interpretation of the Evidence." *International Tax and Public Finance* 5(2): 205–233.

Chernick, Howard. 1999. "The Effect of Matching Grants on Public Assistance Spending: A Replication Analysis." Photocopy, Hunter College, New York.

Coe, Norma B., Gregory R. Acs, Robert I. Lerman, and Keith Watson. 1998. *Does Work Pay? A Summary of the Work Incentives under TANF.* The Urban Institute, Series A, no. A-28, December.

Coughlin, Teresa, Leighton Ku, and John Holahan. 1994. *Medicaid since 1980: Costs, Coverage, and the Shifting Alliance between the Federal Government and the States.* Washington, D.C.: The Urban Institute Press.

Craig, Steven G. 1993. "Redistribution in a Federalist System: Can the Federal Government Alter State Government Behavior?" Photocopy, Department of Economics, University of Houston, September.

Craig, Steven, and Robert Inman. 1986. "Education, Welfare, and the New Federalism: State Budgeting in a Federalist Public Economy." In *Studies in State and Local Public Finance*, Harvey S. Rosen, ed. Chicago: University of Chicago Press.

Dye, Richard F., and Therese J. McGuire. 1998. "Block Grants and the Sensitivity of State Revenues to Recession." *Proceedings of the National Tax Association's Ninetieth (1997) Annual Conference*, Washington, D.C.: National Tax Association, pp. 15–23.

Dye, Richard F., and Therese J. McGuire. Forthcoming. "Fiscal Systems and Business Cycles: What Will Happen to State Welfare Spending When the Next Recession Occurs?" Urban Institute policy brief.

Figlio, David N., Van Wolpin, and William Reid. 1998. *Asymmetric Policy Interaction among Subnational Governments: Do States Play Welfare Games?* Institute for Research on Poverty discussion paper no. 1154-98, University of Wisconsin-Madison.

Figlio, David N., and James P. Ziliak. 1998. "Welfare Reform, the Business Cycle, and the Decline in AFDC Caseloads." Photocopy, Joint Center for Poverty Research, Evanston, Illinois.

Gramlich, Edward, and Deborah Laren. 1984. "Migration and Income Redistribution Responsibilities." *Journal of Human Resources* 19: 489–511.

Lazere, Ed. 1998. *Unspent TANF Funds in Federal Fiscal Year 1998.* Center on Budget and Policy Priorities, Washington, D.C., November.

Levine, Phillip B., and David J. Zimmerman. 1995. *An Empirical Analysis of the Welfare Magnet Debate Using the NLSY.* NBER working paper no. 5264, National Bureau of Economic Research, Cambridge, Massachusetts, September.

Levine, Phillip B. 1998. "Cyclical Welfare Costs in the Post-Reform Era: Will There Be Enough Money?" Photocopy, Joint Center for Poverty Research, Evanston, Illinois.

Levine, Phillip B., and Diane M. Whitmore. 1998. "The Impact of Welfare Reform on the AFDC Caseload." *Proceedings of the National Tax Association's Ninetieth (1997) Annual Conference*, Washington, D.C.: National Tax Association, pp. 24–33.

Liebman, Jeffrey. 1996. "The Impact of the Earned Income Tax Credit on Labor Supply and Taxpayer Compliance." Unpublished doctoral dissertation, Harvard University, September.

Mattoon, Richard H., and William A. Testa. 1992. "State and Local Governments' Reaction to Recession." *Economic Perspectives* (Federal Reserve Bank of Chicago) 16(2): 19–27.

Moffitt, Robert. 1990. "Has State Redistribution Policy Grown More Conservative?" *National Tax Journal* 43: 123–42.

Moffitt, Robert, David Ribar, and Mark Wilhelm. 1998. "The Decline of Welfare Benefits in the U.S.: The Role of Wage Inequality." *Journal of Public Economics* 68(3): 421–4528.

Powers, Elizabeth T. 1998. "Block Granting Welfare: The Outlook for State Budgets." *Proceedings of the National Tax Association's Ninetieth (1997) Annual Conference*, Washington, D.C.: National Tax Association, pp. 34–43.

Ribar, David, and Mark Wilhelm. 1994. *The Effects of Costs, Resources, Interstate and Interprogram Competition, and Redistributional Preferences on AFDC Expenditures.* Working paper no. 1-94-1, Pennsylvania State University, November.

Ribar, David, and Mark Wilhelm. 1999. "The Demand for Welfare Generosity." *Review of Economics and Statistics* 81: 96–108.

Saavedra, L. 1998. "A Model of Welfare Competition with Empirical Evidence from AFDC." Photocopy, Department of Economics, University of Illinois.

Shroder, Mark. 1995. "Games States Don't Play: Welfare Benefits and the Theory of Fiscal Federalism." *Review of Economics and Statistics* 77: 183–91.

Sobel, Russell S., and Randall G. Holcombe. 1996. "Measuring the Growth and Variability of Tax Bases over the Business Cycle." *National Tax Journal* 49(4): 535–552.

U.S. Bureau of the Census. 1998. *Statistical Abstract of the United States 1998.* Washington, D.C.: U.S. Government Printing Office.

U.S. House of Representatives. 1996. *1996 Green Book: Background Material and Data on Programs within the Jurisdiction of the Committee on Ways and Means.* Washington, D.C.: U.S. Government Printing Office.

Walker, J.R. 1994. *Migration among Low Income Households: Helping the Witch Doctors Reach Consensus.* Institute for Research on Poverty, University of Wisconsin-Madison.

Wallis, John Joseph, and Wallace E. Oates. 1988. "The Impact of the New Deal on American Federalism." In *The Defining Moment: The Great Depression and the American Economy in the Twentieth Century,* Michael D. Bordo, Claudia Goldin, and Eugene N. White, eds. Chicago: University of Chicago Press.

Author Index

Headnote: Following the page locators, an italic *t* indicates a table, and an "n" precedes note numbers.

Subject Index

Headnote: Following page locators, an "n" precedes chapter note numbers, and an italic *f* and *t* indicate that subject information is within a figure or table, respectively, on that page.

318

About the Institute

The W.E. Upjohn Institute for Employment Research is a nonprofit research organization devoted to finding and promoting solutions to employment-related problems at the national, state, and local levels. It is an activity of the W.E. Upjohn Unemployment Trustee Corporation, which was established in 1932 to administer a fund set aside by the late Dr. W.E. Upjohn, founder of The Upjohn Company, to seek ways to counteract the loss of employment income during economic downturns.

The Institute is funded largely by income from the W.E. Upjohn Unemployment Trust, supplemented by outside grants, contracts, and sales of publications. Activities of the Institute comprise the following elements: 1) a research program conducted by a resident staff of professional social scientists; 2) a competitive grant program, which expands and complements the internal research program by providing financial support to researchers outside the Institute; 3) a publications program, which provides the major vehicle for disseminating the research of staff and grantees, as well as other selected works in the field; and 4) an Employment Management Services division, which manages most of the publicly funded employment and training programs in the local area.

The broad objectives of the Institute's research, grant, and publication programs are to 1) promote scholarship and experimentation on issues of public and private employment and unemployment policy, and 2) make knowledge and scholarship relevant and useful to policymakers in their pursuit of solutions to employment and unemployment problems.

Current areas of concentration for these programs include causes, consequences, and measures to alleviate unemployment; social insurance and income maintenance programs; compensation; workforce quality; work arrangements; family labor issues; labor-management relations; and regional economic development and local labor markets.